the SCOTCH-IRISH

by

William and Mary Durning

Editor

Margaret Harris

Cover Design

Clayton Clark III

The Irish Family Names Society
P.O. Box 2085, La Mesa, CA 91943-2095

ii

Copyright © 1991

By William and Mary Durning

Library of Congress Catalogue Number 91- 72478
International Standard Book Number 0-9601868-2-4
Printed in the United States of America
Original Printing 1991

Published directly from the authors manuscript by:

The Irish Family Names Society
P.O. Box 2095
La Mesa, California 91943-2095

TABLE OF CONTENTS

DONEGAL CASTLE
COUNTY DONEGAL

DISCOVERING THE PAST
IN COUNTY DOWN

SEARCHING THE RECORDS
IN BELFAST

HOME. LONG AGO

INTRODUCTION

This is a chronicle of the colonists who, in the years 1610 to 1750 came from England, Scotland and other parts of Europe to make their home in Ireland's province of Ulster. Many of their descendants in later years moved on to the New World. The migration to the American Colonies began after 1700. The distinctive accent of the newcomers amused the older American colonists who nicknamed them, "The Scotch-Irish." The majority were Presbyterians but their ranks included Baptists, Methodists, Huguenots, and Quakers.

The earlier Plantation schemes in Ireland gained limited success in the late 1500s. The real opportunity to colonize Ulster came with the departure of the Northern Irish Chiefs in 1607. The English King moved quickly to replace the chiefs with overlords of his own choice. These new landlords in turn brought over farmers from the Scottish Lowlands and less desirables from London.

The Scot-Irish (a more correct term), were close-mouthed, secretive people who left few records or historical documents. The authors have, from old annals or records, and oral tradition, attempted to pinpoint the earliest known abode of immigrants during the early years of the plantation. The information brought together in this book includes a brief account of the people, the political, church and land divisions of the country including the COUNTIES of Ulster, (roughly the equivalent of a North American state or province), the BARONIES (equivalent to an American county), the PARISH (an American city), and finally the TOWNLAND. The latter does not refer to a town but to a division of property (similar to the naming of a farm or of a city street. The townland is as close as we can come to the actual plot of ground where persons of a chosen surname lived. This however, is the basic information necessary to begin the search for an ancestor in Ireland. The text and tables in this book should serve as the STARTING point for your ancestral search. Please read the book from the beginning to better understand the information that follows.

THE ASH TREE BY THE CABIN

By an old mountain cabin there grows a wild ash,
'Twas planted by nature I'm told.
The storms of winter may rave and may lash,
It's roots firmly anchored still hold.

Often with comrades I rambled along,
And sheltered 'neath the old ash tree,
Then repaired to the cabin where music and song,
whiled the night by with mirth-making glee.

Long years have rolled by since I strolled on that hill,
To the cabin I long loved to see.
The cabin is in ruins but there is still memory and thrill,
When I stand 'neath that old ash tree.

By Billy Durning, Donegal poet and farmer
1885 - 1979

HISTORY: A LIMITED DESCRIPTION OF ACTUAL EVENTS USUALLY BIASED

HISTORY IN THE MAKING

One of the earliest accounts of Scotland is part of Irish oral tradition. The tribe we call the Gaelic Irish are said to have been cattle herders who came from the central planes of Europe which are now a part of Russia. The Druids predicted that their future lay in an island far to the west. Leaving their first abode and after many adventures, these enterprising pioneers reached "The Green Island."

Some years after the Gaels had established themselves in the new land, a number of boats loaded with new immigrants arrived and sought permission to join them. These clansmen spoke a language similar to, but not the same as, old Gaelic. Thrace (part of present day Bulgaria and Turkey) was their homeland. The Gaels treating them as kindred advised that the upper portion of the big island, eastward of Ireland, was unoccupied and that they might take up residence there. The Gaels offered them wives upon a promise that the kingly line should pass through the wife rather than the husband. This was agreed. So, according to this tradition, the Picts of Scotland were, in origin, half Gaelic Irish.

Twelve to thirteen miles of open water separate the eastern coast of Ireland from the Kintyre Coast of Scotland. In all probability, an exchange has always existed between the two peoples.

Ireland has been called by many names. The Gaels named the Green Island, "Scota's Land" in honor of their first queen. Scotland was called "Alba" and bore that name until an Irishman named Fergus, son of Earc, established a kingdom in the land of the Picts. Later Kenneth MacAlpin successfully joined the Picts and

Irish into a single nation. From that time on the northern part of the big island was called "Scota's Land" or "Scotland."

The Romans, having successfully occupied much of Europe-as far as it's western coast, now set their sights on conquering the big island to the west. About 43 A.D., Emperor Claudius landed on the big island now called "Great Britain." The Celtic speaking Britons mounted a heroic defense but the Romans, with years of military experience and superior weapons, easily subdued the natives and ruled the island for 350 years. Evidence of their occupation is still visible today.

Departure of the Roman Legions left the native Britons unable to defend themselves against raids by the Irish and the Picts. In desperation, they sought help from the warlike Angle, Jute and Saxon mercenaries living opposite them on the European Coast. A *temporary* visit by these Germanic warriors became an invasion and occupation. The older inhabitants were forced to move west and north, later to be joined by some of the Anglo-Saxons. Thus, the lower part of the big island became known as "Angle-land." This new name denoted a change, in both ethnic make-up and language. The new language became the oldest form of English.

Far to the north an inventive Scandinavian shipbuilder developed a new type of sailing craft capable of withstanding the dangerous storms of the North Atlantic. The northern mariners of the open sea were called "Vikings." Odin was their chief ancestor god. He was a god of war. To die in battle was the highest honor. Victims of Viking raids were considered to be a sacrifice to Odin. In time, the Vikings formed settlements on the islands along Scotland's west coast. There they mixed with the resident Irish and the Picts creating a new people, who in turn, became the Highland Clans. The Vikings founded colonies and towns in Ireland also. A subject covered in our earlier work, "A Guide to Irish Roots."

The southern tribes, pressing northward against Scotlands border, were a mixture of Briton, Welch and Saxon, most of whom now spoke the new English language. Following the Norman invasion of England in 1066 many of the English along Scotlands border crossed over into the lowlands of Scotland.

Alexander, King of the Scots, died in 1286. King Edward of England had been waiting for an opportunity to invade the northern kingdom. Thus began the wars which laid waste the borderlands. Both English and Scots plundered the border residents without mercy. As a final indignity, Edward took possession of the Stone of Scone. This Stone, long used in Ireland for the coronation of its kings, had been loaned to the Scots for the same purpose. Tradition says this is the same stone now cradled below the seat of the coronation chair in London's Westminster Abbey.

Compared to England, Scotland was a poor and undeveloped country. In 1326, Scots seeking outside help to improve their lot, formed an alliance with France and permitted the introduction of feudalism into their land. The Highland Scots resisted the restriction Feudalism placed on their independence. The lowlanders were more submissive and traded their freedom for the protection offered by the new Feudal Lairds.

The lowland Scot has been analyzed by many informed historians. Most agree that the women were healthy, strong and patiently performed the chores expected of them, while bearing as many as 20 children. The men were said to be inflexible, unable to express their feelings, and did not make good neighbors. On the positive side, they were hardworking, thrifty, patient and persistent.

So it was, the people of the lowlands became a hardened and submissive race following their Laird without question, regardless of the hardships imposed upon them.

In earlier times, the lowlands were thickly wooded, but by the 1600s much of the woodland had been cut down creating cleared farmland ideal for pillage by hungry soldiers and marauders. Much of the land, however, was poorly drained bog. The most fertile soil lay along the southeastern Scottish border, directly in the path of marching armies and border raiders.

The Norman Barons from Wales, with the help of an Irish king, gained a foothold in Ireland in 1169. The English King Henry II believed the only way to prevent the Normans from setting up a rival kingdom was to invade Ireland himself, which he proceeded to do.

The Irish had two customs which worked well among themselves but were poor foreign policy. When an Irish king succeeded in becoming more powerful than his neighbors, it was the custom for the lesser nobles to submit to his authority. Sometimes this was a matter of choice or election, but more often than not it was submission due to military superiority. When Henry II arrived with an obviously superior military force, the Leinster and Munster kings accepted his offer to protect them from the invading Normans. The second custom dealt with the length of an agreement. A treaty agreed upon by Irish chiefs remained in force only as long as all parties abided by it. Failure to do so by either party voided the agreement.

Irish culture was based on oral tradition. Few, if any, agreements were in writing. The English kings, however, viewed a written concordat as a totally binding contract. The king was supreme. His accords remained in force until he saw fit to change them. His treaty with the Irish kings required them to surrender title to Irish lands which under their own laws they had no right to do. Henry then regranted these lands to them to be held at his pleasure.

The Irish kings did not comprehend (I believe), that by

signing this document they were giving away their country. The English considered any violation of the treaty, real or supposed, an opportunity to foreclose and replace the Irish kings with tenants of their own choice. Furthermore, the English king had at his command an army capable of enforcing his interpretation of the agreement.

The Irish chiefs in Ulster were among the last to submit to English domination. The beginning of the end of independent Ulster came with the decision of Conn O'Neill to give up his title of "THE" O'Neill; submit to the English and accept the English title of "Baron of Dungannon."

From time to time the native leaders disagreed with English policy. The result was confrontation, appeasement, military conflicts, intrigues, and assassinations. Finally, in 1607 the principal northern chiefs boarded a ship and left Ireland forever. The English government was now free to plant Northern Ireland with English and Scots whom the government believed would more easily accept their plan for Ireland.

THE CLANS

The Scots have had more success in promoting their image than either the English or Irish. The word "Scot" immediately brings to mind a big, burley fellow dressed in a kilt, purse bulging with gold, dagger in stocking and in the act of tossing the Caber. The Highlander inherited the lusty genes of the Vikings along with those of the Irish and the Picts. He felt most at home when quarreling with friends, neighbors and foes. He was an Old Irish Catholic having received his religion from the Irish Prince Columba, who established a monastery on the Island of Iona off the west coast of Scotland.

We all have a need to belong to something, be it family, country or in the case of the Scot, the Clan. The Clan system continued to be the local governing body of the Highlanders until the early 1600s. With the breaking up of this tribal system, the people were required to take surnames similar to those of the English. This change created many of the surnames found in the name lists associated with each of the Scot Highland chiefs. The Irish maintained a close relationship with the Highland Scots, particularly Clan Donald of Kintyre and that part of Scotland nearest Ireland.

Since the Highlander was perfectly willing to fight and die just for the love of it, the Irish chiefs soon recognized their value as mercenary soldiers who could aid them in their skirmishes with each other and the English. These hardy fighting men were called the "Gallowglass," (Gaelic - Galloglaigh, a heavily armed soldier). Many married Irish women and settled down in Donegal and the Glens of Antrim.

The Highlanders were a rough and ready Clan satisfied with the simplest of comforts. It is quite probable that they were among the first North Europeans to adopt the concept of guerrilla warfare, (Spanish - Little War).

Romantic as the Highlanders were, they are not the people Americans call the Scotch-Irish. In fact, representatives of these Highland Clans probably came to the new world at an earlier date than our Scot-Irish ancestors.

THE LOWLAND SCOTS

Compared to England, Scotland in the 1500s was a poor and undeveloped country. Roads were few to non-existent. Most of the Scots who would later go to Ireland lived off the land. They planted grain crops and tended cattle. Their farming methods were far more primitive than those of the English farmer.

In early times, the Laird was a law unto himself. The national government was weak. The king was in many ways, the subservient to the desires of the Lairds. There was no organized police force nor system for keeping the peace. Many undesirable persons roamed the border area robbing and pillaging.

The lowlander was totally submissive to his Laird. He was always at the Lairds service, tilling his fields, tending his cattle and following him in battle. The Laird, for his part, was responsible for the welfare of his people. He listened to their complaints, settled arguments, and saw to it that their basic needs were met. The Laird was close to his people and served as a sort of father figure. By the 1600s, the lowlander had acquired a character quite different from the Highland Scot.

The poor farmer living on the border made most of his household furnishings of wood, with the exception of the kettle over the fire. The house itself was fashioned from available materials, sometimes stone, but more often from poles stuck in the ground, branches woven between and the whole plastered with mud. The roof, made of branches and straw was seldom weatherproof. The dirt floor served as the family bed.

The best land lay in the counties of Berwick and Roxburgh along the chosen path of invading armies. Most invasions came at harvest. The farmer was lucky if he lost only his crops. Usually his house was burned as well.

Adding to the poor farmers misery was the tug-of-war between Scot and English governments and between the national churches. In the mid 1500s, Presbyterianism became the established religion of Scotland.

James VI of Scotland be came James I of both England and Scotland after the death of Queen Elizabeth in 1603. The new king encouraged the border Scots to migrate to Northern Ireland as a way to solve the border problems. The term "lowlander" now referred to those practicing Presbyterianism, as well as a part of the country.

Although some Scots moving to Ireland came from as far north as Inverness and Aberdeen, most were from the present-day counties south of Stirling.

IRISH LANDS IN ENGLISH HANDS

To be a king or queen of England during this period in history was not quite as romantic as the movies would have us believe. Castles were drafty, cold and filthy. Meats were frequently tough or near spoilage. Drought, pestilence, and disease were ever present. Then as today, a king's most pressing problem was financial. Greed often was one of his traits. A formal tax system, as we know it, did not exist. Money did not enjoy the wide circulation it does today. The king very often was forced to accept taxes in the form of produce and services. Persistent wars kept the government in debt to the land holders and the merchants. During the Plantation period the sovereign, and later the Protector, viewed the parceling out of Irish lands to new tenants one way to solve financial problems.

The death of Queen Elizabeth and the ascent of James I, together with the departure of the Irish chiefs, made the plantation of Ulster with Scot and English tenants a certainty.

Prior to James plan for Ireland, two great Scottish Lairds named Montgomery and Hamilton came into possession of Irish property in an unusual way. An Irish chief's lust for wine and a desire to be hospitable, provided the fateful opportunity.

In 1602, Con O'Neill ordered a shipment of wine from Spain. Delivery was held up for some reason by the port authorities at Belfast. A confrontation with the English customs officials ended with the death of a soldier. The authorities decided hanging Con would be a proper punishment. Con's wife made an appeal to a Scottish friend named Montgomery, who through relatives had influence with James, now King of England and Scotland. While Con was confined in prison, another Montgomery relative, supplied the prison guards with wine from Con's detained stocks and thereby accomplished his escape and flight to Scotland. To secure a pardon for Con required the services of yet another Scotsman named Hamilton. For their help, Montgomery and Hamilton received the greater part of Con's tribal lands. Account books, and other records from the estates of Hamilton and Montgomery, have come down to us and contribute interesting details of farm life and management during the 1600s. Details of which can be found in the Hamilton and Montgomery papers, portions of which have been printed by the National Manuscripts Commission.

Farm records are important because they contain the names of tenants and names of the townlands they farmed.

Townlands varied in size from less than an acre to a thousand acres or more. The Montgomery-Hamilton venture probably was a model for the government plan which followed a few years later.

As already mentioned, the English kings were usually short of funds. King James shrewdly took advantage of this lust for dignity by instituting the order of Baronet as a method of defraying expenses. For a mere one thousand pounds (a laborer was paid one pound for a months work), a commoner could be entitled to be addressed as "SIR" so and so, and also entitled to an official "Coat of Arms." Following the Cromwellian invasion of Ireland, large sums of money were due to private parties, government employees, military personnel and suppliers in London. The government confiscated more Irish land to satisfy these debts.

The right to hold and use land was, during this period, one of the best revenue producers. Many, to whom the government owned money or favors, made application for lands in Ireland. The Irish whom the government considered to be in agreement with it's policy had small portions of their lands regranted. The remainder was given in tracts of 1000 acres or more to the applicants mentioned above. Other parcels were set aside for the official church, schools and towns. To qualify some applicants were required to meet certain conditions, among them were: Funds to build a fortified house surrounded by a wall. Transport to Ireland a sufficient number of English or Scot tenants to farm the property and serve as military reserves when necessary. Only good farmland was counted as part of the grant. Forest and boglands were left for the expelled Irish tenants.

The English government did not understand or care that the Gaelic Irish were culturally a different people, nor did they understand that dividing the land and setting property boundaries violated a basic right of freedom of movement. The English also did not understand that under certain circumstances these extremely individualistic people would act in unison. Thus the government's new plantation program was in trouble from the beginning.

RECRUITING NEW TENANTS

Land around what is now the city and county of Londonderry was granted to businesses in London who furnished supplies to the government. Leaving city life in London to become a farmer did not appeal to the more sophisticated English who had been enticed to make the move to Ireland. As a result, many who came over took up residence in the new city of Londonderry, rather than living on the farm. The London companies, unable to attract English farmers, quietly allowed the Irish to reoccupy the lands under their control.

The Scot planters fared much better. Under feudalism, tenants had looked to their local Laird and followed him without question. Many, particularly in the western border counties, eagerly moved to Ireland in anticipation of better land. The new land was exceedingly productive and the Scots quickly learned new farming methods from their English country neighbors. Still there were some Scot planters who were less than successful in recruiting tenants in Scotland. They too soon invited the Irish to reoccupy their grants.

Plots of land were also set aside for the official church which now became known as the Church of Ireland. The church received income from it's lands but also had the right to levy tithes on all individuals, whether members of the church or not. Thus each tenant ultimately paid the landlord for the use of the land, and a tithe to the established church. The tithe could be forcefully collected by the church using the office, the sheriff and sometimes the military.

Although Montgomery and Hamilton had made a success of their plantation venture, the government attempt was less successful. Some of the people selected for grants could not qualify. Others took one look at their holdings and withdrew. Still others sold their rights without making any improvement. Isolated settlements became the focus of raids by the deposed Irish. The occupation could not have survived without the help of the military.

The chief uniting factor among the colonists appears to have been their religious faith. The Presbyterian church soon became the cultural center of each community. It brought the colonists together, fulfilled their spiritual needs, organized schools and fostered peace and tranquility among the members. The Presbyterians and other dissenters resisted unwise government policy and through it's social communion the members helped each other.

The Presbyterian church in Ireland soon developed it's own character and a shortage of ministers paved the way for the introduction of laymen as pastors. The Irish congregations were by nature more independent than the church in Scotland, due in part no doubt, to the infusion of protestant worshippers with roots in other denominations.

FREEDOM, INDEPENDENCE AND THE CHURCH

From the beginning of the plantation, the deposed Irish and the newcomers had two things in common: A dislike for English politics and the right of the English church to make certain demands and to enforce them. Resisting these policies led the English to believe that in time the Irish and the Scots might combine against them. By design or otherwise, the policy of the government became one of "divide and conquer."

English policy was quite fluid and changed frequently. From time to time catholics, protestants, or both were severely restricted in their freedom of movement, participation in government and the right to sell their produce. At various times, a marriage was invalid unless performed by a Church of Ireland minister. For this reason, the genealogist may experience difficulty in locating marriage and baptismal records. The Church of Ireland, as the national church, was subject to government regulation. To further complicate matters, many Church of Ireland records were transferred to Dublin and lost in fires during the struggle for independence. Gravestones, if they exist, may now be the only remaining record of some of our ancestors.

Viscount Wentworth's enforcement of English trade laws (1633-40) prohibiting the export of Irish goods which might adversely affect English trade was vigorously opposed by the the Scottish settlers. Restrictive governmental control over the lives of individuals who were for the first time beginning to enjoy some personal freedom set the stage for the rebellion of 1641.

DAILY LIFE ON AN IRISH PLANTATION

Prosperous English and Scottish farmers and tradesmen found the Irish climate and the destitute condition of the country depressing and offered little hope for immediate profit. Some returned to their former homes or migrated to the south of Ireland. Those who remained as tenants were simple farming folk of humble origin who were quite comfortable in their thatched roof cottage of wattle and daub. Dwellings were grouped together for protection and as close to the landlords fortified house as possible. Most garments were woven from coarse wool, and in later times, of linen. Personal items were few and hung from pegs around the room. Early dwellings were mostly single room structures with a firehole in the dirt floor. An opening in the roof served as a chimney.

In the beginning, the Presbyterian church had minimal influence. Services during the early years were conducted by laymen with little formal training. The church, however, soon became the center of social life and in a relatively short time attracted preachers from Scotland. As the church gained influence, Presbyterian doctrine brought into line even the most disreputable characters. Within two generations the church was firmly established and fell under close government scrutiny.

Within a few years, agricultural and cattle products began to compete with those produced in England. English merchants and farmers urged the government to impose restrictions on Irish goods and products shipped to England or the New World. Loss of income sent a stream of tenants across the channel to Scotland. Many others hearing of opportunities in the New World began to think of going there. Most tenants had been induced to move to Ireland by an offer of a "Lifetime lease." These leases began to expire in the 1630s. Greedy landlords or their agents raised the cost of lease renewals beyond what the tenants believed were acceptable levels. Some Scots refused to pay, and were replaced with Irish tenants who found living on the land and paying an unreasonable rent preferable to living in the woods.

From about 1640 on, Scottish tenants began to be replaced by the deposed Irish.

ESTATE PAPERS

Hugh Montgomery's estate in County Down was established before the Great Plantation. He founded the cities of Donaghadee (currently a community of 3000 people) and Newtownards (13,000 people). Excerpts from family papers and account books have been published in "Analecta Hibernica" and tell us much about the daily life of the people. The Hamilton Estate papers have also been printed in the same publication and contain names of several hundred tenants. Copies of these documents may be available in your university library.

Nine years after the founding of the Great Ulster Plantation in 1610, Nicholas Pynnar was commissioned to report on its progress. His report lists the grantees, their progress and occasionally the names of tenants.

About this same time, Faynes Moryson made a tour of Ireland. He was an aristocrat and his opinion of the Irish people is somewhat biased by his status, nevertheless, his account also can be found in many university libraries and is worth reading.

One of the requirements of undertakers was the equipping and training tenants who could be called into military service. About 1630, a military census of Ulster was taken. Landlords were listed by their location and the names of persons capable of answering a call to arms. Lists for Cavin, Donegal and County Fermanagh have been made available and again can be found in most university libraries.

Other important documents are the "Hearth Money Rolls." These are lists of persons who could be taxed because they were wealthy enough to afford a fireplace. This listing is available for parts of Counties Cavin, Donegal, Fermanagh, Londonderry, Louth, Monaghan, Sligo, and Tyrone. Dates are 1663-5. Unfortunately, those too poor will not be included in this list.

During a later period, Church of Ireland pastors were requested to take a census of their parishes, including a segregated listing of the religious preference of all persons therein. Some did reluctantly, others not at all. The lists for 1740 have not been printed, although private compilations have been donated to certain libraries, notably the Family History Library in Salt Lake City and The Ulster-Scot Historical Foundation, 66 Balmoral Avenue, Belfast, BT9 6NY, North Ireland.

The unsettled status of Ulster generated a variety of records unique to Ireland. If all had survived, Ireland could boast a collection of documents of unequalled importance. When all surviving records are published, at some future date, Ireland will possess one of the world's most varied collections of genealogical lore.

NAMING THE LAND

Little more than three generations ago most North Americans lived on the farm. Country lanes were unnamed and houses in the smaller towns were without numbers.

A thousand years earlier, Ireland was already divided into provinces. From time to time provincial boundaries were moved about but each of the four (formally five) provinces have the general shape they had in 1169 when the Normans came to Ireland. The Normans brought with them a system of "shires" and sheriffs. The shires are called "counties" on present day maps. Within the counties were older Irish tribal property divisions which the Normans named "baronies," a unit often mentioned in old property transactions. Another and smaller division introduced by the Normans in the 1200s was called a "parish." Most of our ancestors in coming to the New World gave as their place of origin either "Ireland" or the name of their parish. Immigrants arriving after 1840 usually gave the location of their parish church. There is a problem, however, for there were THREE different "parish divisions." The church parish introduced by the Normans. The Church of Ireland parish and a governmental division called a "parish." Unfortunately, the boundaries of these territorial divisions have not always been in agreement.

During the plantation period, it was common practice to name both the land and the grantee. For example, Ardgart was the property of Sir John Home, Tallanal of John Archdale, Balliranell of Thomas Roche and so on. The survey of property lines was less than exact and arguments frequently resulted.

A smaller territorial division of the 1600s was the "Townland." Earlier property divisions were the Bailebo (Lit. "The Home of a Cow") and the Taite, (sixty Irish acres), most of which were later renamed Townlands. The Irish Townlands index of 1851 lists over 62,000 of these property divisions. The following is an illustration of the difficulty in determining a precise location using ancient records.

In County Down lies the townland of Ballyvalley. In the early 1700s, 71 acres of this property was leased to brothers John and Gilbert Seawright. By 1775 this same property was let to 15 individuals who's land now varied from a large plot of just over 12 acres down to the smallest of only four. Fortunately, the estate book of the grantee, Solomon Whyte, exists with the names of his new tenants.

Another problem arises from the change of property and city names. The town of Lisburn, for example, was once called Lisnagarvey. Londonderry is so called in the north but is usually referred to as Derry in the republic. In some old Presbyterian records, Blaris is mentioned as though it might be a little town. Today, the designation is that of a small property unit southeast of Lisburn. With so many variations, changes and duplications of townland names, (for example, forty five townlands in Ireland are named Ballynamona), it is quite understandable why a professional genealogist will ask for a precise location and date of an ancestor. It is our purpose in this book to provide examples of locational property names which were "home" for more than 2000 families. It should be remembered that Scottish families were large and that relatives may have settled in other locations. Also, the families in Ireland continued to be large. In general, however, a pattern can be found. Later we will explain how a modern Irish telephone book plus the information in this one can be joined to discover a central location for present-day residents of a particular surname.

Finally, the Province of Ulster in the 1600s included nine northern counties. With the founding of the Republic only six counties were joined in what is now called North Ireland.

WAR AND POLITICS

Although political activities are not a prime consideration in this book. It must be noted that the policies of Cromwell were instrumental in the migration of native Irish to the New World. The period from 1641 to 1652 was especially difficult for them. The city of Drogheda was devastated and its occupants massacred. Yet Cromwell had one of his own soldiers put to death for stealing a fowl from a native. On the other hand, he was quick to provide advancement in his own military. A shoemaker, via acts of bravery, was promoted to the rank of Colonel. A poor preacher was made an officer. Some of the natives in the Irish military were given the right to leave the country to join foreign armies. Others who were less fortunate, both civilian and military, were banished to the plantations in Barbados. Many of the old chiefs were deprived of their lands and herded into the province of Connacht. Cromwell's visit to Ireland was for everyone, an unsettling experience. The genealogist may find it worthwhile to read the history of the Cromwellian period in the records of the time.

Shortly after 1660, Charles II forbade the Presbyterians in Scotland to hold family worship when anyone outside the family was in the house. This act was another incentive for many Scots to leave their homeland for the New World. In Ireland, the uprisings of 1689 and adverse legislation of the early 1700s, sent streams of protestant folk from there to the western hemisphere.

Since the government and the official church were closely allied, the governmental policy as it developed in Ireland, brought them into even closer union. By the early 1700s only members of the Church of Ireland could teach school, become a civil servant, serve in the military, or even be officially married. The catholics answered this challenge with their "Hedge Schools" and the protestants with defiance.

MIGRATION TO THE NEW WORLD

The purpose of this book is to aid those wishing to discover surname origins in Ireland, however, it is proper to include some information on migration to the New World.

Saving for the venture was no easy matter. Most of the migrants to the New World were simple farm folk who had either sold their lease or departed upon its expiration. "Salesmen" representing ship owners traveled through the country seeking passengers. Promised sailing dates were often delayed eating into migrants meager savings. In the early days, passengers brought their own food and supplies. The ship provided water sometimes inadequate and almost always foul tasting. Passage in the early 1700s was reasonable, however. Five English pounds (money) was the usual fare for adults and under a pound for children (remember a pound equalled a months work for a laborer). If the ships were not filled at sailing time, the captain often offered free passage to anyone agreeing to sell themselves as a contract laborer. The contract was in turn sold to someone upon arrival in the New World. The term was usually from one to five years.

Occasionally, due to bad navigation or storms, passengers might find their ship making landfall anywhere along the east coast. After a trip lasting from three weeks to three months, most were glad to land at any port.

Pennsylvania was the choice colony while Delaware, New Jersey, and North Carolina were also favored. Those wishing to go inland tried for Baltimore from which, after 1755, they could travel on Braddocks Military Road which would its way westward to Fort Pitt. Forbes Road, an alternate route, was opened in 1758.

A family arriving at their destination with twenty pounds were considered well off. They could support themselves for a year or use it for transport to an inland destination with money to spare.

Going to the New World was the trip into ocean space almost as dangerous as the voyages of todays astronauts.

The blood of the Gael coursed through the veins of both the Irish and the Scots. They were an adventurous people and it was their destiny to push the frontier ever westward as they sought out their place in the New World. Perhaps they were motivated by the inherited genes from their ancestors who drove their herds across the plains of Central Europe.

PLANTATION HOUSES LATE 1600's

THE BEGINNING

In ancient times, young children in Ireland knew their relationship to the local King. When asked, they would happily recite the King's name first, then each succeeding ancestor down to themselves. We follow a similar method in this book, proceeding from older generations to the present. The maps and charts are designed to help locate the farmsteads of Ulster, immigrants from Scotland and other lands during the 16 and 1700s. In the following pages, we will also suggest ways to locate living persons in Ireland with the surname you are researching. They may be able to provide information to assist in your ancestoral hunt. An explanation of how this system works begins with a discussion of the maps.

THE MAPS

The first two maps cover all of Ireland and Scotland. Both maps are divided into counties which are named and numbered. The county numbers also appear in the charts which follow. Chart, Column I, refers to the Irish map, and Chart, Column S, refers to the Scottish map.

Two sets of Chart pages are included in this book. The first set of charts is grouped by surname and county. Preceding each county is a county map on which parishes mentioned in the charts are shown by number. For clarity only, those parishes relevant to the surnames are identified on these maps. More detailed maps of Ireland may be available free from your local travel agent or by writing to: The Northern Irish Tourist Board, 40 West 57th Street, 3rd Floor, New York, NY 10019. Request a free map and information regarding the County of interest. For a map of the Republic, contact: The Irish Tourist Board, 757 Third Avenue, New York, NY 10017. Your local bookstore may be able to order commercial maps for you.

MORE DETAILED MAPS

The best maps are those issued by the Ordinance Survey of Northern Ireland and the Republic. The one inch per mile scale names the townlands and small communities. The North Ireland Ordinance Survey office is located at 83 Landas, Belfast 6. The Ordinance Survey for the Republic is in Phoenix Park, Dublin 8. Your college or university may have the maps you need, if not, the maps in this book will get you started.

The old Province of Ulster contained nine counties. The Government Act of Partition, in 1920 reduced this number to the following six counties: Antrin, Armagh, Down, Fermanagh, Londonderry, and Tyrone. In this work, we have included the old counties of Cavin, Donegal and Monaghan, as well as counties Mayo and Sligo. The latter two counties were added because some people of the later Plantation Period resided there along with the disposed Irish.

THE CHARTS

These tables offer an exciting new approach to discovering the counties in Scotland from whence immigrants came, and the place in the North of Ireland where they settled. The content of the charts will help answer the fundamental questions always asked by professional researchers, and can provide essential information needed to do your own research.

If you plan to employ a genealogist to work for you, this book, plus your own ancestral knowledge, can provide some of the basic information the researcher will require. It will, however, be more fun and less costly to do as much research as possible on your own.

Many changes, political and geographical, took place in Ireland between 1600 and 1750. Even boundaries were moved. The language changed also, as did the spelling of names of places. Persons receiving land grants sometimes sold or abandoned their properties.

Early in the research process it was deemed wise to select a comparative standard to serve as a bridge between past and present spelling of place names. "The Index of Townlands and Towns, Parishes and Baronies of Ireland" proved to be the ideal choice. In addition to naming property divisions as they existed in 1851, The Index includes the cities where the "Poor Law" of 1857 was administered. The Townlands Index was originally published by Alexander Thom of Dublin in 1861, and reprinted by the Genealogical Publishing Company of Baltimore in 1984.

HOW TO USE CHART NUMBER 2 AS AN INDEX

Turn to Chart 2, which also serves as an index. Search for surnames of interest, then read the instructions below.

1.   This chart contains most, but not all, of the surnames arriving in Ireland at the beginning of the Plantation. Sometimes a surname is listed more than once, an indication that several persons of this name came to Ireland.

Columns following the surname contain information needed to begin the search for an ancestral line in Ulster. Jot down the contents of each column, reading from left to right.

2. Column R is a listing of the religious preference of the oldest person of this surname so far discovered:
    C = Catholic, H = Huguenot, I = Church of Ireland, P = Protestant. Although a religious preference is indicated here, from time to time marriages, baptisms and christenings were not legal unless performed by clergy of the Church of Ireland, thus, your research should ALWAYS include available documents of the Church of Ireland during the time period of your research.

3. Moving over to Column I, note the number, then locate the same number on the All Ireland map. There you'll find the county where a person of this name lived during the early Plantation Period.

4. Column S contains both numbers and letters, each number represents a county on the Scottish map. A letter in this column is an indication of nationality. For example:
    D = a person of Danish or Norse origin, E = English origin, F = French or Norman origin, G = German, H = Huegenot, I = Irish, S = Scotland, and W = Welsh (when the county of origin for this surname is unknown). All of these folk, except those from England and Wales, may have arrived in Ireland via Scotland.

5. TOWNLAND: The word "Townland" relates to a division of property rather than a built-up community. Townland

boundaries and names have been subject to considerable change. There are, for example, three townlands with the strange name of "Moodoge." One of these lies in the Parish of Ballymore, near Banbridge in County Armagh, a small parcel of 181 acres. In early times, this bit of land was called "Muddocke". A map dated 1609 entitles the property Ballymoydogh. In the 1756 census, this same land is labeled "Moydog". Townlands range in size from a few acres to more than a thousand acres. Except in cities, a townland is as close as one can come to the actual abode of an individual in the late 1600s.

6.   BARONY: The "Barony" is an older land division which came into use before counties were formed. It was created in Medieval times and based originally on the territory of a local Irish king. Many old records name the barony as the primary territorial unit. It is one of the five divisions found in the "Townland Index" of 1851.

7.   THE PLACE-PARISH: Arriving in the New World, our ancestors, when asked, often gave the name of the parish as their place of residence. The parish is a smaller land division than the barony, but larger than the townland. Parish names were reasonably stable during the time period covered by this book, but when written down varied in spelling. It should be noted that old parish boundaries often overlap county boundaries.

8.   Some surnames in the charts are followed by an "*". This mark identifies early grantees of the Plantation Period. The same mark may also follow the name of a townland,

indicating that this listing identifies an entire grant, or is the name of a townland which no longer exists under this name. Blank spaces occasionally appear in each category, an indication that the needed information has not yet been discovered.

O' NAMES

Both name lists in this book contain O' names. At first glance, it might seem unusual to find them listed among the Protestant surnames. In most cases, O' names will fall into one of three categories. 1) the requirement during certain periods for marriages, baptisms and christenings to be performed by a church of Ireland minister. 2) conversion of persons of a given surname to membership in a Protestant church. 3) native Irish Subchiefs considered loyal to the English government who were regranted portions of their original lands.

Now turn to Chart 1 and look for the name chosen from Chart 2.

HOW TO USE CHART NUMBER 1

Chart 1 is similar in content to Chart 2, but has been arranged alphabetically by surname within each county. Choose the county number in the Chart 1 pages which corresponds to the county number opposite your surname in Chart 2.

If your surname appears in this new list, look for other surnames in the same townland, these folk may have been neighbours. Marriage between families could have taken place. Persons of your name may have acted as witnesses or otherwise helped their neighbours. Thus, you will want to write down their names to be included in your search. If your surname was alone in the townland, check nearby townlands in the same parish.

Completion of this search brings you as close as possible to identifying the homeland of one family in Ireland between 1600 and 1750. Your objective, however, is to narrow the search to the time period of your immediate ancestor prior to leaving Ireland. If Irish records had not been lost, an investigation could be carried forward in the usual manner. In most cases, however, it will be necessary to use whatever sources are immediately available. Try your local library first. Check the index in EVERY book dealing with Ireland, England and Scotland. Look first for your surname, then for the community nearest where persons of that name might have lived. Nothing? Not unusual, your local library is designed to provide a broad base of general information rather than genealogical data. Next, expand your search to a larger city library, genealogical, college or university library. Here you may find one or more books listed in the Bibliography.

GOING BEYOND THE CHARTS IN THIS BOOK

DOCUMENTS AFTER 1600: Library holdings will vary, but be sure to look for Sir William Petty's CENSUS of IRELAND, recorded in 1659 and published in 1939. Here you will find the names of lease holders and the surnames of tenants within each parish or townland. Counties Cavin and Tyrone were not included in this document.

The "SPINNING WHEEL INDEX" of 1665 is a list of farmers receiving flax seed or other items, in exchange for growing flax. This list is readily available on microfiche at many Family History Libraries.

The "HEARTH MONEY ROLLS" lists, by county and parish, persons wealthy enough to have at least one fireplace. The fireplace was a taxable item in the mid 1600s. The rolls make up a fairly extensive record of householders, with dates at least from 1663 to 1669, but varying by county. Most are available in the Public Record office of Northern Ireland. Some have been printed or microfilmed.

Records for the 1700s are sketchy. A helpful listing of them can be found in a book called; "Irish Genealogy, A Record Finder," published by Heraldic Artists LTD., Trinity Street, Dublin 2, Republic of Ireland.

Probably the most widely used document of the 1800s is Sir Richard Griffith's "PRIMARY VALUATION of IRELAND", 1848-1864. Data is compiled by County, Barony, Poorlaw Union, Parish and Townland. Named is the person holding the townland lease and the tenant occupying it. Since this document was created around the time of the famine, it can be quite valuable in finding the location of family names during that time period.

THE CENSUS of 1901: This is the earliest complete census of persons present when it was taken. It contains a wealth of detail, including approximate ages of individuals, and even the number of rooms in the dwelling. A valuable resource, the original for all Ireland, is kept in the Public Record Office in Dublin. Microfilm of this document is rather widely distributed. There is a copy in The Family History Library in Salt Lake.

The 1911 Census is available in Ireland and can be used to check the name and location of persons in the census of 1901.

If the "Luck of the Irish" is with you, a trail of your surname has been discovered down to fairly recent times. If your interest is like the author's, now is the time to go to Ireland, but before you go take one more step which could lead you directly to living persons who may hold the answers to unsolved problems.

IRISH TELEPHONE BOOKS

As you can see, it may be possible to trace a surname in Ireland using other than the conventional methods, a source which should not be overlooked, the present day Irish Telephone Book!

The telephone book makes possible a system which may work for you. In it you may find the residential address of a person of your surname. It is possible, even after 300 years, that like named individuals may be living in or near the same townland once occupied by your ancestors. Although less than one in four families in Ireland have telephones, this search is still worthwhile. If three or more listings of your chosen surname are found in the same community or nearby, that spot is likely to have been the homeland of the family from older times.

Telephone books from all over the world are now available in most large university libraries and some genealogical societies. AT&T distributes foreign telephone books in the U.S. This firm publishes an "International Telephone Directory Price List". Foreign telephone books are fairly expensive and it might be more practical to make a donation to your local library and ask them to purchase it for you. The phone number of the Directory Department changes on occasion, but try calling 1-800-432-6600 for information.

Should you decide to write to someone in Ireland, enclose three Postal Reply Coupons. Coupons are available from your local Post Office. In your first letter, ask only one easily answered question. Remember, you may or may not receive a reply. If you do, more questions can be asked in another letter. When writing to churches for information one should always include a small contribution.

So, begin your search - we wish you complete success.

The Public Record office,
one source of plantation
documents

BIBLIOGRAPHY

The ensuing reading list may be helpful in your search. Following the reading list will be the name and location of major libraries containing documents dealing with the history of Ireland. Some books may be available via inter-library loan. You might also want to write directly to a distant source. Send along a postpaid envelope.

THE FOLLOWING IS A LIMITED LIST
OF RESOURCES RELATING TO THE PROVINCE OF ULSTER
AND THE PLANTATION PERIOD

BAPTIST BIBLIOGRAPHY, W.T. Whitley, London, 1916

BIRTH of ULSTER (THE), C. Falls, London, 1936

BOOK of IRISH NAMES, Ronan Coghlan, Ida Grehan, P.W. Joyce, Sterling, New York, 1989

COLONIAL RECORDS of PENNSYLVANIA, 1683-1790, Harrisburg, PA, 1851

CREW MSS#630, Lambeth Palace Library, London, England

DICTIONARY of SCOTTISH SETTLERS IN NORTH AMERICA 1625-1825, Genealogical Publishing Company, Baltimore, 1986

GENERAL DESCRIPTION of THE SHIRE of RENFREW (A), G. Crawford, J. Nelson, 1818

HARRIS COLLECTANEA MSS. National Library of Ireland, Dublin 2, Ireland

HEARTH MONEY ROLLS of COUNTY DONEGAL, J.C. Mac Donagh, The Donegal Annual, Donegal, Ireland, 1953

HEARTH MONEY ROLLS of LISBURN, Down & Donnor Historical Society Journal, 1936

HEARTH MONEY ROLLS of COUNTY LOUTH, 1663, J.R. Garstin, Journal of the County Louth Archaeological Society, 1926

HISTORICAL NOTES of LIMAVADY, E.M. Boyle, Ulster, Journal of Archaeology, Belfast, 1902

HISTORY of THE BORDER COUNTIES, G. Douglas, Edinburgh, 1899

HISTORY of COUNTY DOWN (A), A. Knox, Dublin, 1875

HISTORY of THE HOUSE OF HAMILTON (A), G. Hamilton, Edinburgh, 1933

HISTORY of IRELAND, R. Cox, London, 1689

HISTORY of METHODISM in IRELAND, C.H. Crookshank, Belfast, 1895

HISTORY of TWO ULSTER MANORS, Lord Belmore, London, 1903

INDEX to the TOWNLANDS and TOWNS, PARISHES and BARONIES of IRELAND, 1861. Reprint, Genealogical Publishing Company, Baltimore, 1984

IRISH GENEALOGY - A RECORD FINDER, Donal F. Begley, Heraldic Artists, Dublin, 1981

LAGAN VALLEY (THE), E.R. Green, London, 1949

LIST of TOWNLANDS IN COUNTY LOUTH, A. Thom, His Majesty's Stationary Office, Dublin, 1911

MEDIEVAL SCOTLAND, R.W. Cochran-Patrick, Glasgow, 1892

NOTES on BAWNES, A.T. Lee, Ulster Journal of Archeology, 1858

PARISH of DEVENISH, W.B. Steele, The Fermanagh Times, Enniskillen

QUAKERS of IRELAND, 1654-1900, Isabell Grubb, London, 1927

REFORMED CHURCH of IRELAND (THE), 1537-1889, J.T. Ball, 1890

SCOTCH-IRISH in AMERICA, J.W. Dismore, Chicago, 1906

SCOT in ULSTER (THE), J. Harrison, Blackwood, Edinburgh, 1888

SCOTS, MERCENARY FORCES IN IRELAND, 1565-1603, Hayes-Mc Coy, London, 1937

SEANCHAS ARDMHABCHA, M. Glancy, Wexford, 1954

TOPOGRAPHICAL DICTIONARY of IRELAND (A), Samuel Lewis, London, 1837

MAJOR RESEARCH LIBRARIES
HOLDING IRISH DOCUMENTS

ALLEN COUNTY PUBLIC LIBRARY, P.O. Box 2270, Fort Wayne, IN 46801

COUNTY DONEGAL HISTORICAL SOCIETY, 61 Cluain Barrow, Ballyshannon, Republic of Ireland

COLLEGE of SAINT THOMAS, O'Shaughnessy Library, 2115 Summit Avenue, St. Paul, MN 55105-1096

EDINBURGH CENTRAL LIBRARY, George IV Bridge, Edinburgh, EH1 1EG, Scotland

FAMILY HISTORY CENTER, 50 Northwest Temple, Salt Lake City, UT 84150

FAMILY HISTORY CENTER, 10741 Santa Monica Boulevard, Los Angeles, CA

GENEALOGICAL OFFICE, Office of Arms, Dublin 2, Republic of Ireland

KENTUCKY STATE LIBRARY, 300 Coffee Tree Road, P.O. Box 537, Frankfort, KY 40602-0537

UNIVERSITY of CALIFORNIA LIBRARY, Irvine, CA

NATIONAL ARCHIVES, RECORD SERVICE, Washington, DC 20408

U.S. NATIONAL ARCHIVES BRANCHES, Nationwide
380 Trapelo Road, Waltham, MA 02154

Building 22, MOT Bayonne, Bayonne, NJ 07002

5000 Wissahickon Avenue, Philadelphia, PA 19144

3758 S. Polaski Road, Chicago, IL 60629

1557 St. Joseph Avenue, East Point, GA 30344

2306 E. Bannister Road, Kansas City, MO 64131

4900 Hemphill Street, Fort Worth, TX 76115

Building 48, Denver Federal Center, Denver, CO 80225

1000 Commodore Drive, San Bruno, CA 94066

24000 Avila Road, Laguna Niguel, CA 92677

6125 Sand Point Way N.E., Seattle, WA 98115

NATIONAL SOCIETY of the DAUGHTERS of the AMERICAN REVOLUTION, 1776 "D" Street N.W., Washington, DC 20006

NATIONAL LIBRARY of IRELAND, Kildare Street, Dublin 2, Ireland

NEW YORK CITY PUBLIC LIBRARY, 5th Avenue at 42nd Street, New York City, NY 10016

NEWBERRY LIBRARY, 60 West Walton Street, Chicago, IL 60610

PUBLIC ARCHIVES of CANADA, 395 Wellington Street, Ottawa, Ontario, K1A 0N3, Canada

SOCIETY of FRIENDS (QUAKERS) HISTORICAL LIBRARY, 6 Eustace Street, Dublin 2, Ireland

SUTRO LIBRARY, A BRANCH OF THE CALIFORNIA STATE LIBRARY, 480 Winston Drive, San Francisco, CA 94132

TEXAS STATE LIBRARY, Box 12927, Capitol Station, Austin, TX 78711

ULSTER HISTORICAL FOUNDATION, 66 Balmoral Avenue, Belfast BT9 6NY, North Ireland

UNIVERSITY COLLEGE, Folklore Department, Belfield, Dublin 4, Republic of Ireland

Charts Part I

HOW TO USE CHART NUMBER ONE

GO TO PAGE 119 BEFORE USING THIS CHART.

Surnames in this section are alphabetical by county.

The county number under "I" in the "R I S" column
is the same as a county number on the Irish map.   (Page 39).

Turn to the numbered county chosen from chart number TWO.
If your names are found in this chart proceed as follows:

Look for other surnames which have the same Townland or
Parish. If your Townland was a small one these folk could be
neighbours. It is possible that marriage or other records may
include them them also. Copy those names to be part of your
search.

The Scots often migrated to the New World as a group led by
their pastor. No formal records of their arrival in the U.S.were
kept until 1820. Prior to that time consult Colonial, Provincial
or state records.

The first U.S. Census was taken in 1790.

You have now come as close as possible to finding the homeland
of persons of your surname in the North of Ireland during the
1600's.

Map of Scotland

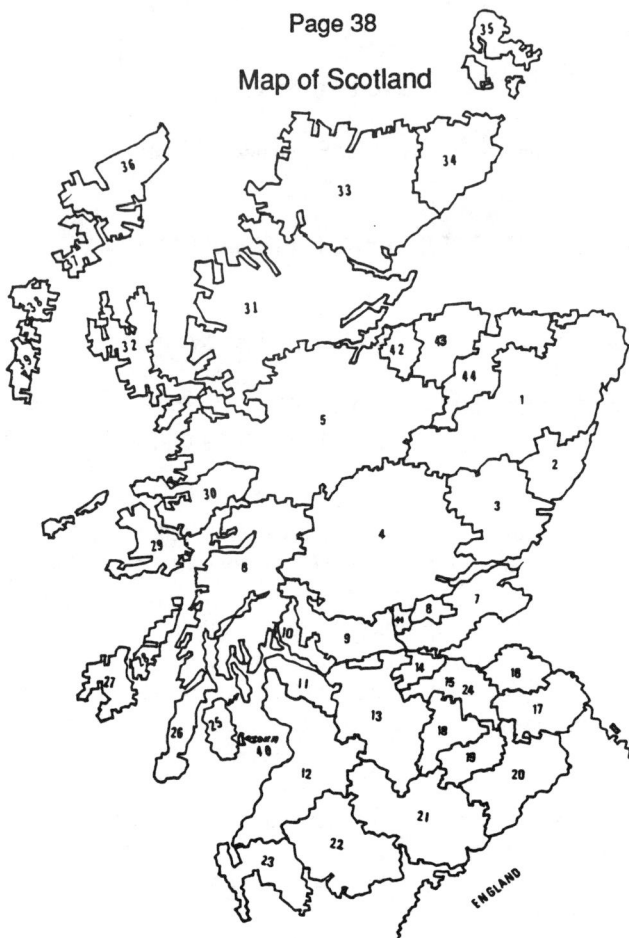

1. ABERDEEN	16. EAST LOTHIAN	31. ROSS & CROMARTY
2. KINCARDINE	17. BERWICK	32. SKYE
3. ANGUS	18. PEEBLES	33. SUTHERLAND
4. PERTH	19. SELKIRK	34. CATHNESS
5. INVERNESS	20. ROXBURGH	35. ORKNEY
6. ARGYLL	21. DUMFRIES	36. LEWIS
7. FIFE	22. KIRKCUDBRIGHT	37. HARRIS
8. KINROSS	23. WIGTON	38. NORTH UIST
9. STERLING	24. MIDLOTHIAN	39. SOUTH UIST
10. DUNBARTON	25. BUTE	40. IONA
11. RENFREW	26. KINTYRE	41. CLACAMANNAN
12. AYR	27. ISLAY	42. NAIRN
13. LANARK	28. JURA	43. MORAY
14. WEST LOTHIAN	29. MULL	44. BANFF
15. EDINBURGH CITY	30. MORUEN	

Map of Ireland

Map of Donegal

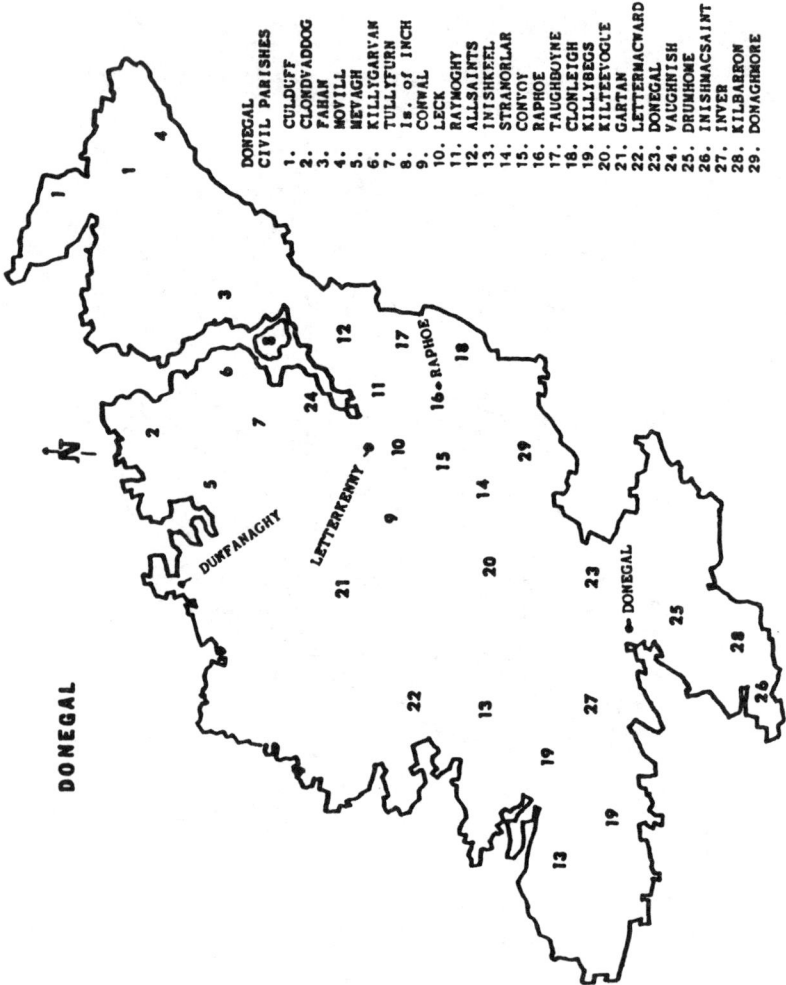

DONEGAL

N

DONEGAL
CIVIL PARISHES

1. CULDUFF
2. CLONDVADDOG
3. FABAN
4. MOVILL
5. MEVAGH
6. KILLYGARVAN
7. TULLYFURN
8. Is. of INCH
9. COWAL
10. LECK
11. RAYMOGHY
12. ALLSAINTS
13. INISHKEEL
14. STRANORLAR
15. CONVOY
16. RAPHOE
17. TAUGHBOYNE
18. CLONLEIGH
19. KILLYBEGS
20. KILTEEVOGUE
21. GARTAN
22. LETTERMACWARD
23. DONEGAL
24. VAUGHNISH
25. DRUMHOME
26. INISHMACSAINT
27. INVER
28. KILBARRON
29. DONAGHMORE

DUNFANAGHY

LETTERKENNY

RAPHOE

DONEGAL

Surname	R	I	S	Townland	Barony	Place-Parish
Alexander	P	1	12		Raphoe	Raphoe
Allis	P	1	1	Drimahy *	Banagh	Inishkeel
Allison	P	1	12		Raphoe	Leck
Anderson	I	1	18	Toome	Boylagh	Lettermcward
Arckley	P	1	3	Portlough	Raphoe	Allsaints
Arkless	I	1	E	Cloghro	Raphoe	Convoy
Armour	P	1	13	Croghan	Raphoe	Clonleigh
Arrell	P	1	4	Monfad	Raphoe	Allsaints
Ash	I	1	E		Raphoe	Convoy
Babington	I	1	E	Portlough	Raphoe	Allsaints
Balfoure	I	1	E	Kildrum L.	Raphoe	Allsaints
Ballentine	P	1	9	Dromore	Raphoe	Leck
Balmann	P	1	2	Portlough	Raphoe	Allsaints
Barclay	I	1	E	Ballybogan	Raphoe	Clonleigh
Bates	I	1	E	Toome	Kilmacrenan	Clondavaddog
Baxter	P	1	7	Moness	Raphoe	Taughboyne
Benson	P	1	7	Drumboe	Raphoe	Stranorlar
Bigley	I	1	E		Tirhugh	Drumhome
Blackburn	I	1	E	Argory *	Raphoe	
Blair	P	1	7		Raphoe	Raphoe
Blare	P	1	7	Portlough	Raphoe	Allsaints
Boggs	I	1	E	Monglass	Raphoe	Allsaints
Bolton	C	1	21	Toome	Kilmacrenan	Clondavaddog
Bonar	C	1	I	Ballybofey	Raphoe	Stranorlar
Bonner	Q	1	4	Portlough	Raphoe	Allsaints
Boveard	P	1	H		Raphoe	Leck
Boyce	I	1	7	Devlin	Kilmacrenan	Mevagh
Boyce	I	1	7	Doagh	Kilmacrenan	Mevagh
Boyce	I	1	7	Tullagh	Kilmacrenan	Mevagh
Boyle	P	1	12	Drumlackagh	Kilmacrenan	Mevagh
Bready	P	1	9	Altacaskin *	Raphoe	Taughboyne
Breedy	P	1	9		Raphoe	Raphoe
Brisland	C	1	I		Inishowen	Moville
Brison	C	1	I	Clonmany *	Inishowen	
Broadley	C	1	I			
Brogan	C	1	I	Drumies *	Kilmacrenan	Mevagh
Brown	P	1	17		Raphoe	Raphoe
Buchanan	P	1	9		Raphoe	Raphoe

Surname	R	I	S	Townland	Barony	Place-Parish
Burd	P	1	1	Croghan	Raphoe	Clonleigh
Burnside	P	1	7	Castletorris	Raphoe	Convoy
Burnside	P	1	2		Raphoe	Raphoe
Bustard	I	1	E		Tirhugh	Donegal
Caldwell	I	1	E		Raphoe	Raphoe
Calhoone	P	1	10	Letterkenny	Kilmacranan	Conwal
Camble	P	1	6		Raphoe	Raphoe
Cannon	C	1	I	Ardbane	Kilmacrenan	Mevagh
Cannon	C	1	I	Dundooan	Kilmacrenan	Mevagh
Canny	C	1	I		Inishowen E.	Culdaff
Carre	P	1	S	Inver	Banagh	Inver
Carson	P	1	21		Raphoe	Raphoe
Caughlan	C	1	I		Raphoe	Raphoe
Chisime			1	Momeen	Raphoe	Taughboyne
Cock	P	1	13	Cargins *	Raphoe	
Coken	P	1	4		Raphoe	Raphoe
Coll	I	1	6		Kilmacrenan	Mevagh
Colquhon *	P	1	10	Corkagh *	gh	
Conor	C	1	I	Doagh	Kilmacrenan	Mevagh
Conyngham	P	1	9	Monargan Glebe	Banagh	Killybegs
Cowen	P	1	12	St.Johnstown	Raphoe	Taughboyne
Coyle	I	1	I	Ardbane	Kilmacrenan	Mevagh
Coyle	I	1	I	Dundooan	Kilmacrenan	Mevagh
Coyle	I	1	I	Glenkoe	Kilmacrenan	Mevagh
Coyle	I	1	I	Tullagh	Kilmacrenan	Mevagh
Crawford	C	1	12	Letterkenny	Kilmacrenan	Conwal
Crogan	C	1	I		Raphoe	Raphoe
Crookshanks	P	1	1	Raphoe	Raphoe	Raphoe
Cudbertson	P	1	18	Shannon	Raphoe	Taughboyne
Cullin	C	1	I	Carrickart	Kilmacrenan	Mevagh
Cullin	I	1	I	Dundooan	Kilmacrenan	Mevagh
Cullin	I	1	I	Glenkoe	Kilmacrenan	Mevagh
Cunningham *	P	1	12	Donboy *	Raphoe	Allsaints
Cunningham *	P	1	12	Portlough	Raphoe	Allsaints
Daugherty	C	1	I	Dundooan	Kilmacrenan	Mevagh
Daugherty	I	1	I	Glenkoe	Kilmacrenan	Mevagh
Daugherty	I	1	I	Meenlaragh	Kilmacrenan	Mevagh
Davison	P	1	20		Raphoe	Raphoe

Surname	R	I	S	Townland	Barony	Place-Parish
Deazley		1			Raphoe	Stranorlar
Denning	I	1	E	Dromore	Raphoe	Leck
Denniston	I	1	E	Drumdutton	Kilmacrenan	Mevagh
Dick	P	1	15		Raphoe	Raphoe
Diver	C	1	I	Ardbane	Kilmacrenan	Mevagh
Dixon	I	1	E	Rawros	Kilmacrenan	Mevagh
Doack	C	1	I		Raphoe	Taughboyne
Dogherty	C	1	I	Carrickart	Kilmacrenan	Mevagh
Dredan	C	1	15		Raphoe	Raphoe
Drummond	P	1	4	Rathmelton	Kilmacrenan	Aughnish
Duffy	C	1	I	Carrickart	Kilmacrenan	Mevagh
Dunbar *	P	1	23	Kilkerhan *	Boylagh	
Duncan	P	1	31		Raphoe	Raphoe
Dunkin	P	1	17	Portlough	Raphoe	Allsaints
Durning,Chas.		1	I		Raphoe	Conwal
Durning,Edw.		1	I		Inishowen	Is. of Inch
Edmiston	P	1	13	Trienmullen*	Raphoe	Taughboyne
Elder	P	1	1	Portlough	Raphoe	Allsaints
Ellue	H	1	F		Kilmacrenan	Killygarvan
Ewing	P	1	12		Raphoe	Raphoe
Faucett	I	1	E	Derrycassan	Kilmacrenan	Mevagh
Faucitt	I	1	E	Meenacross	Kilmacrenan	Mevagh
Ferry	I	1	E	Carrickart	Kilmacrenan	Mevagh
Filson	I	1	E	Maghribue *	Raphoe	Leck
Fleming	P	1	18	Drumboy	Raphoe	Clonleigh
Flood	I	1	E	Meenlaragh	Kilmacrenan	Mevagh
Flood	I	1	E		Raphoe	Raphoe
Forrest	P	1	21	Gortnesk	Raphoe	Raphoe
Forsythe	P	1	9		Raphoe	Raphoe
Fould	P	1	21	Portlough	Raphoe	Allsaints
Frederick,J.	I	1	E		Kilmacrenan	
Fulsan	I	1	E	Drumerdagh	Raphoe	Leck
Gallagher	C	1	I	Ardbane	Kilmacrenan	Mevagh
Gallagher	I	1	I	Tullagh	Kilmacrenan	Mevagh
Gallaugher	I	1	I	Derrycassan	Kilmacrenan	Mevagh
Gamble	I	1	E		Raphoe	Raphoe
Garvill	H	1	F	Lurgybrack	Kilmacrenan	Clondavaddog
Gilgour	P	1	7	Ratein *	Raphoe	Taughboyne

Surname	R	I	S	Townland	Barony	Place-Parish
Gilliece	P	1	21	Ballyshannon	Tirhugh	Inishmacsaint
Gillies	P	1	43	Portlough	Raphoe	Allsaints
Gooleand	P	1	11	Glassegowen *	Raphoe	
Gordon *	P	1	S	Mullaghveagh *	Boylagh	
Gourland	P	1	S	Momeen	Raphoe	Taughboyne
Graham	P	1	9	Carrickart	Kilmacrenan	Mevagh
Graham	P	1	4	Devlin	Kilmacrenan	Mevagh
Gray	I	1	E		Raphoe	Raphoe
Greenham	I	1	E	Tonage	Raphoe	Taughboyne
Grier	P	1	21	Big Park	Tirhugh	Drumhome
Hansard	I	1	E	Monyn	Raphoe	Raphoe
Haran	C	1	I	Ballyshannon	Tirhugh	Inishmacsaint
Harighty	C	1	I	Derrycassan	Kilmacrenan	Mevagh
Harran *	I	1	E	Carrick	Raphoe	Donaghmore
Hart	P	1	15	Taughboyne	Raphoe	Taughboyne
Harvy	I	1	E	Carshoe	Raphoe	Raphoe
Henderson	P	1	7	Loughros	Kilmacrenan	Tullyfern
Heney	C	1	I	Toome	Kilmacrenan	Clondavaddog
Hesson	C	1	I	Toome	Kilmacrenan	Clondavaddog
Hoard	I	1	E	Portlough	Raphoe	Allsaints
Hogshead	P	1	S	Ballybogan	Raphoe	Clonleigh
Hood	I	1	E	Portlough	Raphoe	Allsaints
Hood	I	1	E	Momein	Raphoe	Taughboyne
Howat	I	1	E	Tullirapp	Raphoe	Taughboyne
Hyneman	I	1	E	Beltany L.	Kilmacrenan	
Irwin	I	1	E	Toome	Kilmacrenan	Clondavaddog
Isaic	H	1	G	Portlough	Raphoe	Allsaints
Jervis	P	1	9	Donagh	Kilmacrenan	Clondavaddog
Jessop	I	1	E	Portlough	Raphoe	Allsaints
Johnston	P	1	S		Raphoe	Raphoe
Jonken	Q	1	D	Toome	Kilmacrenan	Clondavaddog
Kelly	C	1	I	Ardbane	Kilmacrenan	Mevagh
Kinkead	P	1	S		Raphoe	Allsaints
Kirkwood	I	1	E	Trimra	Raphoe	Leck
Knee	P	1	S		Raphoe	Leck
Knox	P	1	S		Raphoe	Raphoe
Kyle	C	1	I		Raphoe	Raphoe
Kyle	C	1	I		Kilmacrenan	Tullyfern

Surname	R	I	S	Townland	Barony	Place-Parish
Laird	P	1	S	Assmoyne*	Raphoe	Raphoe
Lata		1		Taghboyne	Raphoe	Clonleigh
Lawrey	P	1	S		Raphoe	Raphoe
Leaky	I	1	E		Bannagh	Inishkeel
Lennox	P	1	10	Portlough	Raphoe	Allsaints
Letch	I	1	E	Cullin	Raphoe	Leck
Lieper		1		Cargins*	Raphoe	
Lockhart	P	1	15	Creevesmith	Raphoe	Leck
Logue	C	1	I	Carrickart	Kilmacrenan	Mevagh
Logue	C	1	I	Downies	Kilmacrenan	Mevagh
Logue	C	1	I	Drimfin	Kilmacrenan	Mevagh
Logue	P	1	I	Dundooan	Kilmacrenan	Mevagh
Longpill	I	1	E	Portlough	Raphoe	Allsaints
Mac Carran	C	1	I		Raphoe	Raphoe
Mac Cleery	C	1	I		Raphoe	Raphoe
Mac Erlain	P	1	12	Toome	Kilmacrenan	Clondavaddog
Mac Fadin	P	1	29	Carrickart	Kilmacrenan	Mevagh
Mac Gill	C	1	I	Toome	Kilmacrenan	Clondavaddog
Mac Guire	C	1	I		Raphoe	Raphoe
Mac Kelvey	P	1	12		Raphoe	Raphoe
Mac Lorian	P	1		Toome	Kilmacrenan	Clondavaddog
Mac Williams	P	1	23	Toome	Kilmacrenan	Clondavaddog
Macanally	P	1	10	Toome	Kilmacrenan	Clondavaddog
Machan	P	1	I	Ardchilly	Raphoe	Convoy
Magovern	P	1	I		Tirhugh	Inishmacsaint
Mandy	P	1	W	Carrickart	Kilmacrenan	Mevagh
Maris	I	1	E		Raphoe	Raymoghy
Marmaduke	I	1		Raphoe	Raphoe	Raphoe
Martin	I	1	E	Carrickart	Kilmacrenan	Mevagh
Mason	I	1	E		Raphoe	Raymoghy
Maxfield	I	1	E	Portlough	Raphoe	Allsaints
Maxwell	I	1	E	Raforty	Banagh	Inver
Mc Adoe	P	1	S	Portrush	Raphoe	Allsaints
Mc Aulay *	P	1	10	Ballyweagh*	Raphoe	Allsaints
Mc Award	P	1	I	Meenlaragh	Kilmacrenan	Mevagh
Mc Bride	C	1	I	Ardbane	Kilmacrenan	Mevagh
Mc Bride	P	1	I	Carrickart	Kilmacrenan	Mevagh
Mc Bride	P	1	S	Derrycassan	Kilmacrenan	Mevagh

Surname	R	I	S	Townland	Barony	Place-Parish
Mc Bride	P	1	S	Devlinreagh	Kilmacrenan	Mevagh
Mc Bride	C	1	I	Glenoory	Kilmacrenan	Mevagh
Mc Caferty	I	1	I	Ardbane	Kilmacrenan	Mevagh
Mc Clintoc	P	1	S		Raphoe	Raphoe
Mc Clure	P	1	23	Drumlackagh	Kilmacrenan	Mevagh
Mc Clure	P	1	23		Raphoe	Raphoe
Mc Coach	P	1		Rawros	Kilmacrenan	Mevagh
Mc Connel	C	1	I	Island Roy	Kilmacrenan	Mevagh
Mc Connell	C	1	I		Raphoe	Raphoe
Mc Corkill	P	1	S	Portlough	Raphoe	Allsaints
Mc Corkle	P	1	S	Ballehesky	Raphoe	
Mc Cue	C	1	I	Glenkoe	Kilmacrenan	Mevagh
Mc Culloch	P	1	23	Mullaghveagh	Boylagh & B.	
Mc Culloch *	P	1	23	Cargie	Boylagh	
Mc Cutchon	C	1	32	Portlough	Raphoe	Allsaints
Mc Dade	P	1	4	Killarhel		
Mc Elhar	C	1	I	Devlin	Kilmacrenan	Mevagh
Mc Elhar	I	1	I	Devlinreagh	Kilmacrenan	Mevagh
Mc Elhar	C	1	I	Glenoory	Kilmacrenan	Mevagh
Mc Elhinney	C	1	I	Island Roy	Kilmacrenan	Mevagh
Mc Elhinney	C	1	I	Maghera Beg	Kilmacrenan	Mevagh
Mc Elhir	C	1	I	DerryCassan	Kilmacrenan	Mevagh
Mc Fadin	I	1	I	Carrickart	Kilmacrenan	Mevagh
Mc Fadin	I	1	I	Doagh	Kilmacrenan	Mevagh
Mc Fadin	C	1	I	Glenieragh	Kilmacrenan	Mevagh
Mc Farlan	P	1	10	Portlough	Raphoe	Allsaints
Mc Garvey	I	1	I	Drimfin	Kilmacrenan	Mevagh
Mc Garvey	C	1	I	Mgrymagrn	Kilmacrenan	Mevagh
Mc Getigan	P	1	S	Drumlackagh	Kilmacrenan	Mevagh
Mc Getigan	C	1	I	Glenieragh	Kilmacrenan	Mevagh
Mc Ginly	C	1	I	Derrycassan	Kilmacrenan	Mevagh
Mc Ginly	C	1	I	Meenformal	Kilmacrenan	Mevagh
Mc Grody	P	1	S	Ardbane	Kilmacrenan	Mevagh
Mc Hugh	C	1	I	Tullagh	Kilmacrenan	Mevagh
Mc Intire	C	1	I	Dundooan	Kilmacrenan	Mevagh
Mc Kee	P	1	12	Cargie	Boylagh & B.	
Mc Kee *	P	1	12	Cargie	Boylagh	
Mc Kinney	P	1	11	Glenoughly	Raphoe	Leck

Surname	R	I	S	Townland	Barony	Place-Parish
Mc Laferty	P	1	26	Derrycassan	Kilmacrenan	Mevagh
Mc Neale	P	1	15	Toome	Kilmacrenan	Clondavaddog
Mc Neevein	P	1	S	Tullyrap	Raphoe	Taughboyne
Mc Nevin	I	1	E		Raphoe	Raphoe
Mc Nulty	C	1	I	Carrickart	Kilmacrenan	Mevagh
Mc Robb	P	1	4	Drumenan	Raphoe	Conwal
Mc Ward	C	1	I	Glenkoe	Kilmacrenan	Mevagh
Menzes	P	1	S		Bannagh	Inishkeel
Mickey	P	1	S		Raphoe	Conwal
Mills	P	1	1		Raphoe	Raymoghy
Mitchell	P	1	S		Raphoe	Raphoe
Moody	I	1	E		Raphoe	Raphoe
Moore	P	1	I	Carrickart	Kilmacrenan	Mevagh
Moore	I	1	E	Island Roy	Kilmacrenan	Mevagh
Moryson	P	1	37	Portlough	Raphoe	Allsaints
Murray	P	1	S	Mullaghveagh	Boylagh & B.	
Murray	P	1	S		Raphoe	Raphoe
Murray *	P	1	23	Kilkerhan	Boylagh	
Myegah	I	1		Carshoe	Raphoe	Raphoe
Nearne	C	1	I	Tullyrap	Raphoe	Taughboyne
Neesson	C	1	I	Toome	Kilmacrenan	Clondavaddog
Nesbit	I	1	E		Raphoe	Raphoe
Nevin	I	1	E		Raphoe	Raphoe
Nixon	Q	1	S		Tirhugh	Inishmacsaint
Noble	I	1	E	Cashell	Raphoe	Kilteevoge
O' Donnell	C	1	I	Meenformal	Kilmacrenan	Mevagh
O' Donnell	C	1	I	Meenlaragh	Kilmacrenan	Mevagh
O' Neale	C	1	I	Toome	Kilmacrenan	Clondavaddog
Packenham	I	1	E	Kilbarron	Tirhugh	Kilbarron
Park	P	1	17	Devlin	Kilmacrenan	Mevagh
Pedin	I	1	E	Cloghfin	Raphoe	Clonleigh
Peebles	P	1	7	Lifford	Raphoe	Clonleigh
Peoples	P	1	7	Maghera Beg	Kilmacrenan	Mevagh
Pettigrew	H	1	F	Glassegowan*	Raphoe	
Porterfield	I	1	E	Ballylennon	Raphoe	Taughboyne
Quale	C	1	I	Raphoe	Raphoe	Raphoe
Rankin	P	1	1	Corcamon	Raphoe	Donaghmore
Rees	P	1				

Surname	R	I	S	Townland	Barony	Place-Parish
Roper	I	1	E	Knockfare	Raphoe	Stranorlar
Sands	C	1	7	Moneymore	Raphoe	Raymoghy
Scott	P	1	15	Tullymore	Kilmacrenan	Gartan
Scott	P	1	S	Ardara	Banagh	Killybegs
Semple	P	1	E	Letterkenny	Kilmacrenan	Conwal
Shiels	P	1	20	Ardbane	Kilmacrenan	Mevagh
Shiels	C	1	20	Drumies	Kilmacrenan	Mevagh
Shiels	C	1	15	Derrycassan	Kilmacrennan	Mevagh
Simms	I	1	E	Rawros	Kilmacrenan	Mevagh
Simson	P	2	15	Toome	Kilmacrenan	Clondavaddog
Snodgrass	P	1	S	Beltany	Raphoe	Raphoe
Speir(Speer)	P	1	4	Kill	Kilmacrenan	Mevagh
Starrit	I	1	E	Drumlackagh	Kilmacrenan	Mevagh
Stincean	P	1	S	Leganathraw	Raphoe	Taughboyne
Storrett	P	1	S	Gortlush	Raphoe	Allsaints
Strain	C	1	I	Downies	Kilmacrenan	Mevagh
Sweeney	C	1	I	Carrickart	Kilmacrenan	Mevagh
Sweeney	C	1	I	Glenkoe	Kilmacrenan	Mevagh
Sweeney	P	1	I	Meenformal	Kilmacrenan	Mevagh
Syms	I	1	E	Baractcla*		
Torenline	I	1	E	Drumore	Raphoe	Leck
Triwews	I	1	E	Carnshannagh	Raphoe	Taughboyne
Tyford	I	1	E	Raphoe	Raphoe	Raphoe
Vaughn	P	1	W	Buncrana	Inishowen W.	Fahan L.
Ward	C	1	I	Glenkoe	Kilmacrenan	Mevagh
Warke	I	1	E	Drumore	Raphoe	Leck
Watson	P	1	7	Rawros	Kilmacrenan	Mevagh
Wigton *	P	1	S	Raphoe	Raphoe	Raphoe
Wilky	I	1	E	Ardaganna	Raphoe	Leck
Williams	I	1		Carrickart	Kilmacrenan	Mevagh
Willock	I	1	E	Cloghfin	Raphoe	Clonleigh
Wilson	I	1	E	Drumlackagh	Kilmacrenan	Mevagh
Wilson	I	1	E	Maghera Beg	Kilmacrenan	Mevagh
Worisky	I	1	E	Kill	Kilmacrenan	Mevagh

Map of Derry

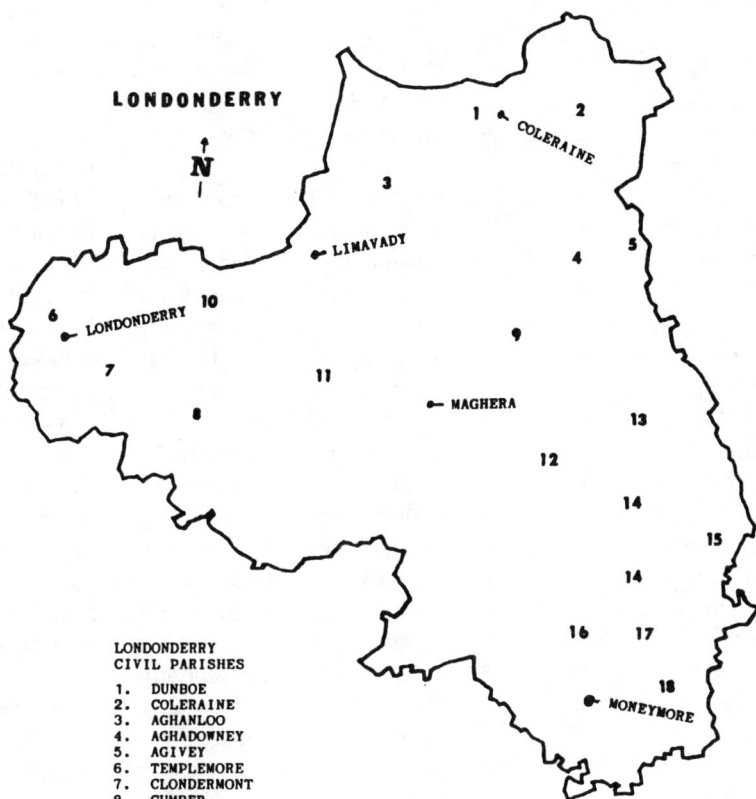

LONDONDERRY

N

1. COLERAINE
2.
3.
LIMAVADY
4. 5.
6. LONDONDERRY 10
7. 11
8.
9.
MAGHERA
13
12
14
15
14
16 17
18 MONEYMORE

LONDONDERRY
CIVIL PARISHES

1. DUNBOE
2. COLERAINE
3. AGHANLOO
4. AGHADOWNEY
5. AGIVEY
6. TEMPLEMORE
7. CLONDERMONT
8. CUMBER
9. ERRIGAL
10. FAUGHANVALE
11. BOVEGA
12. KILLELAGH
13. TAMLAGHT O'
14. MAGHERA
15. BALLYSCULLION
16. DESERTMARTIN
17. MAGHERAFELT
18. ARTREA

Name	R	I	S	Townland	Barony	Place-Parish
Abercromby	P	2	7	Desertmartin	Loughinsholin	Desertmartin
Adams	I	2	E	Ballymoney	Coleraine	Dunboe
Adams	I	2	E	Culmore	Keenaght	Tamlaght O'
Allisob	I	2	E	Londonderry	Londonderry	Templemore
Apton	I	2	E	Londonderry	Londonderry	Templemore
Arbutton	I	2	2	Londonderry	Londonderry	Templemore
Ardock	I	2	E	Londonderry	Londonderry	Templemore
Armsteed	I	2	E	Londonderry	Londonderry	Templemore
Asbisson		2		Londonderry	Londonderry	Templemore
Ash	I	2	E	Londonderry	Londonderry	Templemore
Babington	I	2	E	Londonderry	Londonderry	Templemore
Baker	I	2	E	Moneymore	Loughinsholin	Artrea
Baldrich	I	2	E	Londonderry	Londonderry	Templemore
Balfour	I	2	7	Desertmartin	Loughinsholin	Desertmartin
Bar	P	2		Lissaghmore	Coleraine	Agivey
Bateson	P	2	7	Londonderry	Londonderry	Templemore
Bayley	I	2	E	Londonderry	Londonderry	Templemore
Beaman	I	2	E	Londonderry	Londonderry	Templemore
Bennett	I	2	20	Colerane	Coleraine	Colerane
Bennett	P	2	20	Londonderry	Londonderry	Templemore
Betts	P	2	7	Londonderry	Londonderry	Templemore
Black	P	2	6	Londonderry	Londonderry	Templemore
Blair	P	2	7	Londonderry	Londonderry	Templemore
Blair	P	2	7	Londonderry	Londonderry	Templemore
Bonner	Q	2	4	Londonderry	Londonderry	Templemore
Boyd	P	2	12	Londonderry	Londonderry	Templemore
Britton	I	2	E	Magherafelt	Loughinsholin	Magherafelt
Brolly	C	2	I		Keenaght	Bovevagh
Broome	I	2	E	Londonderry	Londonderry	Templemore
Brown	P	2	13	Bellaghy	Loughinsholin	Ballyscullion
Brunett	P	2	18	Londonderry	Londonderry	Templemore
Buchanan	P	2	9	Londonderry	Londonderry	Templemore
Burnett	I	2	E		Loughinsholin	Artrea
Campbell	P	2	6	Londonderry	Londonderry	Templemore
Campse	P	2	9	Londonderry	Londonderry	Templemore
Campsie	P	2	9	Londonderry	Londonderry	Templemore
Canning	I	2	E	Lissaghmore	Coleraine	Agivey

Page 51

Name	R	I	S	Townland	Barony	Place-Parish
Canning	I	2	E	Garvagh	Coleraine	Errigal
Carr	P	2	17	Londonderry	Londonderry	Templemore
Chamberlyn	I	2	E	Lissaghmore	Coleraine	Agivey
Church	I	2	E	Lissaghmore	Coleraine	Agivey
Clandinning	-	2	-	Drummaney	Tirkeeran	Faughanvale
Clarke	P	2	7	Londonderry	Londonderry	Templemore
Clements	P	2	10	Londonderry	Londonderry	Templemore
Cocken	P	2	7	Londonderry	Londonderry	Templemore
Collon	P	2		Lissaghmore	Coleraine	Agivey
Cott	P	2	4	Londonderry	Londonderry	Templemore
Coulburn	P	2	7	Londonderry	Londonderry	Templemore
Crofton	C	2	I	Londonderry	Londonderry	Templemore
Curling	P	2	S	Londonderry	Londonderry	Templemore
Cust	I	2	E	Londonderry	Londonderry	Templemore
Darcus	I	2	E	Londonderry	Londonderry	Templemore
Davis	P	2	W	Corlackie	Loughinsholin	Killelagh
Davyes	P	2	1	Londonderry	Londonderry	Templemore
de Blaquiere	P	2	F	Ardkill	Tirkeeran	Clondermot
Deglees		2		Londonderry	Londonderry	Templemore
Denning	I	2	E	Londonderry	Londonderry	Templemore
Dennison	P	2	11	Londonderry	Londonderry	Templemore
Dent	I	2	E	Londonderry	Londonderry	Templemore
Dixon	I	2	E	Lissaghmore	Coleraine	Agivey
Douglas	P	2	21			
Downing	I	2	E	Bellaghy	Loughinsholin	Ballyscullion
Downing	I	2	E	Londonderry	Londonderry	Templemore
Duckett	I	2	E	Londonderry	Londonderry	Templemore
Duddle	I	2	E	Londonderry	Londonderry	Templemore
Dyermond	I	2	E		Tirkeeran	Cumber
Dysart	P	2	7	Londonderry	Londonderry	Templemore
Eady	P	2	1	Londonderry	Londonderry	Templemore
Ebbitt	I	2	E	Londonderry	Londonderry	Templemore
Entrikin		2		Londonderry	Londonderry	Templemore
Fane	I	2	E	Londonderry	Londonderry	Templemore
Fane	I	2	E	Londonderry	Londonderry	Templemore
Faulkner	I	2	E	Londonderry	Londonderry	Templemore
Fawcett	I	2	E	Londonderry	Londonderry	Templemore

Name	R	I	S	Townland	Barony	Place-Parish
Fenny	C	2	I	Londonderry	Londonderry	Templemore
Ferrier	H	2	F	Londonderry	Londonderry	Templemore
Ffyliff	I	2	E	Londonderry	Londonderry	Templemore
Fibs		2		Londonderry	Londonderry	Templemore
Fifield	I	2	E	Londonderry	Londonderry	Templemore
Figsby	I	2	E	Londonderry	Londonderry	Templemore
Fisher	I	2	E	Londonderry	Londonderry	Templemore
Flemin	Q	2	18	Londonderry	Londonderry	Templemore
Forward	I	2	E	Londonderry	Londonderry	Templemore
Fuller	P	2	15	Londonderry	Londonderry	Templemore
Fullerton	P	2	12	Londonderry	Londonderry	Templemore
Fulton	P	2	12	Londonderry	Londonderry	Templemore
Gailbraith	P	2	26	Londonderry	Londonderry	Templemore
Galtworth	I	2	E	Londonderry	Londonderry	Templemore
Gardner	I	2	E	Londonderry	Londonderry	Templemore
Garnet	I	2	E	Londonderry	Londonderry	Templemore
Garven	P	2		Lissaghmore	Coleraine	Agivey
Gemett	C	2	I	Londonderry	Londonderry	Templemore
Gilbraith	P	2	26	Londonderry	Londonderry	Templemore
Godfrey	I	2	E	Londonderry	Londonderry	Templemore
Goodlett	P	2	7	Londonderry	Londonderry	Templemore
Gordon	P	2	22	Londonderry	Londonderry	Templemore
Gorrey	P	2	4	Londonderry	Londonderry	Templemore
Gould	I	2	E	Lissaghmore	Coleraine	Agivey
Graham	P	2	9	Londonderry	Londonderry	Templemore
Greer *	C	2	21	Maghera *	Loughinsholin	Magherafelt
Gregg	P	2	7	Londonderry	Londonderry	Templemore
Grigson	I	2	E	Londonderry	Londonderry	Templemore
Grove	I	2	E	Londonderry	Londonderry	Templemore
Hagan *	C	2	I		Loughinsholin	Artrea
Hall	I	2	E	Desertmartin	Loughinsholin	Desertmartin
Hallart	I	2	E	Desertmartin	Loughinsholin	Desertmartin
Hamilton	P	2	11	Moneymore	Loughinsholin	Artrea
Hammon	C	2	I	Desertmartin	Loughinsholin	Desertmartin
Harris	I	2	E	Desertmartin	Loughinsholin	Desertmartin
Heatherton	I	2	E	Desertmartin	Loughinsholin	Desertmartin
Hicks	I	2	E		Loughinsholin	Desertmartin

Name	R	I	S	Townland	Barony	Place-Parish
Hilhouse	P	2	12	Ballycastle	Keenaght	Aghanloo
Hilhouse	P	2	12	Londonderry	Londonderry	Templemore
Hill	I	2	E	Londonderry	Londonderry	Templemore
Hilton	P	2	17		Londonderry	Templemore
Hinkell	H	2	G	Londonderry	Londonderry	Templemore
Hipson	P	2	21	Desertmartin	Loughinsholin	Desertmartin
Hitchin	I	2	E	Londonderry	Londonderry	Templemore
Horner	P	2	12	Desertmartin	Loughinsholin	Desertmartin
Hosh	I	2	E	Desertmartin	Loughinsholin	Desertmartin
Houston	P	2	13	Desertmartin	Loughinsholin	Desertmartin
Howden	P	2	20	Desertmartin	Loughinsholin	Desertmartin
Hoy	C	2	12	Desertmartin	Loughinsholin	Desertmartin
Humes	P	2	17	Derry	Londonderry	Templemore
Hurst	I	2	E	Desertmartin	Loughinsholin	Desertmartin
Islen	I	2	E	Londonderry	Londonderry	Templemore
Jenny	I	2	E	Londonderry	Londonderry	Templemore
Johnston	P	2	20	Moneymore	Loughinsholin	Artrea
Johnston	P	2	21	Derry	Londonderry	Templemore
Kaey	P	2	15	Desertmartin	Loughinsholin	Desertmartin
Kidd	I	2	E	Moneymore	Loughinsholin	Artrea
Kinade	P	2	15	Desertmartin	Loughinsholin	Desertmartin
King	I	2	E	Londonderry	Londonderry	Templemore
Kitchen	I	2	E	Desertmartin	Loughinsholin	Desertmartin
Kmow	P	2	S	Londonderry	Londonderry	Templemore
Lane	C	2	I	Londonderry	Londonderry	Templemore
Larmock	P	2	1	Desertmartin	Loughinsholin	Desertmartin
Law *	P	2	S	Garvagh	Coleraine	Errigal
Leacock	P	2	15	Desertmartin	Loughinsholin	Desertmartin
Lee	I	2	E	Desertmartin	Loughinsholin	Desertmartin
Leeson	I	2	E	Londonderry	Londonderry	Templemore
Lithgow	P	2	S	Clondermont	Tirkennedy	Clendermot
Logan	P	2	15	Derry	Londonderry	Templemore
Lough	C	2	I	Desertmartin	Loughinsholin	Desertmartin
Lundy	I	2	E	Londonderry	Londonderry	Templemore
Lyndsie	P	2		Londonderry	Londonderry	Templemore
Mac Cory	C	2	I	Moneymore	Loughinsholin	Artrea
Mac Elhone	C	2	I	Moneymore	Loughinsholin	Artrea

Name	R	I	S	Townland	Barony	Place-Parish
Mac Guide	C	2	I	Moneymore	Loughinsholin	Artrea
Mac Gulpin	C	2	I	Moneymore	Loughinsholin	Artrea
Mac Loinan	C	2	I	Moneymore	Loughinsholin	Artrea
Mac Neal	P	2	31	Moneymore	Loughinsholin	Artrea
Mac Neil	P	2	15	Desertmartin	Loughinsholin	Desertmartin
Mac Peake	C	2	I	Londonderry	Londonderry	Templemore
Mac Quig	P	2	I	Moneymore	Loughinsholin	Artrea
Mac Sparron	C	2	I	Moneymore	Loughinsholin	Artrea
Mackedow	P	2	S		Londonderry	Templemore
Macool	C	2	I	Desertmartin	Loughinsholin	Desertmartin
Maghlin	P	2	I	Londonderry	Londonderry	Templemore
Magorran	C	2	I	Desertmartin	Loughinsholin	Desertmartin
Magory	C	2		Desertmartin	Loughinsholin	Desertmartin
Magullion	C	2	I	Desertmartin	Loughinsholin	Desertmartin
Makilly	C	2	I	Desertmartin	Loughinsholin	Desertmartin
Maleer	I	2	E	Desertmartin	Loughinsholin	Desertmartin
Mallon	P	2	S	Moneymore	Loughinsholin	Artrea
Manson	I	2	E	Londonderry	Londonderry	Templemore
Mardock	I	2	E	Desertmartin	Loughinsholin	Desertmartin
Matters	P	2	1	Desertmartin	Loughinsholin	Desertmartin
Mauleverer	I	2	E	Londonderry	Londonderry	Templemore
Maxwell	I	2	E	Londonderry	Londonderry	Templemore
Mc Alister	P	2	6	Desertmartin	Loughinsholin	Desertmartin
Mc Cafer	C	2	I		Londonderry	Templemore
Mc Causland	P	2	10	Dreenagh		
Mc Cayne	P	2	S	Desertmartin	Loughinsholin	Desertmartin
Mc Clhenny	P	2	S	Londonderry	Londonderry	Templemore
Mc Culloch	P	2	6	Londonderry	Londonderry	Templemore
Mc Gilahattan	I	2	I		Londonderry	Templemore
Mc Glaggan	C	2	I	Londonderry	Londonderry	Templemore
Mc Hatten	C	2	I	Londonderry	Londonderry	Templemore
Mc Hilbrown		2		Londonderry	Londonderry	Templemore
Mc Kelvey	P	2	21	Desertmartin	Loughinsholin	Desertmartin
Mc Lean	P	2	29	Moneymore	Loughinsholin	Artrea
Mc Linnan	C	2	S	Desertmartin	Loughinsholin	Desertmartin
Mc Loghlin	C	2	I	Desertmartin	Loughinsholin	Desertmartin
Mc Lorinan	C	2	I	Moneymore	Loughinsholin	Artrea

Name	R	I	S	Townland	Barony	Place-Parish
Mecue	C	2	I	Desertmartin	Loughinsholin	Desertmartin
Megart	P	2	21	Desertmartin	Loughinsholin	Desertmartin
Megue	C	2	I	Desertmartin	Loughinsholin	Desertmartin
Mitchel	P	2	12	Moneymore	Loughinsholin	Artrea
Moffett	P	2	21	Londonderry	Londonderry	Templemore
Moncreiff	P	2	S	Londonderry	Londonderry	Templemore
Monday	C	2	I		Tirkeeran	Cumber
Monry	I	2	E	Londonderry	Londonderry	Templemore
Montgomery	P	2	11	Desertmartin	Loughinsholin	Desertmartin
Moody	P	2	E	Londonderry	Londonderry	Templemore
Moore	I	2	E	Londonderry	Londonderry	Templemore
Morgan	P	2	W	Londonderry	Londonderry	Templemore
Morovonagh	P	2	S	Desertmartin	Loughinsholin	Desertmartin
Morrow	I	2	E	Londonderry	Londonderry	Templemore
Mulholland	C	2	I	Londonderry	Londonderry	Templemore
Mullan	C	2	I	Desertmartin	Loughinsholin	Desertmartin
Murphy	C	2	I	Moneymore	Loughinsholin	Artrea
Nevins	I	2	E	Moneymore	Loughinsholin	Artrea
Newcomb	I	2	E	Londonderry	Londonderry	Templemore
Newton	I	2	E	Londonderry	Londonderry	Templemore
Noble	P	2	10	Desertmartin	Loughinsholin	Desertmartin
Noble	I	2	E	Londonderry	Londonderry	Templemore
Nogher	C	2	I	Desertmartin	Loughinsholin	Desertmartin
O' Kain	P	2	I	Desertmartin	Loughinsholin	Desertmartin
O' Kane	C	2	I	Moneymore	Loughinsholin	Artrea
O' Larkion	C	2	I	Moneymore	Loughinsholin	Artrea
Orr	P	2	12	Desertmartin	Loughinsholin	Desertmartin
Orr	P	2	11	Londonderry	Londonderry	Templemore
Ourvis	P	2	S	Desertmartin	Loughinsholin	Desertmartin
Owns	P	2	W	Desertmartin	Loughinsholin	Desertmartin
Phelan	C	2	I	Moneymore	Loughinsholin	Artrea
Phillips	I	2	21	Londonderry	Londonderry	Templemore
Pollock	P	2	11	Londonderry	Londonderry	Templemore
Ponsonby	C	2	E	Londonderry	Londonderry	Templemore
Portus	P	2	18	Desertmartin	Loughinsholin	Desertmartin
Poslitt	P	2	E	Londonderry	Londonderry	Templemore
Pots	P	2	15	Desertmartin	Loughinsholin	Desertmartin

Name	R	I	S	Townland	Barony	Place-Parish
Poulton	I	2	E	Londonderry	Londonderry	Templemore
Purvey	C	2	17	Moneymore	Loughinsholin	Artrea
Quigley	C	2	I	Moneymore	Loughinsholin	Artrea
Ramsey	P	2	3	Moneymore	Loughinsholin	Artrea
Ramsey	P	2	3	Londonderry	Londonderry	Templemore
Rankin	P	2	12	Desertmartin	Loughinsholin	Desertmartin
Rankin	P	2	S	Londonderry	Londonderry	Templemore
Reed	I	2	E	Aghadowey	Coleraine	Aghadowey
Reston	P	2	12	Desertmartin	Loughinsholin	Desertmartin
Rice	P	2	W	Londonderry	Londonderry	Templemore
Riddle	P	2	12	Londonderry	Londonderry	Templemore
Robinson	P	2	7	Moneymore	Loughinsholin	Artrea
Robinson	P	2	11	Londonderry	Londonderry	Templemore
Rod	I	2	E	Aghadowey	Coleraine	Aghadowey
Rogers	C	2	E	Londonderry	Londonderry	Templemore
Rossgrow	I	2	E	Desertmartin	Loughinsholin	Desertmartin
Rowley	P	2	20	Londonderry	Londonderry	Templemore
Rullack	P	2	E	Londonderry	Londonderry	Templemore
Rutherford	P	2	5	Moneymore	Loughinsholin	Artrea
Sadler	P	2	20	Londonderry	Londonderry	Templemore
Sanderson	P	2	5	Londonderry	Londonderry	Templemore
Schoales	I	2	E	Londonderry	Londonderry	Templemore
Semple	P	2	E	Londonderry	Londonderry	Templemore
Sharp	P	2	4	Desertmartin	Loughinsholin	Desertmartin
Shiry	I	2	E	Desertmartin	Loughinsholin	Desertmartin
Shoyough		2		Londonderry	Londonderry	Templemore
Sidney	I	2	E	Londonderry	Londonderry	Templemore
Simpson	P	2	12	Moneymore	Loughinsholin	Artrea
Simson	P	2	15	Toome	Kilmacrenan	Clondavaddog
Skinner	P	2	20	Londonderry	Londonderry	Templemore
Skipton	I	2	E	Londonderry	Londonderry	Templemore
Slavin	C	2	E	Desertmartin	Loughinsholin	Desertmartin
Smith	P	2	E	Moneymore	Loughinsholin	Artrea
Smith	I	2	E	Desertmartin	Loughinsholin	Desertmartin
Smyth	P	2	11	Londonderry	Londonderry	Templemore
Spire	I	2	E	Aghadowey	Coleraine	Aghadowey
Spottswood	P	2	17	Londonderry	Londonderry	Templemore

Name	R	I	S	Townland	Barony	Place-Parish
Spratt	I	2	E	Moneymore	Loughinsholin	Artrea
Spraule	P	2	13	Londonderry	Londonderry	Templemore
Squire	I	2	E	Londonderry	Londonderry	Templemore
Steward	P	2	S	Londonderry	Londonderry	Templemore
Stewart	P	2	11	Londonderry	Londonderry	Templemore
Stiles	I	2	E	Londonderry	Londonderry	Templemore
Stockman	I	2	E	Desertmartin	Loughinsholin	Desertmartin
Stoller	H	2	G	Londonderry	Londonderry	Templemore
Stoope	P	2	E	Londonderry	Londonderry	Templemore
Stout	I	2	E	Londonderry	Londonderry	Templemore
Stoyle		2		Londonderry	Londonderry	Templemore
Stoyle		2		Londonderry	Londonderry	Templemore
Sturdyr	P	2	G	Desertmartin	Loughinsholin	Desertmartin
Sturgeon	I	2	E	Londonderry	Londonderry	Templemore
Suden	P	2	N	Londonderry	Londonderry	Templemore
Suden	P	2	N	Londonderry	Londonderry	Templemore
Sullivan	C	2	I	Desertmartin	Loughinsholin	Desertmartin
Taylor	P	2	6			
Tichburn	I	2	E	Desertmartin	Loughinsholin	Desertmartin
Tilford	I	2	E	Londonderry	Londonderry	Templemore
Tobias	I	2	E	Londonderry	Londonderry	Templemore
Tome	I	2	E	Londonderry	Londonderry	Templemore
Tomkins	I	2	E	Londonderry	Londonderry	Templemore
Toomouth	I	2	E	Desertmartin	Loughinsholin	Desertmartin
Tracy	C	2	I	Desertmartin	Loughinsholin	Desertmartin
Truman	I	2	E	Londonderry	Londonderry	Templemore
Tuck	I	2	E	Londonderry	Londonderry	Templemore
Tuckey	I	2	E	Londonderry	Londonderry	Templemore
Veach	I	2	E	Desertmartin	Loughinsholin	Desertmartin
Vildone	H	2	G	Desertmartin	Loughinsholin	Desertmartin
Walker	I	2	E	Londonderry	Londonderry	Templemore
Walker	P	2	17	Londonderry	Londonderry	Templemore
Wallis	P	2	5	Desertmartin	Loughinsholin	Desertmartin
Ward	I	2	E	Aghadowey	Coleraine	Aghadowey
Waterson	P	2	12	Desertmartin	Loughinsholin	Desertmartin
Wetsor	P	2	S	Desertmartin	Loughinsholin	Desertmartin
White	I	2	E	Londonderry	Londonderry	Templemore

Name	R	I	S	Townland	Barony	Place-Parish
Whittlo	I	2	E	Londonderry	Londonderry	Templemore
Whittlo	I	2	E	Londonderry	Londonderry	Templemore
Wilkin	P	2	S	Desertmartin	Loughinsholin	Desertmartin
Wilkins	I	2	E	Londonderry	Londonderry	Templemore
Will *	P	2		Clondermot	Tirkeeran	Clondermot
Wilson	P	2	S	Moneymore	Loughinsholin	Artrea
Woodgate	I	2	E	Londonderry	Londonderry	Templemore
Woodside	I	2	E	Londonderry	Londonderry	Templemore
Woodward	I	2	E	Londonderry	Londonderry	Templemore
Wooley	I	2	E	Londonderry	Londonderry	Templemore
Woore		2		Londonderry	Londonderry	Templemore
Wooten	I	2	E	Londonderry	Londonderry	Templemore
Workman	P	2	E	Moneymore	Loughinsholin	Artrea
Wright	P	2	S	Moneymore	Loughinsholin	artrea
Wytty	I	2	E	Aghadowey	Coleraine	Aghadowey
Young	C	2	I	Londonderry	Londonderry	Templemore

DUNGIVEN CASTLE
LONDONDERRY 1617

Map of Antrim

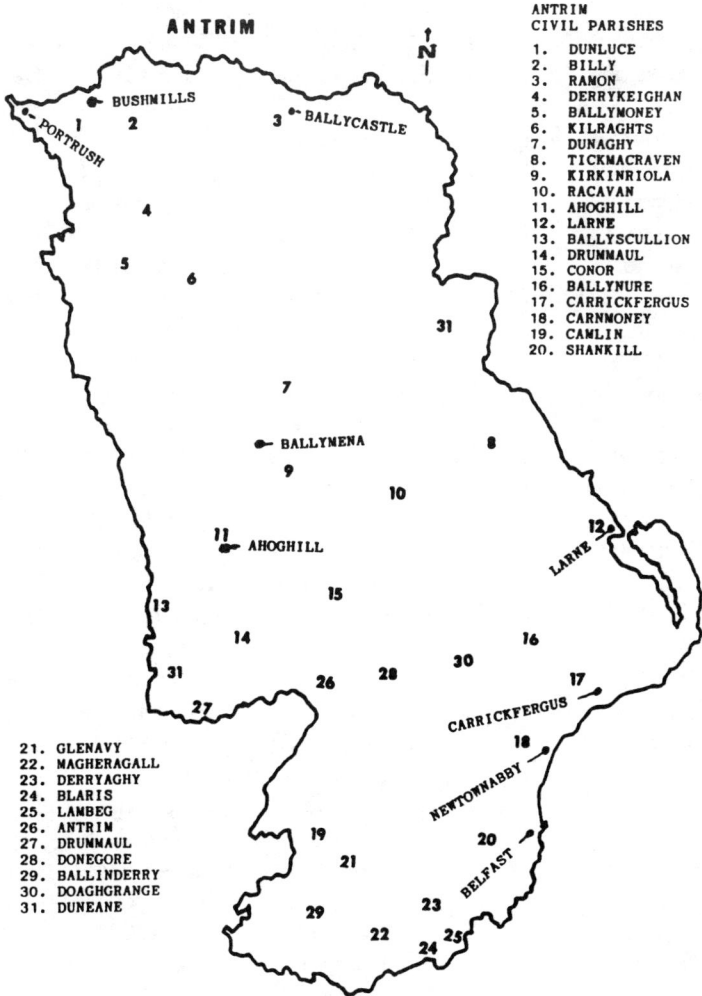

ANTRIM

N

PORTRUSH

BUSHMILLS

BALLYCASTLE

BALLYMENA

AHOGHILL

LARNE

CARRICKFERGUS

NEWTOWNABBY

BELFAST

ANTRIM CIVIL PARISHES

1. DUNLUCE
2. BILLY
3. RAMON
4. DERRYKEIGHAN
5. BALLYMONEY
6. KILRAGHTS
7. DUNAGHY
8. TICKMACRAVEN
9. KIRKINRIOLA
10. RACAVAN
11. AHOGHILL
12. LARNE
13. BALLYSCULLION
14. DRUMMAUL
15. CONOR
16. BALLYNURE
17. CARRICKFERGUS
18. CARNMONEY
19. CAMLIN
20. SHANKILL

21. GLENAVY
22. MAGHERAGALL
23. DERRYAGHY
24. BLARIS
25. LAMBEG
26. ANTRIM
27. DRUMMAUL
28. DONEGORE
29. BALLINDERRY
30. DOAGHGRANGE
31. DUNEANE

Surname	R	I	S	Townland	Barony	Place-Parish
Achey	I	3	7	Derryaghy	Belfast U.	Derryaghy
Adair	C	3	23	Ballymena	Toome	Kirkinriola
Agar	I	3	E	Belfast	Belfast	Shankill
Agnew	C	3	23	Larne	Glenarm	Larne
Aiken	P	3	12	Ballymena	Toome	Kirkinriola
Alderdice	I	3	E	Derryaghy	Belfast U.	Derryaghy
Allot	P	3	S		Dunluce L.	Kilraghts
Armour	P	3	17	Bushmills	Dunluce L.	Dunluce
Armstrong	P	3	21	Crumlin	Massereene	Camlin
Atkinson	I	3	1		Massereene	Derryaghy
Bailey	I	3	13	Derryaghy	Belfast U.	Derryaghy
Banister	I	3	E		Massereene	Derryaghy
Barr	P	3	11	Belfast	Belfast	Shankill
Barron	P	3	21	Antrim	Antrim U.	Antrim
Baxter	P	3	13	Larne	Glenarm	Larne
Beggs	C	3	I	Carrickfergus	Carrickfergus	Carrickfergus
Bell	P	3	21	Ballinderry	Massereene	Ballinderry
Belshaw	I	3	E	Magheragall	Massereene	Magheragall
Bennard	P	3	4	Bushmills	Dunluce L.	Dunluce
Bennett	P	3	20	Carrickfergus	Carrickfergus	Carrickfergus
Bickerstaffe	I	3	E		Massereene	Derryaghy
Blackburn	I	3	E	Derryaghy	Belfast U.	Derryaghy
Blackhall	I	3	E		Belfast U.	Derryaghy
Blackly	I	3	E		Belfast U.	Derryaghy
Blakney	P	3	12	Bushmills	Dunluce L.	Dunluce
Bolton	I	3	21	Glenavey	Massereene	Glenavey
Boyd	P	3	12	Ballygrooby	Toome U.	Drummaul
Boyd	P	3	12	Bushmills	Dunluce L.	Dunluce
Boys	I	3	E	Derryaghy	Belfast U.	Derryaghy
Branah	C	3	I	Derryaghy	Belfast U.	Derryaghy
Brannagh	C	3	I	Ballinderry	Massereene	Ballinderry
Breadley	P	3	I	Derryaghy	Belfast U.	Derryaghy
Brown	P	3	1	Derryaghy	Belfast U.	Derryaghy
Bullmer	I	3	E	Derryaghy	Belfast U.	Derryaghy
Burris	I	3	E	Derryaghy	Belfast U.	Derryaghy
Buttle	I	3	E	Ballymena L.	Belfast	Ballynure
Calkey	I	3	E		Dunluce L.	Billy
Calshinder	I	3	E	Derryaghy	Belfast U.	Derryaghy

Surname	R	I	S	Townland	Barony	Place-Parish
Cannel		3		Derryaghy	Belfast U.	Derryaghy
Cathcart	P	3	11	Randalstown	Toome	Drummaul
Chesnut	I	3	E		Dunluce L.	Derrykeighan
Christian	I	3	E	Derryaghy	Belfast U.	Derryaghy
Christie		3	7	Lisburn	Massereene	Blaris
Clagg	H	3	F	Derryaghy	Belfast U.	Derryaghy
Close	I	3	E	Derryaghy	Belfast U.	Derryaghy
Cobreth	I	3		Derryaghy	Belfast U	Derryaghy
Coburn	P	3	20	Derryaghy	Belfast U.	Derryaghy
Cohoon	P	3	10	Derryaghy	Belfast U.	Derryaghy
Collins	I	3	E	Derryaghy	Belfast U.	Derryaghy
Comberland	I	3	E	Derryaghy	Belfast U.	Derryaghy
Conway	P	3	W	Lisburn	Massereene	Blaris
Corkin	I	3	E	Derryaghy	Belfast U	Derryaghy
Cormichil	P	3	13	Derryaghy	Belfast U.	Derryaghy
Corr	C	3	I	Derryaghy	Belfast U.	Derryaghy
Courtney	I	3	E	Grange Pk.	Toome	Ballyscullion
Crawford	P	3	12	Donegore	Antrim	Donegore
Croan	C	3	I	Derryaghy	Belfast U.	Derryaghy
Cromlin	Q	3	F	Derryaghy	Belfast U.	Derryaghy
Crooks	P	3	13	Ballykelly	Massereene	Ballinderry
Cumming	P	3	1	Kilraghts	Dunlance	Kilraghts
Cunningham *	P	3	12	Broadisland*		
Cushnahan	C	3	I	Derryaghy	Belfast U.	Derryaghy
Dawson	P	3	5			
De Balquiere	H	3	F	Lisburn	Massereene	Blaris
De La Cherois	H	3	F	Lisburn	Massereene	Blaris
Dein	P	3	1	Derryaghy	Belfast U.	Derryaghy
Dela Brentone	P	3	F	Belfast	Belfast	Shankill
Dewart	P	3	15	Connor	Antrim L.	Connor
Dimon	I	3	E	Derryaghy	Belfast U.	Derryaghy
Douglass	P	3	13	Broughshane	Antrim L.	Racavan
Drake	I	3	E	Derryaghy	Belfast U.	Derryaghy
Duncan	P	3	1	Derryaghy	Belfast U	Derryaghy
Dunlap	I	3	12	Derryaghy	Belfast U.	Derryaghy
Dunlop	P	3	12	Ballymena	Toome	Kirkinriola
Eager	I	3	17	Derryaghy	Belfast U.	Derryaghy
Eiles	I	3	E	Derryaghy	Belfast U.	Derryaghy

Surname	R	I	S	Townland	Barony	Place-Parish
Farril	C	3	I	Derryaghy	Belfast U.	Derryaghy
Fleming	P	3	18	Glenarm	Glenarm L.	Tickmacrevan
Foreman	I	3	E	Derryaghy	Belfast U.	Derryaghy
Forsythe	P	3	9	Rosedermot	Kilconway	Dunaghy
Frizill	I	3	E	Derryaghy	Belfast U.	Derryaghy
Fullerton	P	3	12	Ballynure	Belfast	Ballynure
Fulton	P	3	12	Carnmoney	Belfast	Carnmoney
Galley	I	3	33	Derryaghy	Belfast U.	Derryaghy
Gayer	I	3	E	Derryaghy	Belfast U.	Derryaghy
Geneste	H	3	F	Lisburn	Massereene	Blaris
George	P	3	E	Moyrusk	Massereene	Magheragall
Getty	Q	3	E	Belfast	Belfast	Shankill
Gibson	Q	3	21	Belfast	Belfast	Shankill
Glenfield	I	3	E	Derryaghy	Belfast U.	Derryaghy
Golether	C	3	I	Derryaghy	Belfast U.	Derryaghy
Gordon	C	3	17	Carnlough	Glenarm	Ardclinis
Gormley	C	3	I	Magheragall	Massereene	Magheragall
Goyer	H	3	F	Lisburn	Massereene	Blaris
Graham	C	3	9			
Grahams	I	3	4	Derryaghy	Belfast U.	Derryaghy
Grainger	P	3	20	Derryaghy	Belfast U.	Derryaghy
Green	C	3	I	Derryaghy	Belfast U.	Derryaghy
Gribib	H	3	F	Derryaghy	Belfast U.	Derryaghy
Grimbs	I	3	E	Derryaghy	Belfast U.	Derryaghy
Grogan	C	3	I	Derryaghy	Belfast U.	Derryaghy
Guillot	H	3	F	Lisburn	Massereene	Blaris
Hamel	I	3	12		Messereene	Derryaghy
Hamilton	P	3	23	Bushmills	Dunluce L.	Dunluce
Hannah	I	3	E		Belfast	Derryaghy
Harper	I	3	E	Bushmills	Dunluce L.	Dunluce
Harrison	I	3	E	Bushmills	Dunluce L.	Dunluce
Hart	I	3	E	Derryaghy	Belfast U.	Derryaghy
Hastings	I	3	20		Massereene	Derryaghy
Hay	I	3	23	Derryaghy	Belfast U.	Derryaghy
Heney	C	3	I	Moyrusk	Massereene	Magheragall
Hodsmyth	I	3	E	Derryaghy	Belfast U.	Derryaghy
Hogg	I	3	4	Derryaghy	Belfast U.	Derryaghy
Hogsyard *	P	3	11			

Surname	R	I	S	Townland	Barony	Place-Parish
Holden	I	3	E	Ballyclare	Antrim U.	Dona Grange
Howard	I	3	E	Derryaghy	Belfast U.	Derryaghy
Hudson	I	3	E	Derryaghy	Belfast U.	Derryaghy
Hueston	P	3	31	Creggan	Toome U.	Duneane
Huey	P	3	6		Belfast	Derryaghy
Hunter	I	3	11	Derryaghy	Belfast U.	Derryaghy
Hunter	P	3	12	Ballygrooby	Toome	Drummaul
Hutchison	P	3	1	Bushmills	Dunluce L.	Dunluce
Johnson	I	3	21	Derryaghy	Belfast U.	Derryaghy
Kennedy	P	3	12	Glengormley	Belfast	Carnmoney
Kennedy	P	3	S	Templepatrick	Belfast	Templepatrick
Ker	P	3	20	Ballymoney	Belfast	Shankill
Kernahan	C	3	I	Derryaghy	Belfast U.	Derryaghy
Kerney	C	3	I	Derryaghy	Belfast U.	Derryaghy
Keyes	I	3	E	Bushmills	Dunluce L.	Dunluce
Keyes	I	3	E	Belfast	Belfast	Shankill
Kidd	P	3	E	Derryaghy	Belfast U.	Derryaghy
Killpatrick	I	3	10	Derryaghy	Belfast U.	Derryaghy
Kirrigan	C	3	I	Derryaghy	Belfast U.	Derryaghy
Knox	P	3	11	Balleymoney	Dunlance	Ballymoney
La Vallade	H	3	F	Lisburn	Massereene	Blaris
Lamont	P	3	6			
Lamour	I	3	E	Ballinderry	Massereene	Ballinderry
Land	I	3	E	Derryaghy	Belfast U.	Derryaghy
Laverty	C	3	I	Derryaghy	Belfast U.	Derryaghy
Lawson	I	3	21	Derryaghy	Belfast U.	Derryaghy
le Burt	P	3	F	Belfast	Belfast	Shankill
Lennox	P	3	10	Ballygrooby	Toome	Drummaul
Linn	P	3	12	Magheragall	Massereene	Magheragall
Litter	I	3	E	Derryaghy	Belfast U.	Derryaghy
Little	P	3	1	Bushmills	Dunluce L.	Dunluce
Logan	P	3	13	Carrickfergus	Carrickfergus	Carrickfergus
Logen	I	3	13	Derryaghy	Belfast U.	Derryaghy
Loggan	P	3	12	Ahoghill	Toome	Ahoghill
Longmoor	I	3	E	Bushmills	Dunluce L.	Dunluce
Love	P	3	11	Dunlance	Dunlance	Ballymoney
Lun	I	3		Derryaghy	Belfast U.	Derryaghy
Mac Clelland	P	3	22	Ballycastle	Cary	Ramoan

Surname	R	I	S	Townland	Barony	Place-Parish
Machlin	P	3	S	Derryaghy	Belfast U.	Derryaghy
MacKine	C	3	I	Ballygrooby	Toome	Drummaul
Madole	C	3	I	Bushmills	Dunluce L.	Dunluce
Magee	C	3	I	Bushmills	Dunluce L.	Dunluce
Mains	P	3	S	Bushmills	Dunluce L.	Dunluce
Marsden	I	3	E		Belfast	Derryaghy
Marshall	P	3	15	Bushmills	Dunluce L.	Dunluce
Martin	P	3	7	Bushmills	Dunluce L.	Dunluce
Mathes	I	3	E	Derryaghy	Belfast U.	Derryaghy
May	C	3	I	Ballinderry	Massereene	Ballinderry
Mc Alester	I	3	21		Belfast	Derryaghy
Mc Bride	C	3	I	Bushmills	Dunluce L.	Dunluce
Mc Call	P	3	S	Derryaghy	Belfast U.	Derryaghy
Mc Cartney	P	3	21			
Mc Chesney	P	3	2	Bushmills	Dunluce L.	Dunluce
Mc Clean	C	3	12	Derryaghy	Belfast U.	Derryaghy
Mc Clemens	P	3	S	Bushmills	Dunluce L.	Dunluce
Mc Cloy	P	3	10	Carrickfergus	Carrickfergus	Carickfergus
Mc Cloyster	P	3	I	Derryaghy	Belfast U.	Derryaghy
Mc Clune	P	3	12	Bushmills	Dunluce L.	Dunluce
Mc Clurg	P	3	12	Bushmills	Dunluce L.	Dunluce
Mc Comb	P	3	23	Belfast	Belfast	Shankill
Mc Cracken	P	3	I	Derryaghy	Belfast U.	Derryaghy
Mc Creery	P	3	5	Belfast	Belfast	Shankill
Mc Creight	C	3	23		Massereene	Derryaghy
Mc Crusky	P	3	23	Lisburn	Belfast	Lambeg
Mc Cublagh	I	3	S	Derryaghy	Belfast U.	Derryaghy
Mc Farlin	P	3	10	Bushmills	Dunluce L.	Dunluce
Mc Fee	I	3	6	Derryaghy	Belfast U.	Derryaghy
Mc Ginnahty	C	3	I	Ballygrooby	Toome	Drummaul
Mc Golphin	P	3	I	Derryaghy	Belfast U.	Derryaghy
Mc Gregor	P	3	4	Bushmills	Dunluce L.	Dunluce
Mc Guckin	C	3	6	Ballygrooby	Toome	Drummaul
Mc Guffin	P	3	1	Bushmills	Dunluce L.	Dunluce
Mc Ilroy	I	3	12	Derryaghy	Belfast U.	Derryaghy
Mc Kee	P	3	26	Bushmills	Dunluce L.	Dunluce
Mc Kelvey	P	3	21	Bushmills	Dunluce L.	Dunluce
Mc Keon	P	3	S	Lisabany		

Surname	R	I	S	Townland	Barony	Place-Parish
Mc kever	I	3	I	Derryaghy	Belfast U.	Derryaghy
Mc Kibbin	P	3	6		Lecale	Saul
Mc Kitrick	P	3	21	Belfast	Belfast	Shankill
Mc Lean	P	3	29		Massereene	Derryaghy
Mc Levenny	I	3	I		Belfast	Derryaghy
Mc Loan	I	3	S	Derryaghy	Belfast U.	Derryaghy
Mc Lroy	P	3	12	Derryaghy	Belfast U.	Derryaghy
Mc Lure	P	3	12	Derryaghy	Belfast U	Derryaghy
Mc Manis	P	3	S	Derryaghy	Belfast U.	Derryaghy
Mc Mullen	C	3	S	Derryaghy	Belfast U.	Derryaghy
Mc Murran	I	3	23	Derryaghy	Belfast U.	Derryaghy
Mc Nabs	P	3	4	Derryaghy	Belfast U.	Derryaghy
Mc Night	P	3	22	Bushmills	Dunluce L.	Dunluce
Mc Night	C	3	I	Glenavey	Massereene	Glenavey
Mc Watters	P	3	S	Rasham		
Mc Whiney	P	3	12	Derryaghy	Belfast U.	Derryaghy
Meculloch	P	3	21		Belfast	Derryaghy
Mephet	I	3	E	Derryaghy	Belfast U.	Derryaghy
Mercer	Q	3	E	Whiteabbey	Belfast	Carnmoney
Mercer	P	3	4	Bushmills	Dunluce L.	Dunluce
Mexwell	P	3	S	Derryaghy	Belfast U.	Derryaghy
Montgomery	P	3	11	Belfast	Belfast	Shankill
Morison	I	3	E	Derryaghy	Belfast U.	Derryaghy
Morrell	I	3	E	Belfast	Belfast	Shankill
Morrow	I	3	E	Bushmills	Dunluce L.	Dunluce
Morton	P	3	21			
Murgan	I	3	E	Derryaghy	Belfast U.	Derryaghy
Murra	P	3	1		Belfast	Derryaghy
Musen	H	3	G	Massereene	Massereene	Derryaghy
Musgrave	I	3	E	Bushmills	Dunluce L.	Dunluce
Mussen	H	3	G	Derryaghy	Belfast U.	Derryaghy
Nesbitt	I	3	E	Glenarm	Glenarm	Tickmcrevan
Nevel	I	3	E	Derryaghy	Belfast U.	Derryaghy
Newell	P	3	22	Bushmills	Dunluce L.	Dunluce
Norret	P	3	S	Bushmills	Dunluce L.	Dunluce
O' Green	I	3	I		Belfast	Lambeg
O' Lavery	I	3	I	Derryaghy	Belfast U.	Derryaghy
O' Merran	C	3	I	Carrickfergus	Carrickfergus	Carrickfergus

Surname	R	I	S	Townland	Barony	Place-Parish
Osbourah	I	3	E	Derryaghy	Belfast U.	Derryaghy
Patten	P	3	7	Derryaghy	Belfast U.	Derryaghy
Patterson	P	3	1	Lisburn	Massereene	Blaris
Patterson	P	3	1	Derryaghy	Belfast U.	Derryaghy
Patterson	P	3	9	Bushmills	Dunluce L.	Dunluce
Peake	I	3	E	Derryaghy	Belfast U.	Derryaghy
Peel	P	3	21	Bushmills	Dunluce L.	Dunluce
Pepper	P	3	11	Derryaghy	Belfast U.	Derryaghy
Perrin	I	3	E	Lisburn	Massereene	Blaris
Petticrew	P	3	13	Bushmills	Dunluce L.	Dunluce
Philips	P	3	21	Derryaghy	Belfast U	Derryaghy
Phillips	I	3	E	Derryaghy	Belfast U.	Derryaghy
Pohgue	I	3	E	Derryaghy	Belfast U.	Derryaghy
Pottinger	P	3	35	Larne	Glenarm	Larne
Potts	I	3	E	Derryaghy	Belfast U.	Derryaghy
Preistman	P	3	18	Derryaghy	Belfast U	Derryaghy
Ray	P	3	9	Derryaghy	Belfast U.	Derryaghy
Ray	P	3	34	Derryaghy	Belfast U.	Derryaghy
Rea	I	3	1	Carrickfergus	Carrickfergus	Carrickgergus
Rennet	H	3	F	Derryaghy	Belfast U.	Derryaghy
Resnison	P	3		Derryaghy	Belfast U.	Derryaghy
Rice	P	3	W	Derryaghy	Belfast U.	Derryaghy
Richardson	P	3	10	Derryaghy	Belfast U.	Derryaghy
Richey	P	3	12	Derryaghy	Belfast U.	Derryaghy
Rines	P	3	I	Derryaghy	Belfast U.	Derryaghy
Robinson	P	3	4	Bushmills	Dunluce L.	Dunluce
Robison	P	3	21	Bushmills	Dunluce L.	Dunluce
Rockbourah	I	3	E	Derryaghy	Belfast U.	Derryaghy
Rodgers	P	3	4	Derryaghy	Belfast U.	Derryaghy
Rosbothom	I	3	E	Derryaghy	Belfast U.	Derryaghy
Rossbotham	I	3	E	Derryaghy	Belfast U.	Derryaghy
Rowan	I	3	E	Dunaghy	Dunluice	Ballymoney
Rowan	P	3	12	Lisburn	Massereene	Blaris
Ruddagh	P	3	1	Ballygrooby	Toome	Drummaul
Russel	P	3	1	Bushmills	Dunluce L.	Dunluce
Russell	P	3	S	Lisburn	Massereene	Blaris
Rutherford	P	3	20	Bushmills	Dunluce L.	Dunluce
Saurin	P	3	F	Ardagh	Cary	Ramoan

Surname	R	I	S	Townland	Barony	Place-Parish
Scot	P	3	7	Derryaghy	Belfast U.	Derryaghy
Scott	P	3	12	Ballygrooby	Toome	Drummaul
Scott	P	3	12	Belfast	Belfast	Shankill
Seeds	I	3	12 E		Massereene	Derryaghy
Seeds	I	3	E	Derryaghy	Belfast U.	Derryaghy
Sefton	I	3	E	Magheragall	Massereene	Magheragall
Shaw	P	3	12	Gemeway		
Shaw	P	3	12	Ahoghill	Toome Lower	Ahoghill
Shaw	P	3	20	Carnmoney	Belfast L.	Carnmoney
Shean	P	3	12	Derryaghy	Belfast U .	Derryaghy
Shearer	P	3	12	Belfast	Belfast	Carnmoney
Shiel	I	3	E	Ballygrooby	Toome	Drummaul
Simpson	P	3	35	Ballyclare	Belfast	Ballynure
Simpson	P	3	1	Bushmills	Dunluce L.	Dunluce
Simpson	P	3	12	Ballymena	Lower Toome	Kirkinriola
Sincler	P	3	34	Derryaghy	Belfast U.	Derryaghy
Skelly	P	3	I	Bushmills	Dunluce L.	Dunluce
Skelton	I	3	E	Derryaghy	Belfast U.	Derryaghy
Strowde	P	3	S	Lisburn	Massereene	Blaris
Stueart	P	3	7	Derryaghy	Belfast U.	Derryaghy
Tate	P	3	35	Derryaghy	Belfast U.	Derryaghy
Thirkhill	P	3	N		Massereene	Derryaghy
Thompson	I	3	E	Lisburn	Massereene	Blaris
Thompson	P	3	21	Derryaghy	Belfast U.	Derryaghy
Tucker	P	3	E	Derryaghy	Belfast U.	Derryaghy
Vance	P	3	S	Bushmills	Dunluce L.	Dunluce
Venables	P	3	W		Massereene	Derryaghy
Vicars	I	3	E	Derryaghy	Belfast U.	Derryaghy
Walker	P	3	15	Derryaghy	Belfast U.	Derryaghy
Walker	I	3	E	Bushmills	Dunluce L.	Dunluce
Waring	I	3	E	Derryaghy	Belfast U.	Derryaghy
Watson	P	3	E	Bushmills	Dunluce L.	Dunluce
Watt	P	3	E	Bushmills	Dunluce L.	Dunluce
Watts	Q	3	E	Whiteabbey	Belfast	Carnmoney
Weir	P	3	13	Bushmills	Dunluce L.	Dunluce
White	I	3	E	Derryaghy	Belfast U.	Derryaghy
White *	P	3	S	Fannet*		
Whygam	P	3	S	Bushmills	Dunluce L.	Dunluce

Surname	R	I	S	Townland	Barony	Place-Parish
Wier	I	3	E	Derryaghy	Belfast U.	Derryaghy
Wilkinson	I	3		Derryaghy	Belfast U.	Derryaghy
Willas	I	3	E		Massereene	Derryaghy
Willas	I	3	E	Derryaghy	Belfast U.	Derryaghy
Williams	I	3	E	Derryaghy	Belfast U.	Derryaghy
Wilson	P	3	34	Bushmills	Dunluce L.	Dunluce
Wolfden	I	3	E	Derryaghy	Belfast U	Derryaghy
Wolfenden	I	3	E	Derryaghy	Belfast U.	Derryaghy
Woods	I	3	E	Derryaghy	Belfast U.	Derryaghy
Woods	P	3	S	Ballygrooby	Toome	Drummaul
Wyley	P	3	S	Bushmills	Dunluce L.	Dunluce
Young	P	3	S	Bushmills	Dunluce L.	Dunluce

BALLYGALLEY CASTLE
ANTRIM 1625

Map of Tyrone

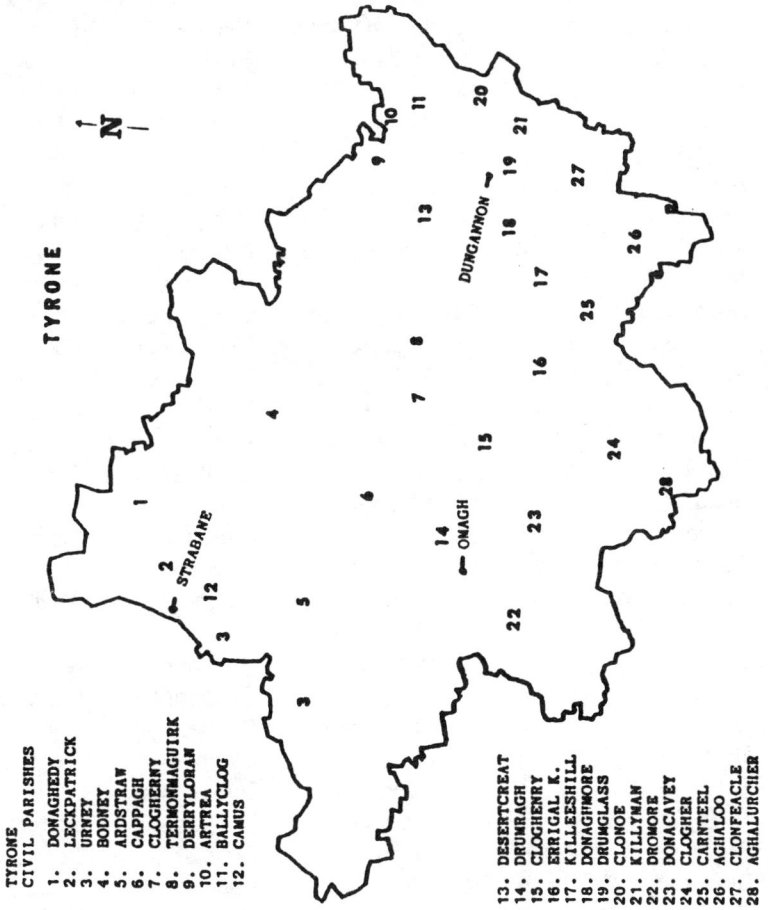

TYRONE
CIVIL PARISHES

1. DONAGHEDY
2. LECKPATRICK
3. URNEY
4. BODNEY
5. ARDSTRAW
6. CAPPAGH
7. CLOGHERNY
8. TERMONMAGUIRK
9. DERRYLORAN
10. ARTREA
11. BALLYCLOG
12. CAMUS

13. DESERTCREAT
14. DRUMRAGH
15. CLOGHERNY
16. ERRIGAL K.
17. KILLEESHILL
18. DONAGHMORE
19. DRUMGLASS
20. CLONOE
21. KILLYMAN
22. DROMORE
23. DONACAVEY
24. CLOGHER
25. CARNTEEL
26. AGHALOO
27. CLONFEACLE
28. AGHALURCHER

Surname	R	I	S	Townland	Barony	Place-Parish
Abernathy	P	4	13	Minterburn*		
Adamson	P	4	17	Omagh	Omagh	Drumragh
Alcorn	P	4	21		Omagh	Drumragh
Alexander	I	4	13	Clogher	Clogher	Clogher
Alexander	I	4	12	Fivemiletown	Clogher	Clogher
Alexander	P	4	12	Dullerton *	Strabane L.	Donaghedy
Algier	P	4	12		Strabane L.	Ardstraw
Allen	P	4	10	Nurchossy	Clogher	Clogher
Anderson	P	4	1		Omagh	Termonmaguirk
Angle	I	4	E		Dungannon	Derryloran
Anguish	P	4	15		Dungannon	Aghaloo
Arbuckle	P	4	13		Strabane	Donaghedy
Archibald	I	4	E		Strabane L.	Ardstraw
Armstrong	P	4	20	Dungannon	Dungannon	Drumglass
Armstrong	P	4	21	Bogane	Dungannon	Killyman
Art	C	4	I	Tullyveagh	Dungannon	Artrea
Art	C	4	I	Dungannon	Dungannon	Drumglass
Atkinson	I	4	12	Lisgallon	Dungannon	Donaghmore
Bailey	P	4	14	Clogher	Clogher	Clogher
Baird	P	4	13	Clogher	Clogher	Clogher
Barbor	I	4	E		Strabane L.	Ardstraw
Barkley	P	4	13	Ardstraw	Strabane L.	Ardstraw
Barnett	I	4	15	Ballagh	Clogher	Clogher
Barnett *	P	4	15	Mullybaney*		
Barnhill	P	4	12	Ardstraw	Strabane L.	Ardstraw
Barrett	I	4	E		Dungannon	Aghaloo
Baxter	I	4	7	Edernagh	Dungannon	Artrea
Baxter	P	4	7	Fivemiletown	Clogher	Clogher
Baxter	P	4	13	Dungannon	Dungannon	Drumglass
Beatty	P	4	21	Dungannon	Dungannon	Drumglass
Betty	P	4	E	Lurganboy	Clogher	Donacavey
Bigger	P	4	13		Dungannon	Arboe
Bincher	I	4	E		Omagh	Dromore
Bird	I	4	E			
Birney	P	4	15	Clogher	Clogher	Clogher
Birney	P	4	15	Fivemiletown	Clogher	Clogher
Birsben	I	4	E		Strabane L.	Ardstraw
Bisland	P	4	9		Strabane L.	Ardstraw

Surname	R	I	S	Townland	Barony	Place-Parish
Bisland	P	4	9		Strabane	Leckpatrick
Bleakley	I	4	E	Clogher	Clogher	Clogher
Bloomfield	I	4	E	Slatmore *	Clogher	Clogher
Bounty	P	4	E	Ardstraw	Strabane L.	Ardstraw
Boyd	P	4	12	Timpany	Clogher	Aghalurcher
Boyd	P	4	12	Edernagh	Dungannon	Artrea
Boyd	P	4	12	Annagh	Dungannon	Clonfecale
Boyd	P	4	12	Dungannon	Dungannon	Drumglass
Boyd *	P	4	12	Seein	Strabane	Urney
Boyle	P	4	21	Ballynahone	Dungannon	Artrea
Boyle	P	4	12	Dungannon	Dungannon	Drumglass
Brisban	P	4	11	Dungannon	Dungannon	Drumglass
Brisben	P	4	11		Strabane L.	Strabane
Brown	P	4	15	Carnteel	Dungannon	Carnteel
Bruse	P	4	19		Strabane L.	Strabane
Bunting	I	4	E		Strabane L.	Strabane
Burley	I	4	E	Carnteel	Dungannon	Carnteel
Burnes	P	4	12	Carnteel	Dungannon	Carnteel
Burns	P	4	6		Dungannon	Aghaloo
Campbell	P	4	6		Dungannon	Aghaloo
Carmichael	P	4	13	Dungannon	Dungannon	Drumglass
Carren	C	4	I		Dungannon	Aghaloo
Carroll	C	4	I	Carnteel	Dungannon	Carnteel
Carson	P	4	10	Dungannon	Dungannon	Drumglass
Chapman	I	4	E			
Chism	P	4	20		Strabane	Donaghedy
Clapham *	P	4	S	Newton*	Strabane	
Clapham *	P	4	S	Lislapp	Strabane	Cappagh
Clarke	P	4	7	Dungannon	Dungannon	Drumglass
Clements	P	4	10	Dungannon	Dungannon	Drumglass
Cole	C	4	I		Dungannon	Aghaloo
Colhoun	P	4	10			
Conely	C	4	I		Dungannon	Aghaloo
Cook	P	4	17	Dungannon	Dungannon	Drumglass
Cooke	I	4	E	Cookstown	Dungannon	Derryloran
Coote	I	4	E	Ballygawley	Clogher	Errigal
Cowan	P	4	12	Dungannon	Dungannon	Drumglass
Cowper	I	4	7	Edernagh	Dungannon	Artrea

Surname	R	I	S	Townland	Barony	Place-Parish
Coyle	P	4	I	Carnteel	Dungannon	Carnteel
Craghead	P	4	1		Strabane L.	Strabane
Craighead *	P	4	1	Donaghmore	Dungannon	Donaghmore
Crawford	P	4	13	Carnteel	Dungannon	Carnteel
Crooks	P	4	13	Cookstown	Dungannon	Derryloran
Crown	I	4	E	Donaghmore	Dungannon	Donaghmore
Cush	P	4	1		Dungannon	Aghaloo
Davidson	P	4	5	Dungannon	Dungannon	Drumglass
Davis	P	4	W	Dungannon	Dungannon	Drumglass
Delap	C	4	I		Strabane	Strabane
Delapp	C	4	I	Moylagh	Omagh	Clogherny
Dennison	P	4	11	Dungannon	Dungannon	Drumglass
Dilry		4			Dungannon	Clonfeacle
Dixon	P	4	17	Carnteel	Dungannon	Carnteel
Doak	C	4	I		Omagh	Ardstraw
Dolly	C	4	I	Carnteel	Dungannon	Carnteel
Donaghy	P	4	6		Dungannon	Aghaloo
Dougall	P	4	12	Dungannon	Dungannon	Drumglass
Dowey	P	4	4	Edernagh	Dungannon	Artrea
Drummond *	P	4	4	Ballymagoieth	Strabane	
Duffin	I	4	26	Dungannon	Dungannon	Dungannon
Duffy	C	4	I	Carnteel	Dungannon	Carnteel
Earlie	I	4	E		Dungannon	Kildress
Easter	I	4	E		Omagh	Cappagh
Ectore		4			Strabane	Urney
Emery	H	4	G	Castlederg	Omagh	Urney
Eskin	P	4	11	Tullyweery	Dungannon	Artrea
Falles	P	4	20	Lisboy	Dungannon	Artrea
Falls	P	4	20	Knocknaroy	Dungannon	Aghaloo
Ferguson	P	4	21	Tullyraw	Dungannon	Artrea
Ferguson	P	4	21	Edernagh	Dungannon	Artrea
Ferguson	P	4	21	Tullyvegah	Dungannon	Artrea
Fisher	I	4	E	Drumlagher	Clogher	Donacavey
Forsythe	P	4	9		Dungannon	Aghaloo
Frederick	I	4	E		Clogher	Clogher
Gibson	P	4	7	Tullyveagh	Dungannon	Artrea
Gildernue	I	4	E		Dungannon	Aghaloo
Gorden	P	4	S		Dungannon	Aghaloo

Surname	R	I	S	Townland	Barony	Place-Parish
Graham	P	4	4	Tulluconnell	Dungannon	Artrea
Greer	P	4	10	Tullyhurken	Dungannon	Artrea
Grierson	P	4	21	Tullylagan *	Dungannon	Desertcreat
Griffin	P	4	W	Edernagh	Dungannon	Artrea
Griffith	P	4	W		Dungannon	Aghaloo
Guy	I	4	E	Carnteel	Dungannon	Carnteel
Haig *	P	4	17	Tiremurtagh*	Strabane	Ardstraw
Hall	P	4	20	Alderwood *	Clogher	Aghalurcher
Hall	P	4	20	Findermore	Clogher	Clogher
Hamill *	P	4	I	Aughnaglough*		
Hamilton	P	4	S	Dirrywoon	Strabane	Ardstraw
Hamilton	P	4	13	Tullyveagh	Dungannon	Artrea
Hamilton	P	4	13	Killycorran	Clogher	Clogher
Hamilton *	P	4	11	Largie C.	Strabane	Ardstraw
Hamilton *	P	4	13	Teadanekilleny	Strabane	Ardstraw
Hance	P	4	13	Tullybroom	Clogher	Clogher
Hanna	P	4	13	Slatbeg	Clogher	Clogher
Hannah	P	4	12		Clogher	Clogher
Hardy	I	4	21	Glenhoy	Clogher	Clogher
Hardy	I	4	21	Eskermore	Omagh	Clogherny
Hardy	I	4	21	Kilgreen	Clogher	Errigal
Harriott	P	4	11	Dungannon	Dungannon	Aghaloo
Harris	I	4	E	Dungannon	Dungannon	Drumglass
Hatton	I	4	E		Strabane	Ardstraw
Hay	P	4	4	Ardstraw	Strabane	Ardstraw
Hector	H	4	F		Strabane	Ardstraw
Hedin	C	4	I	Corick	Clogher	Clogher
Heidin	C	4	I	Corick	Clogher	Clogher
Helan	I	4	E		Strabane	Ardstraw
Hendrick	I	4	E	Ardstraw	Strabane	Ardstraw
Hendricks	I	4	E	Ardstraw	Strabane	Ardstraw
Hepburn *	P	4	S	O'Carragan*		
Heuerat	H	4	G		Strabane	Ardstraw
Higgins	I	4	E	Dungannon	Dungannon	Drumglass
Hill	P	4	13	Ardstraw	Strabane	Ardstraw
Hill	I	4	E	Tullyconnell	Dungannon	Artrea
Hill	I	4	E	Dungannon	Dungannon	Drumglass
Hilles	I	4	E	Edernagh	Dungannon	Artrea

Surname	R	I	S	Townland	Barony	Place-Parish
Hilles	I	4	E	Dungannon	Dungannon	Drumglass
Himpol	I	4	E		Strabane	Ardstraw
Hogg	P	4	4	Ballynahone	Dungannon	Artrea
Holmes	P	4	12	Ardstraw	Strabane	Ardstraw
Holmes	P	4	12	Clogher	Clogher	Clogher
Homes	P	4	1		Omagh	Termonmaguirk
Hood	I	4	E	Mt.Stewart	Clogher	Clogher
Houghy	P	4	12	Tullyconnell	Dungannon	Artrea
Houston *	P	4	13	Castlestewart		
How	I	4	E		Strabane	Ardstraw
Howard	I	4	E	Lurgiboy	Clogher	Donacavey
Howard	I	4	E	Dungannon	Dungannon	Drumglass
Hues	I	4	E		Strabane	Ardstraw
Hughes	P	4	W	Dungannon	Dungannon	Aghaloo
Hurkles	I	4	N	Ardstraw	Strabane	Ardstraw
Hutcheson	I	4	E	Carnteel	Dungannon	Carnteel
Irvine	P	4	21	Mullaghmore	Clogher	Clogher
Irvine	P	4	21	Prolusk	Clogher	Clogher
Irwin	P	4	S	Carnteel	Dungannon	Carnteel
Irwin	P	4	21	Mullaghmore	Clogher	Clogher
Irwin	P	4	21	Drumnamalta	Dungannon	Kildress
Jameson	P	4	1	Shantonagh	Clogher	Clogher
Jamison	P	4	1	Ballyness	Clogher	Clogher
Johnson	P	4	21	Knocknaroy	Dungannon	Aghaloo
Johnson	P	4	21	Knockinarvoer	Dungannon	Artrea
Johnston	P	4	21	Timpany	Clogher	Aghalurcher
Johnston	P	4	20	Tulnavert	Clogher	Clogher
Johnston	P	4	21	Tully	Dungannon	Desertcreat
Johnston	P	4	21	Lisgallon	Dungannon	Donaghmore
Johnston *	P	4	20	Annagarvey	Clogher	Clogher
Kavanagh	C	4	I	Ballyscally	Clogher	Clogher
Kearnes *	C	4	I	Askragh*	Armagh	
Keenan *	C	4	I	Aughnaglough*		
Keene	C	4	I	Ardstraw	Strabane	Ardstraw
Keith	P	4	1	Dungannon	Dungannon	Dungannon
Kelly	P	4	I	Dungannon	Dungannon	Aghaloo
Kelter	H	4	G	Carnteel	Dungannon	Carnteel
Kenitter	P	4	S		Strabane	Ardstraw

Surname	R	I	S	Townland	Barony	Place-Parish
Kennedy	P	4	22	Ballymagowan	Clogher	Clogher
Kennedy *	P	4	22	Gortnaville*		
Kernoghan	C	4	I	Annaloughan	Clogher	Clogher
Kerr	P	4	20	Carnteel	Dungannon	Carnteel
Keyes	I	4	E	5Mi. Town	Clogher	Clogher
Kidd	I	4	E	Tallelar*		
Kidd	P	4	S	Tullyveagh	Dungannon	Artrea
Kiell	-	4	-		Strabane	Ardstraw
King	P	4	E	Mossfield*		
Kinibrough	I	4	E	Tullyraw	Dungannon	Artrea
Kinibrough	I	4	E	Dungannon	Dungannon	Drumglass
Kirkpatrick	P	4	21	Glenhoy	Clogher	Clogher
Kniland	C	4	I		Strabane	Ardstraw
Laird	P	4	17	Carnahinney	Clogher	Clogher
Lamond	P	4	6	Lisboy	Clogher	Clogher
Large	P	4	1	Ardstraw	Strabane	Ardstraw
Latemore	P	4	20	Tullyconnell	Dungannon	Artrea
Latemore	I	4	E	Dungannon	Dungannon	Drumglass
Latimer	P	4	S		Dungannon	Aghaloo
Laughlin	P	4	1	Ardstraw	Strabane	Ardstraw
Law *	P	4	S	Cavanakirk*		
Law *	I	4	E	Latbeg	Clogher	Clogher
Lawrence	I	4	E	Ardstraw	Strabane	Ardstraw
Leamond	P	4	4	Lisboy	Dungannon	Artrea
Learman	I	4	E		Strabane	Ardstraw
Leathers	I	4	E	Tullyraw	Dungannon	Artrea
Lendrum *	P	4	1	Cullenane*		
Lendrum *	P	4	1	Timpany	Clogher	Aghalurcher
Leslie	P	4	7	Clogher	Clogher	Clogher
Leslie	P	4	7		Strabane	Urney
Letty	I	4	E		Strabane	Ardstraw
Ley	P	4	15	Clogher	Clogher	Clogher
Ley	P	4	15	Kilclay	Clogher	Clogher
Liggett	P	4	9	Corbo	Clogher	Clogher
Lilly	I	4	E		Dungannon	Kildress
Lindasy *	P	4	15	Tulloghoge*		
Lindesay	I	4	7	Fardross	Clogher	Clogher
Lindsay	P	4	20	Tullyveagh	Dungannon	Artrea

Surname	R	I	S	Townland	Barony	Place-Parish
Lindsay	P	4	15	Tullyvegah	Dungannon	Artrea
Lindsay	P	4	12	Lisnacrieve	Clogher	Donacravey
Lindsay *	P	4	S	Creighballes*		
Linn	P	4	12	Ardstraw	Strabane	Ardstraw
Little	I	4	E	Slatbeg	Clogher	Clogher
Lochrane	C	4	I	Tullyconnell	Dungannon	Artrea
Loghron	P	4	-	Carnteel	Dungannon	Carnteel
Lomond	P	4	S	Lisboy	Dungannon	Artrea
Lomond	P	4	S	Lisboy	Clogher	Clogher
Long	P	4	21	Augher	Clogher	Clogher
Lowry	P	4	S	Knocknaroy	Aghaloo	Aghaloo
Lowry	P	4	21	Ardstraw	Strabane	Ardstraw
Lowry	P	4	1	Knockinarvoer	Dungannon	Artrea
Lowther	I	4	E	Ardstraw	Strabane	Ardstraw
Luggy	P	4	13		Strabane	Ardstraw
Lynn	P	4	12	Tullyconnell	Dungannon	Artrea
Lyttle	I	4	E	Duffsland	Dungannon	Drumglass
Lyttle	I	4	E	Dungannon	Dungannon	Drumglass
Mac Adam	P	4	12	Edernagh	Dungannon	Artrea
Mac Atagart	C	4	I	Lisgallon	Dungannon	Donaghmore
Mac Canna	C	4	I		Omagh	Termonmaguirk
Mac Colgan	C	4	I		Omagh	Termonmaguirk
Mac Conway	C	4	I		Omagh	Termonmaguirk
Mac Corde	P	4	12	Lisnahull	Dungannon	Donaghmore
Mac Eldoon	C	4	I	Tevena	Dungannon	Artrea
Mac Elhair	C	4	I		Omagh	Termonmaguirk
Mac Ginnahty	C	4	I	Duffsland	Dungannon	Artrea
Mac Ginnahty	C	4	I	Dufless	Dungannon	Artrea
Mac Ginnahty	C	4	I	Tevena	Dungannon	Artrea
Mac Guirk	P	4	S		Omagh	Termonmaguirk
Mac Henry	C	4	I	Tullyveagh	Dungannon	Artrea
Mac Ilbreed	C	4	I		Omagh	Termonmaguirk
Mac Ilduff	P	4	21		Omagh	Termonmaguirk
Mac Lane	P	4	12	Ardstraw	Strabane	Ardstraw
Mac Mahon	C	4	I		Omagh	Termommaguirк
Mac Manus	C	4	I		Omagh	Termonmaguirk
Mac Murphy	C	4	I		Omagh	Termonmaguirk
Mac Rory	P	4	22	Tullyveagh	Dungannon	Artrea

Surname	R	I	S	Townland	Barony	Place-Parish
Mac Rory	P	4	5	Tullyvegah	Dungannon	Artrea
Mac Rory	P	4	5		Omagh	Termonmaguirk
Mac Wornock	P	4	S		Omagh	Termonmaguirk
Mackey	C	4	I	Clogher	Clogher	Clogher
Macklin	P	4	1	Ardstraw	Strabane	Ardstraw
Mahon	C	4	I	Findermore	Clogher	Clogher
Maize	H	4	F	Tullidonell	Dungannon	Drumglass
Mallon	P	4	S	Kilnaheery	Clogher	Clogher
Maloy	C	4	I		Dungannon	Aghaloo
Markey	C	4	I	Ardstraw	Strabane	Ardstraw
Marshall	I	4	E		Dungannon	Aghaloo
Materick	I	4	E		Strabane	Ardstraw
Mathews	P	4	15	Ardstraw	Strabane	Ardstraw
Maynes	P	4	1	Kilnahushogue	Clogher	Clogher
Maynes	P	4	1	Lungs	Clogher	Clogher
Mc Allen	I	4	I	Ardstraw	Strabane	Ardstraw
Mc Ardle	C	4	I	Clogher	Clogher	Clogher
Mc Atagart	C	4	I	Lisgallon	Dungannon	Donaghmore
Mc Cames	C	4	I	Edernagh	Dungannon	Artrea
Mc Cames	P	4	25	Edernagh	Dungannon	Artrea
Mc Cames	P	4	10	Lisboy	Dungannon	Artrea
Mc Cames	C	4	I	Lisboy	Clogher	Clogher
Mc Camon	P	4	I	Carnteel	Dungannon	Carnteel
Mc Cardel	P	4	I	Carnteel	Dungannon	Carnteel
Mc Carney	P	4	15	Altanaverga	Clogher	Clogher
Mc Carney	P	4	15	Fivemiletown	Clogher	Clogher
Mc Carrell	C	4	I			
Mc Carroll	C	4	I	Carntall	Clogher	Clogher
Mc Carroll	C	4	I	Tullybroom	Clogher	Clogher
Mc Caughey	C	4	I	Lismore	Clogher	Clogher
Mc Caugheye	C	4	I	Findermore	Clogher	Clogher
Mc Causland	I	4	10	Ardstraw	Strabane	Ardstraw
Mc Causland	P	4	10	Tullyconnell	Dungannon	Artrea
Mc Causland	P	4	21	Tullyconnell	Dungannon	Artrea
Mc Cawell	C	4	I	Newtownsville		
Mc Cawell	C	4	I	Bolies	Clogher	Clogher
Mc Cawell	C	4	I	Lisgorran	Clogher	Clogher
Mc Cillin	P	4	11	Ardstraw	Strabane	Ardstraw

Surname	R	I	S	Townland	Barony	Place-Parish
Mc Clean	P	4	12	Kilnahushoghe	Clogher	Clogher
Mc Clelland	P	4	12	Clogher	Clogher	Clogher
Mc Clery	P	4	I		Dungannon	Aghaloo
Mc Cobe	P	4	S		Strabane	Ardstraw
Mc Colgah	I	4	I	Ardstraw	Strabane	Ardstraw
Mc Collum	P	4	S	Clogher	Clogher	Clogher
Mc Cowy	P	4	I	Carnteel	Dungannon	Carnteel
Mc Coy	C	4	I	Cess *		
Mc Coy	C	4	I	Altanaverga	Clogher	Clogher
Mc Crabb	P	4	1	Ardstraw	Strabane	Ardstraw
Mc Crea	P	4	12	Townagh	Clogher	Clogher
Mc Creevy	P	4	12	Corcreevy	Clogher	Clogher
Mc Culer	P	4	E		Strabane	Ardstraw
Mc Dermond	P	4	12	Gravaghey	Clogher	Clogher
Mc Dowell	C	4	38	Ardstraw	Strabane	Ardstraw
Mc Dowell	C	4	38	Augher	Clogher	Clogher
Mc Dowell	C	4	38	Clogher	Clogher	Clogher
Mc Dowell	C	4	38	kilrudden	Clogher	Clogher
Mc Elhenney	C	4	I	Shanco	Clogher	Clogher
Mc Elrath	C	4	I	Beltiny	Strabane	Cappagh
Mc Elroy	P	4	I	Springtown		
Mc Elroy	P	4	I	Clogher	Clogher	Clogher
Mc Farlan	P	4	10	Ardstraw	Strabane	Ardstraw
Mc Fetridge	P	4	21	Clogher	Clogher	Clogher
Mc Gahey	C	4	I	Lurgaboyn	Dungannon	Drumglass
Mc Gaogy	I	4	I	Cormore	Clogher	Clogher
Mc Gaogy	I	4	I	Lisnarable	Clogher	Clogher
Mc Gauggey	C	4	I	Fernaghandrum	Clogher	Clogher
Mc Gauvern	P	4	12	Ballymagowan	Clogher	Clogher
Mc Gee	C	4	I	Clogher	Clogher	Clogher
Mc Ginn	C	4	I	Malabaney	Clogher	Clogher
Mc Ginnelly	C	4	I	Tullybroom		
Mc Ginnelly	C	4	I	Beltiny	Strabane	Cappagh
Mc Girr	P	4	21	Clarmore	Clogher	Clogher
Mc Grady	C	4	I	Carnteel	Dungannon	Carnteel
Mc Guire	C	4	I	Altnacerney *		
Mc Gunshenon	P	4	-		Dungannon	Aghaloo
Mc Ilvaney	C	4	I	Ardstraw	Strabane	Ardstraw

Surname	R	I	S	Townland	Barony	Place-Parish
Mc Kasby	P	4	I		Strabane	Ardstraw
Mc Keever	p	4	I	Gortin	Strabane	Bodoney
Mc Kenna	P	4	21	Altnacarney *		
Mc Kenna	P	4	21	Norchossy		
Mc Kenna	C	4	I	Tulnavert *		
Mc Kenna	P	4	I		Dungannon	Aghaloo
Mc Keowan	C	4	I	Ballynaguragh*		
Mc Keown	C	4	I	Ballymagowan	Clogher	Clogher
Mc Kever	P	4	S	Carnteel	Dungannon	Carnteel
Mc Kinney	P	4	22		Omagh	Termonmaguirk
Mc Kinsey	P	4	S		Omagh	Termonmaguirk
Mc Knight	P	4	12	Clogher	Clogher	Clogher
Mc Knight	P	4	12	Glenhoy	Clogher	Clogher
Mc Knight *	P	4	12	Omagh		
Mc Laren	P	4	4			
Mc Laurin	P	4	4	Latbeg		
Mc Leane	P	4	6	Tevena	Dungannon	Artrea
Mc Lough	P	4	S		Strabane	Ardstraw
Mc Mahon	P	4	I		Dungannon	Aghaloo
Mc Mahon	C	4	I		Omagh	Termonmaguirk
Mc Martin	P	4	21		Omagh	Termonmaguirk
Mc Minn	I	4	I			Killyman
Mc Nichol	P	4	31	Tullyveagh	Dungannon	Artrea
Mc Nichol	P	4	32	Tullyvegah	Dungannon	Artrea
Mc Quade	C	4	I		Dungannon	Aghaloo
Mc Tyre	P	4	S		Strabane	Ardstraw
Mc Williams	P	4	23	Kilnahushogue		
Means	C	4	I	Dufless	Dungannon	Artrea
Means	P	4	1	Dufless*	Dungannon	Artrea
Meegan	C	4	I	Mountstewart	Clogher	Clogher
Mellon	C	4	I		Clogher	Clogher
Menaul		4		Clogher	Clogher	Clogher
Merwin	I	4	E	Trilick *		
Meyring	I	4	E	Ardstraw	Strabane	Ardstraw
Middleton	P	4	2	Ardstraw	Strabane	Ardstraw
Millar	P	4	12	Daisey Hill		
Miller	I	4	E	Ardstraw	Strabane	Ardstraw
Miller	I	4	E	Knockinarvoer	Dungannon	Artrea

Surname	R	I	S	Townland	Barony	Place-Parish
Miller	I	4	E	Dungannon	Dungannon	Drumglass
Milligan	P	4	11	Kell		
Mills	P	4	1	Carntall	Clogher	Clogher
Mills	P	4	1	Clogher	Clogher	Clogher
Milygan	P	4	S		Dungannon	Aghaloo
Mitchell	P	4	1	Ardstraw	Strabane	Ardstraw
Mitcheltree	P	4	S	Rahack	Clogher	Aghalurcher
Moderwell	I	4	E		Strabane	Clogher
Moffat	P	4	21	Cormore	Clogher	Clogher
Montcriff	P	4	S		Strabane	Ardstraw
Montgomery	P	4	12	Slatbeg	Clogher	Clogher
Moorcroft	P	4	E	Newtownstewart		
Moore	P	4	S		Dungannon	Aghaloo
Moore	P	4	E	Augher	Clogher	Clogher
Moore	I	4	E	Ballymacan	Clogher	Clogher
Moore	I	4	E	Deanery	Clogher	Clogher
Moore	I	4	E	Donaghmoyne	Clogher	Clogher
Moore	P	4	13	Glenhoy	Clogher	Clogher
Moore	I	4	E	Lislane	Clogher	Clogher
Moore	P	4	I	Lislane	Clogher	Clogher
Moore	I	4	E	Corkhill	Dungannon	Pomeroy
Moorhead	P	4	S	Lisgallon	Dungannon	Donaghmore
Morrow	I	4	E	Kilrudden	Clogher	Clogher
Mossey	I	4	E	Augher	Clogher	Clogher
Mucklewrath	C	4	1	Carnteel	Dungannon	Carnteel
Mudd	I	4	E		Strabane	Ardstraw
Muddy	I	4	E		Strabane	Ardstraw
Mulligan	C	4	21	Orchard Hill*		
Munagh	-	4	-	Aughamullan	Dungannon	Clone
Murrey	P	4	4	Ardstraw	Strabane	Ardstraw
NcGahey	C	4	I	Lurgiboy	Clogher	Donacavey
Neely	C	4	I	Ballymagowan	Clogher	Clogher
Nelson	I	4	E	Carnteel	Dungannon	Carnteel
Nelson	I	4	E	Killyfaddy	Clogher	Clogher
Nelson *	I	4	E	Townagh *		
Nelson *	I	4	E	Carntall	Clogher	Clogher
Nesbit	P	4	17	Ardstraw	Strabane	Ardstraw
Nesmith	I	4	E		Strabane	Ardstraw

Surname	R	I	S	Townland	Barony	Place-Parish
Nicholl	P	4	13	Ardstraw	Strabane	Ardstraw
Noble	P	4	10	Carnahinney	Clogher	Clogher
O' Coogan	C	4	I		Omagh	Termonmaguirk
O' Donnelly	C	4	I		Omagh	Termonmaguirk
O' Gorman	C	4	I		Omagh	Termonmaguirk
O' Heir	P	4	I	Carnteel	Dungannon	Carnteel
O' Hourisky	C	4	I		Omagh	Termonmaguirk
O' Hoyne	C	4	II		Omagh	Termonmaguirk
O' Kelly	C	4	I	Ardstraw	Strabane	Ardstraw
O' Lafferty	C	4	I		Omagh	Termonmaguirk
O' Mullen	P	4	I	Carnteel	Dungannon	Carnteel
O' Mulroomey	C	4	I		Omagh	Termonmaguirk
O' Neill	C	4	I		Omagh	Termonmaguirk
O' Shiel	C	4	I		Omagh	Termonmaguirk
O' Tanny	C	4	I		Omagh	Termonmaguirk
O' Teigue	C	4	I		Omagh	Termonmaguirk
Oliver	I	4	E		Dungannon	Aghaloo
Ore	P	4	S	Ardstraw	Strabane	Ardstraw
Orr *	P	4	12	Prolusk	Clogher	Clogher
Orr *	P	4	12	Tullybroom	Clogher	Clogher
Orr *	P	4	11	Drumhirk	Dungannon	Donaghmore
Osborn	I	4	E	Brigh	Dungannon	Ballylcog
Otterson	P	4	17	Ballynahone	Dungannon	Artrea
Owens	C	4	I	Dromore	Dungannon	Arboe
Patrick	P	4	12	Carnteel	Dungannon	Carnteel
Patterson	P	4	S	Ballygawley	Clogher	Errigal K.
Paul	P	4	7	Ardstraw	Strabane	Ardstraw
Peet	P	4	1	Ardstraw	Strabane	Ardstraw
Perry	I	4	E		Omagh	Termonmaguirk
Peticrue	H	4	F		Dungannon	Aghaloo
Pock	I	4	E	Ardstraw	Strabane	Ardstraw
PoKe	P	4	11	Ardstraw	Strabane	Ardstraw
Porter	I	4	11	Derrygonigan	Dungannon	Artrea
Porter	I	4	E	Clogher	Clogher	Clogher
Potter	P	4	12	Ardstraw	Strabane	Ardstraw
Potter	I	4	E	Carnteel	Dungannon	Carnteel
Potter	P	4	12	Freughmore	Clogher	Donacavey
Pringle	P	4	S		Dungannon	Aghaloo

Surname	R	I	S	Townland	Barony	Place-Parish
Provan	P	4	12	Augher	Clogher	Clogher
Purdon	C	4	N	Ardstraw	Strabane	Ardstraw
Purvice	P	4	17	Derrygonigan	Dungannon	Artrea
Purvice	P	4	17	Tullyvegah	Dungannon	Artrea
Quigley	P	4	19	Carnteel	Dungannon	Carnteel
Rae	P	4	34	Ardstraw	Strabane	Ardstraw
Ramsay	P	4	17	Waterhill*		
Ramsay	P	4	17	Gunnell	Clogher	Clogher
Ramsay	P	4	17	Mullaghtinny	Clogher	Clogher
Ramsay	P	4	17	Beagh	Omagh	Clogherny
Ramsey	P	4	S	Castlegore	Omagh	Urney
Rankin	P	4	12	Ardstraw	Strabane	Ardstraw
Ransay	P	4	3	Castletown	Strabane	Leckpatrick
Ray	P	4	9		Dungannon	Aghaloo
Ray	P	4	23		Dungannon	Aghaloo
Ray	P	4	12	Lisgallon	Dungannon	Donaghmore
Read	I	4	E	Ardstraw	Strabane	Ardstraw
Reily	P	4	I	Carnteel	Dungannon	Carnteel
Renny	P	4	16	Aedstraw	Strabane	Ardstraw
Reynalds	C	4	I	Ardstraw	Strabane	Ardstraw
Rice	P	4	W	Augher	Clogher	Clogher
Richardson	P	4	1	Farnetra*		
Richardson	P	4	1	Augher	Clogher	Clogher
Richardson	P	4	1	Springtown	Clogher	Clogher
Richey	P	4	12	Clarmore	Omagh	Ardstraw
Richey	P	4	12	Carnahinney	Clogher	Clogher
Richey	P	4	12	Fivemiletown	Clogher	Clogher
Richey	P	4	12	Freughmore	Clogher	Donacavey
Robinson	P	4	17	Ardstraw	Strabane	Ardstraw
Russell	P	4	1	Ardstraw	Strabane	Ardstraw
Russell	P	4	S	Dunnamany	Strabane	Donaghedy
Rutledge	I	4	E	Collumbrone*		
Sampson	P	4	13	Carntall	Clogher	Clogher
Sandiford	P	4	7	Ballynahone	Dungannon	Artrea
Sayers	I	4	E	Omagh	Omagh	Drumragh
Scott	P	4	12	Augher	Clogher	Clogher
Scott	P	4	12		Omagh	Termonmaguirk
Seate	I	4	E	Clogher	Clogher	Clogher

Surname	R	I	S	Townland	Barony	Place-Parish
Seaton	I	4	E	Lisnahull	Dungannon	Donaghmore
Shepherd	I	4	18	Clogher	Clogher	Clogher
Sheridan	C	4	I		Dungannon	Aghaloo
Sherry	P	4	I		Dungannon	Aghaloo
Shields	P	4	15	Clogher	Clogher	Clogher
Short	P	4	21	Clogher	Clogher	Clogher
Simpson	I	4	E	Daisey Hill*		
Simpson	P	4	15	Drumhirk	Dungannon	Donaghmore
Simpson	P	4	1	Bloomhill	Clogher	Errigal K.
Simpson	P	4	15	Keady	Clogher	Errigal K.
Simpson	P	4	15	Cullentra	Dungannon	Kileeshil
Sitt	P	4	S	Knockinarvoer	Dungannon	Artrea
Sloane	P	4	15	Tullyconnell	Dungannon	Artrea
Smith	I	4	E	Ardstraw	Strabane	Ardstraw
Smith	I	4	15	Carnteel	Dungannon	Carnteel
Smith	P	4	15	Lisnamaghery	Clogher	Clogher
Smith	I	4	E		Omagh	Termonmaguirk
Smyth	I	4	E	Augher	Clogher	Clogher
Somervil	I	4	17	Ardstraw	Strabane	Ardstraw
Somerville	I	4	E	Augher	Clogher	Clogher
Somerville	I	4	17	Bolies	Clogher	Clogher
Steel	P	4	21	N.Tn.Stewart	Strabane	Ardstraw
Steele	P	4	12	Ardstraw	Strabane	Ardstraw
Steen	C	4	I	Tiercar*		
Steen	P	4	I	Clogher	Clogher	Clogher
Steen	C	4	I	Skelgagh	Clogher	Clogher
Steen	P	4	I	Cornmullagh	Dungannon	Clonfeacle
Stephenson	P	4	12	Findermore	Clogher	Clogher
Stewart	P	4	15	Aughentain*		
Stewart	P	4	15	Aughnaglough*		
Stewart	P	4	11	Daisey Hill*		
Stewart	P	4	7		Dungannon	Aghaloo
Stewart	P	4	15	Clogher	Clogher	Clogher
Stewart	P	4	11	Knocknacarny	Clogher	Clogher
Stewart	P	4	20	Lislane	Clogher	Clogher
Stewart	P	4	7	Killemoonan	Omagh	Donacavey
Stewart	P	4	13	Lisgallon	Dungannon	Donaghmore
Stinson	I	4	E	Travenmore*		

Surname	R	I	S	Townland	Barony	Place-Parish
Stockdale	I	4	E	Beechill*		
Stockdale	I	4	E	Clogher	Clogher	Clogher
Story	P	4	1	Corick	Clogher	Clogher
Taggart	P	4	21	Clogher	Clogher	Clogher
Tanahill	P	4	12	Ardstraw	Strabane	Ardstraw
Taylor	P	4	21	Cranbrooke*		
Taylor	P	4	21	Norchossy*		
Tearney	C	4	I	Corleaghan	Clogher	Clogher
Thompson	P	4	21	Augher	Clogher	Clogher
Todd	P	4	17	Ballynaguragh*		
Treanor	P	4	I	Aughnacloy	Dungannon	Carnteel
Treanor	P	4	I	Killaney	Clogher	Clogher
Treanor	P	4	I	Mount Stewart	Clogher	Clogher
Tremble	P	4	13	Gartmore*		
Trimble	P	4	15	Ballagh*		
Trimble	P	4	E	Lisgawsey?		
Trimble	I	4	E	Tullyweery	Dungannon	Artrea
Trimble	P	4	15	Ballymacan	Clogher	Clogher
Trimble	P	4	15	Clogher	Clogher	Clogher
Trimble	P	4	E	Shanco	Clogher	Clogher
Twigg	I	4	E	Clogher	Clogher	Clogher
Upton	I	4	E	Knockinarvoer	Dungannon	Artrea
Walke	H	4	G	Carnteel	Dungannon	Carnteel
Wallace	P	4	12	Carnteel	Dungannon	Carnteel
Wallis	P	4	5	Ardstraw	Strabane	Ardstraw
Wat	P	4	1	Ardstraw	Strabane	Ardstraw
Watson	P	4	7	Ardstraw	Strabane	Ardstraw
Watson	P	4	E		Omagh	Termonmaguirk
Watt	I	4	11	Carnteel	Dungannon	Carnteel
Waugh	P	4	S	Carnteel	Dungannon	Carnteel
Wenn	P	4	S	Ardstraw	Strabane	Ardstraw
White	P	4	E	Derrygonigan	Dungannon	Arerea
Whitty	I	4		Augher	Clogher	Clogher
Wilcox *	I	4	E	Strangmore*		
Wilke	P	4	S	Tullyconnell	Dungannon	Artrea
Wilkins	I	4	E	Ardstraw	Strabane	Ardstraw
Willoughby	P	4	S		Dungannon	Aghaloo
Willson	P	4	S	Ardstraw	Strabane	Ardstraw

Surname	R	I	S	Townland	Barony	Place-Parish
Wilson	P	4	S	Strabane	Strabane L.	Camus
Wilson	I	4	E	Augher	Clogher	Clogher
Winnan	P	4	S	Lisboy	Dungannon	Artrea
Wood	I	4	E	Ardstraw	Strabane	Ardstraw
Woods	I	4	E		Omagh	Termonmaguirk
Yates	C	4	I	Ardstraw	Strabane	Ardstraw
Young	P	4	S	Ardstraw	Strabane	Ardstraw
Yury	P	4	S	Ardstraw	Strabane	Ardstraw

CASTLE CAULFIELD 1614
TYRONE

Map of Armagh

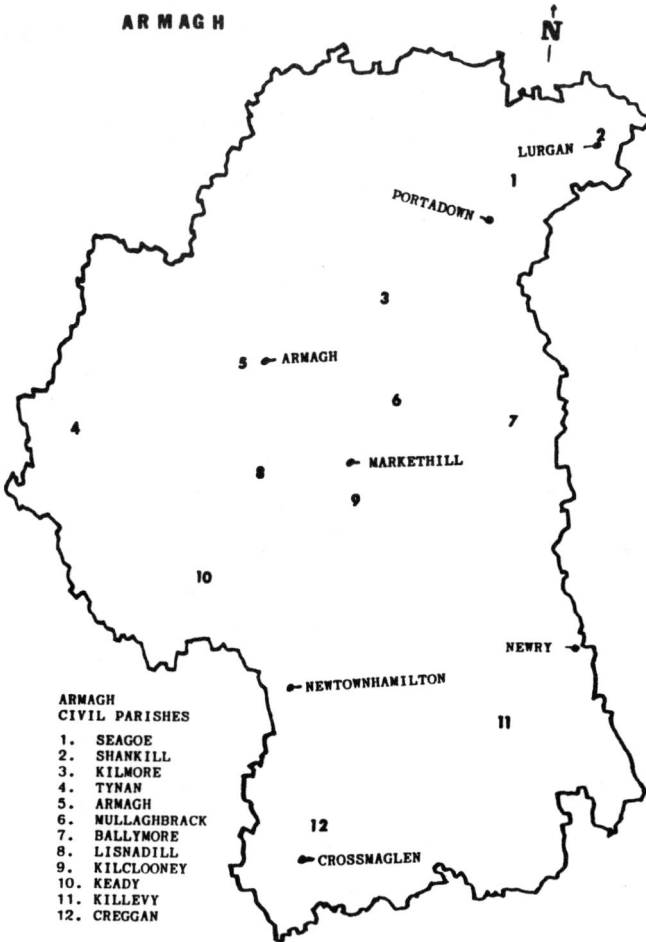

ARMAGH

N

LURGAN 2

1

PORTADOWN

3

5 ARMAGH

6

4

7

8 MARKETHILL

9

10

NEWRY

NEWTOWNHAMILTON

11

ARMAGH
CIVIL PARISHES

1. SEAGOE
2. SHANKILL
3. KILMORE
4. TYNAN
5. ARMAGH
6. MULLAGHBRACK
7. BALLYMORE
8. LISNADILL
9. KILCLOONEY
10. KEADY
11. KILLEVY
12. CREGGAN

12

CROSSMAGLEN

Surname	R	I	S	Townland	Barony	Place-Parish
Acheson *	P	5	15	Coolmillish	Fews	Mullaghbrack
Annett	I	5	E	Tandragee	Orior	Ballymore
Barrow	I	5	E	Lurgan	Oneilland	Shankill
Bayers	I	5	E	Armagh	Armagh	Armagh
Bennerman	I	5	E	Markethill	Fews	Kilclooney
Blizard	P	5		Lurgan	Oneilland	Shankill
Booth	I	5	E	Lurgan	Oneilland	Shankill
Bulla	P	5	E		Armagh	Kilmore
Burch	I	5	E		Armagh	Kilmore
Camack	P	5		Lurgan	Oneilland	Shankill
Care	C	5	I	Markethill	Fews	Kilclooney
Chaloner	P	5	15	Lurgan	Oneilland	Shankill
Charnor	I	5	E	Lurgan	Oneilland	Shankill
Coullow	I	5	E	Lurgan	Oneilland	Shankill
Craig *	P	5	15	Magharyetrim*	Fews	
Cromie	P	5	1			
Crymble	P	5		Lurgan	Oneilland	Shankill
Cuppage		5		Lurgan	Oneilland	Shankill
Cuthbert	C	5	5	Lurgan	Oneilland	Shankill
Dealy	C	5	I		Armagh	Tynan
Delincourt	P	5	F	Armagh	Armagh	Armagh
Dobson	P	5	13	Lurgan	Oneilland	Shankill
Dogan	C	5	I		Oneilland	Armagh
Duke	I	5	E	Armagh	Armagh	Armagh
Fawcet	I	5	E	Loughross	Fews	Creggan
Flory	I	5	E	Lurgan	Oneilland	Shankill
Fowler	I	5	E	Meigh	Orior	Killevy
Gill	I	5	E	Armagh	Armagh	Armagh
Gillpin	I	5	E	Portadown	Oneilland	Seagoe
Glenny	I	5	E	Markethill	Fews	Kilclooney
Goyer	P	5	F	Lurgan	Oneilland	Shankill
Guest	I	5	E	Armagh	Armagh	Armagh
Hamilton *	P	5	11	Fdeneveagh?	Fews	
Hamilton *	P	5	11	Magheryetrim*	Fews	
Hardin	I	5	E	Lurgan	Oneilland	Shankill
Harland	I	5	E	Lurgan	Oneilland	Shankill
Harwood	I	5	E	Armagh	Oneilland	Armagh
Hewett	I	5	E			

Surname	R	I	S	Townland	Barony	Place-Parish
Hobbs	I	5	E	Lurgan	Oneilland	Shankill
Hodson	E	5	E	Armagh	Armagh	Armagh
Hondwon	P	5	-	Lurgan	Oneilland	Shankill
Honoff	I	5	E	Lurgan	Oneilland	Shankill
Hoope	I	5	7	Lurgan	Oneilland	Shankill
Johnson	P	5	21		Armagh	Armagh
Jordan	I	5	E	Lurgan	Oneilland	Shankill
Lauder *	P	5	7	Kilruddan*	Fews	
Leadley	P	5	-	Markethill	Fews	Kilclooney
Loo		5		Lurgan	Oneilland	Shankill
Lougherbee	P	5	-	Armagh	Armagh	Armagh
Mac Ginnahty	C	5	I	Tavanagh	Oneilland	Drumcree
Maziere	H	5	F	Lurgan	Oneilland	Shankill
Mc Cadam	P	5	11		Tiranny	Keady
Mc Camon	P	5	I	Markethill	Fews	Kilclooney
Mc Clinchy	P	5	I	Lurgan	Oneilland	Shankill
Mc Clinshe	C	5	I	Markethill	Fews	Kilclooney
Mc Come	P	5	S		Armagh	Armagh
Mc Creightt	C	5	I	Markethill	Fews	Kilclooney
Mc Elroy	P	5	I	Drumgaw	Fews	Lisnadill
Mc Grane	C	5	I	Armagh	Armagh	Armagh
Mc Ilduff	P	5	21	Lurgan	Oneilland	Shankill
Mc Ilgallogly	C	5	I	Armagh	Armagh	Armagh
Mc Ilrudd	P	5	6	Armagh	Armagh	Armagh
Mc Keever	I	5	I	Armagh	Armagh	Armagh
Mc Lane	I	5	E	Tavanagh	Oneilland	Drumcree
Mc Langly	I	5	E	Lurgan	Oneilland	Shankill
Mc Mackin	C	5	I	Armagh	Armagh	Armagh
Mc Mopne	P	5	-	Armagh	Armagh	Armagh
Mc Quaffye	C	5	I	Armagh	Armagh	Armagh
Mc Roly	P	5	S	Lurgan	Oneilland	Shankill
Mc Sherry	C	5	I	Armagh	Armagh	Armagh
Moggs	P	5	S	Lurgan	Oneilland	Shankill
Nelson	P	5	12			
O' Brainighan	C	5	I	Armagh	Fews	Armagh
O' Dailly	C	5	I	Armagh	Fews	Armagh
O' Heartye	C	5	I	Armagh	Fews	Armagh
O' Lavvan	C	5	I	Armagh	Fews	Armagh

Surname	R	I	S	Townland	Barony	Place-Parish
O' Lue	C	5	I	Armagh	Fews	Armagh
O' Moony	I	5	I	Armagh	Oneilland	Armagh
O' Quyne	C	5	I	Armagh	Fews	Armagh
O' Rugan	C	5	I	Armagh	Fews	Armagh
O' Tonner	C	5	I	Armagh	Fews	Armagh
Ogle	I	5	E	Lurgan	Oneilland	Shankill
Oliver	I	5	E	Markethill	Fews	Kilclooney
Pillow	I	5	E	Armagh	Fews	Armagh
Pooler	P	5	21	Markethill	Fews	Mullaghbrack
Read	I	5	E	Armagh	Oneilland	Armagh
Ruddell	I	5	E	Lurgan	Oneilland	Shankill
Russell	P	5	17	Lurgan	Oneilland	Shankill
Short	H	5	S	Lurgan	Oneilland	Shankill
Short	P	5	21	Lurgan	Oneilland	Shankill
Sinclair	P	5	34			
Tinsly	I	5	E	Lurgan	Oneilland	Shankill
Truman	I	5	E	Lurgan	Oneilland	Shankill
Turbett	I	5	E	Lurgan	Oneilland	Shankill
Turner	P	5	1	Lurgan	Oneilland	Shankill
Usher	I	5	E	Lurgan	Oneilland	Shankill
Webb	I	5	E	Lurgan	Oneilland	Shankill
Wells	I	5	E	Lurgan	Oneilland	Shankill
Whitley	P	5	S	Markethill	Fews	Kilclooney
Wisdom	I	5	E	Lurgan	Oneilland	Shankill
Wood	I	5	E	Lurgan	Oneilland	Shankill

GOSFORD CASTLE
1729

Map of Down

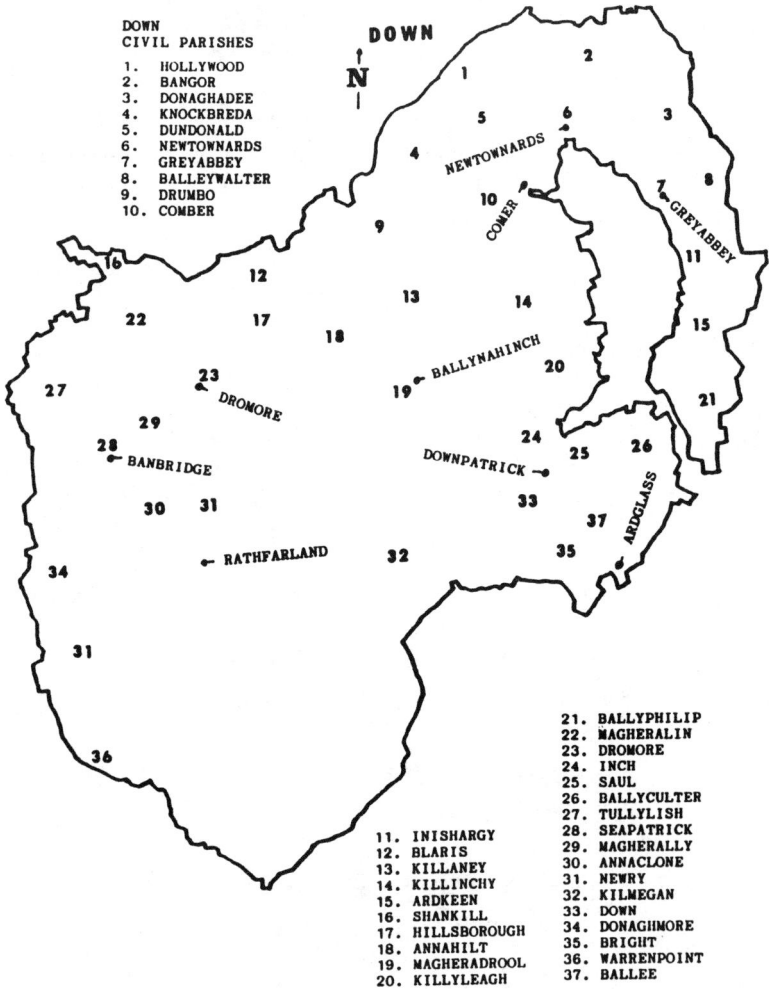

DOWN
CIVIL PARISHES

1. HOLLYWOOD
2. BANGOR
3. DONAGHADEE
4. KNOCKBREDA
5. DUNDONALD
6. NEWTOWNARDS
7. GREYABBEY
8. BALLEYWALTER
9. DRUMBO
10. COMBER

11. INISHARGY
12. BLARIS
13. KILLANEY
14. KILLINCHY
15. ARDKEEN
16. SHANKILL
17. HILLSBOROUGH
18. ANNAHILT
19. MAGHERADROOL
20. KILLYLEAGH

21. BALLYPHILIP
22. MAGHERALIN
23. DROMORE
24. INCH
25. SAUL
26. BALLYCULTER
27. TULLYLISH
28. SEAPATRICK
29. MAGHERALLY
30. ANNACLONE
31. NEWRY
32. KILMEGAN
33. DOWN
34. DONAGHMORE
35. BRIGHT
36. WARRENPOINT
37. BALLEE

Surname	R	I	S	Townland	Barony	Place-Parish
Abernethy	P	6	7	Drumbo	Castlereagh	Drumbo
Adams	P	6	26	Donaghadee	Ards	Donaghadee
Aidy	C	6	17	Downpatrick	Lecale	Down
Allen	P	6	10	Kircubbin	Ards	Inishargy
Allen	P	6	10	Magheralin	Iveagh	Magheralin
Allen	P	6	10		Lecale	Saul
Alsop	I	6	E		Lecale	Ballyculter
Anderson	P	6	21	Aughendarrah	Castlereagh	Killinchy
Annet	I	6	E	Tandragee *	Iveagh	Kilbroney
Anslo	I	6	E		Lecale	Saul
Arbuthnett	P	6	2	Dromore	Iveagh	Dromore
Arbuthnot	P	6	2	Dromore	Iveagh	Dromore
Arnott	P	6	12		Lecale	Saul
Athenleck		6		Dromore	Iveagh	Dromore
Atkinson	I	6	E	Dromore	Iveagh	Dromore
Audley *	I	6	E	Brade(Breda)	Castlereagh	Knockbreda
Bailie	P	6	5	Ardkeen	Ards U.	Ardkeen
Bailie	P	6	14	Inishargy *	Ards	Inishargy
Bailie	P	6	15	Kircubbin	Ards	Inisnargy
Baillie	P	6	15	Bangor	Ards	Bangor
Bane	C	6	I	Dromore	Iveagh	Dromore
Bassett	I	6	E	Downpatrick	Lecale	Down
Baxter *	I	6	E	Aughentaine *	Lecale	Down
Bean	I	6	E		Lecale	Down
Beck	P	6	10	Kircubbin	Ards	Inisnargy
Beers	P	6	10	Killyleagh	Duffrin	Killyleagh
Beggs	P	6	15	Drumbo	Castlereagh	Drumbo
Bell	I	6	E		Lecale	Saul
Benson	P	6	7	Drumbo	Castlereagh	Drumbo
Benson	P	6	7		Lecale	Saul
Bernard	I	6	E	Drumbo	Castlereagh	Drumbo
Betty	C	6	I		Kinelarty	Annahilt
Betty	P	6	20		Lecale	Down
Betty	C	6	I	Hillsborough	Iveagh	Hillsborough
Betty	C	6	I	Ballykeel	Iveagh	Seapatrick
Bigham	I	6	E	Banbridge	Iveagh	Seapatrick
Bingham	P	6	12	Rathfryland	Iveagh	Drumgrath
Bingham	P	6	12		Lecale	Saul

Surname	R	I	S	Townland	Barony	Place-Parish
Birrell	P	6	F	Lisburn	Castlereagh	Blaris
Blackburn	P	6	9	Ballylintagh	Iveagh	Annahilt
Blackwood	P	6	10	Bangor	Ards	Bangor
Blackwood	P	6	13		Lecale	Saul
Blair	P	6	7	Kircubbin	Ards	Inisnargy
Blakley	P	6	12	Bangor	Ards	Bangor
Bodel	P	6	13	Dromore	Iveagh	Dromore
Boileau	P	6	F	Lisburn	Castlereagh	Blaris
Bole	P	6	15	Bangor	Ards	Bangor
Bonner	Q	6	4	Dromore	Iveagh	Dromore
Boyd	P	6	12	Bangor	Ards	Bangor
Boyd	P	6	12	Downpatrick	Lecale	Down
Boyd	P	6	12		Lecale	Saul
Brannon	C	6	I	Bleary	Iveagh	Tullylish
Briggs	I	6	E		Iveragh	Annaclone
Brogton	I	6	E	Dromore	Iveagh	Dromore
Burns	P	6	6	Lurgan	Oneilland	Shankill
Campbell	P	6	6	Rathfryland	Iveagh	Drumgrath
Carr	P	6	17	Kilkeel	Mourne	Kilkeel
Carvill	C	6	I	Downpatrick	Lecale	Down
Casement	C	6	I	Downpatrick	Lecale	Down
Chartres	P	6	F	Lisburn	Castlereagh	Blaris
Clingan	P	6	21		Lecale	Ballee
Coates	P	6	1	Blaris	Massereene	Blaris
Colehy	I	6	E	Dromore	Iveagh	Dromore
Cooper	P	6	7	Killany	Castlereagh	Killaney
Cormac	C	6	I	Bleary	Iveagh	Tullylish
Cornwall	I	6	E	Ballywilliam	Ards	Donaghadee
Cosgrove	C	6	I	Downpatrick	Lecale	Down
Coulter *	P	6	13	Ballycoulter	Lecale	Ballyculter
Coyle	C	6	I	Bleary	Iveagh	Tullylish
Crickard	C	6	I	Downpatrick	Lecale	Down
Crommelin	P	6	F	Lisburn	Castlereagh	Blaris
Croskery	C	6	I	Downpatrick	Lecale	Down
Dalzell	I	6	E	Dundonald	Castlereagh	Dundonald
de la Valade	P	6	F	Lisburn	Castlereagh	Blaris
de Lolme	P	6	F	Lisburn	Castlereagh	Blaris
Debourdieu	P	6	F	Annahilt*		

Surname	R	I	S	Townland	Barony	Place-Parish
Defour	P	6	F	Lisburn	Castlereagh	Blaris
Denvir	I	6	E		Lecale	Bright
Depre	P	6	F	Lisburn	Castlereagh	Blaris
Desbrisay	P	6	F	Lisburn	Castlereagh	Blaris
Dick	P	6	18	Downpatrick	Lecale	Down
Divers	C	6	I	Bleary	Iveagh	Tullylish
Dolling	P	6	F	Magheralin	Iveagh	Magheralin
Domville	P	6	F	Lisburn	Castlereagh	Blaris
Doran	C	6	I	Bleary	Iveagh	Tullylish
Dow	P	6	4	Dromore	Iveagh	Dromore
Drainy	C	6	I	Bleary	Iveagh	Tullylish
Drysdale	P	6	1	Portaferry	Ards	Ballyphilip
Duff	P	6	26	Drumbo	Castlereagh	Drumbo
Dunlop	P	6	12	Kilmore	Iveagh	Shankill
Eadie	P	6	1	Newtownards	Castlereagh	Newtownards
Eakin	P	6	S	Bangor	Ards	Bangor
Edgar	P	6	17	Newtownards	Ards	Newtownards
Ellis	I	6	E	Dromore	Iveagh	Dromore
English	I	6	E	Dromore	Iveagh	Dromore
Fall	P	6	10	Dromore	Iveagh	Dromore
Faloon	P	6	F	Comber	Castlereagh	Comber
Frazier	P	6	31	Bleary	Iveagh	Tullylish
Glass	C	6	7	Dromore	Iveagh	Dromore
Goffe	C	6	I	Dromore	Iveagh	Dromore
Gordon	P	6	17	Comber	Castlereagh	Comber
Greg	P	6	7	Newtownards	Ards	Newtownards
Gregg	P	6	7	Dromore	Iveagh	Dromore
Gussen	P	6	F	Newry	Newry	Newry
Hallyday	P	6	21	Drumbo	Castlereagh	Drumbo
Hamilton	P	6	23	Comber	Castlereagh	Comber
Hannah	P	6	23	Comber	Castlereagh	Comber
Haraford	I	6	E	Market Hill	Fews	Kilclooney
Hardy	P	6	13	Kircubbin	Ards	Inisnargy
Harper	P	6	17	Comber	Castlereagh	Comber
Harvey	I	6	E	Downpatrick	Lecale	Down
Hawthorne	P	6	23	Downpatrick	Lecale	Down
Heather	I	6	E	Market Hill	Fews	Kilclooney
Heer	C	6	I	Dromore	Iveagh	Warrenspoint

Surname	R	I	S	Townland	Barony	Place-Parish
Heron	C	6	21	Killyleagh	Dufferin	Killyleagh
Heslip	P	6	15	Bangor	Ards	Bangor
Hewitt	I	6	E	Bangor	Ards	Bangor
Hinton	I	6	E	Dromore	Iveagh	Warrenspoint
Hogg	P	6	17	Bangor	Ards	Bangor
Hogg	P	6	19		Lecale	Saul
Holland	P	6	19	Bangor	Ards	Bangor
Hone	P	6	12	Downpatrick	Lecale	Down
Huddlestone	P	6	21		Lecale	Saul
Hughes	I	6	E		Lecale	Saul
Hunter	P	6	12	Moneymore	Iveagh	Donaghmore
Hunter	P	6	21	Dromore	Iveagh	Warrenspoint
Hutchinson	P	6	1	Dromore	Iveagh	Warrenspoint
Hutchison	P	6	1	Saintfield	Castlereagh	Saintfield
Hutton	I	6	17	Dromore	Iveagh	Warrenspoint
Innis	C	6	I		Lecale	Saul
Jellet	P	6	F	Dromore	Iveagh	Warrenspoint
Jenjins	P	6	15	Bangor	Ards	Bangor
Jennings	I	6	E	Downpatrick	Lecale	Down
Jillets	I	6	E		Lecale	Saul
Kane	C	6	I	Dromore	Iveagh	Warrenspoint
Kearney	C	6	I	Bleary	Iveagh	Tullylish
Keesh	I	6	E		Lecale	Saul
Kellips	C	6	32	Dromore	Iveagh	Warrenspoint
Kelly	P	6	11		Lecale	Saul
Kennedy	P	6	S	Dromore	Iveagh	Warrenspoint
Kenner	C	6	I		Lecale	Saul
Kewon	P	6	I		Lecale	Bright
Kibon	I	6	E		Lecale	Saul
Kinen	C	6	I	Dromore	Iveagh	Warrenspoint
Kinkead	P	6	9	Drumbo	Castlereagh	Drumbo
Kinner	P	6	1		Lecale	Saul
Kirk	P	6	21	Kircubbin	Ards	Inisnargy
Kirk	P	6	21	Lisburn	Castlereagh	Killaney
Knott	I	6	E		Lecale	Saul
Knox	P	6	11	Dromore	Iveagh	Warrenspoint
Lambert	P	6	17		Lecale	Saul
Landon	P	6	S		Lecale	Saul

Surname	R	I	S	Townland	Barony	Place-Parish
Lascelles	P	6	F	Lisburn	Castlereagh	Blaris
Laughlin	P	6	12	Bangor	Ards	Bangor
Leatherdale	I	6	E		Lecale	Saul
Lemon	C	6	I	Drumbo	Castlereagh	Drumbo
Lenox	P	6	15	Newtownards	Ards	Newtownards
Lewers	P	6	13		Lecale	Ballee
Lilburn	I	6	E	Dromore	Iveagh	Warrenspoint
Lindsay	P	6	12	Bangor	Ards	Bangor
Linton	P	6	20		Lecale	Saul
Livingston	P	6	S	Drumbo	Castlereagh	Drumbo
Lloyd	I	6	E		Lecale	Saul
Lockerby	P	6	21	Drumbo	Castlereagh	Drumbo
Lockhart	P	6	15	Bangor	Ards	Bangor
Long	P	6	15	Bangor	Ards	Bangor
Loughlin	C	6	I	Kircubbin	Ards	Inisnargy
Low	P	6	E	Downpatrick	Lecale	Down
Lowers	I	6	E		Lecale	Saul
Lowery	I	6	E		Lecale	Saul
Lundy	P	6	7	Downpatrick	Lecale	Down
Lyster	I	6	E	Kircubbin	Ards	Inisnargy
Mac Conwell	P	6	S	Bleary	Iveagh	Tullylish
Mac Neale	P	6	S	Dundrum	Lecale	Kilmegan
Mackel	C	6	I	Bleary	Iveagh	Tullylish
Madill	C	6	I		Lecale	Saul
Magill	P	6	S	Downpatrick	Lecale	Down
Magnigain	P	6	I	Bleary	Iveagh	Tullylish
Makky	C	6	I	Dromore	Iveagh	Warrenspoint
Mannis	P	6	20	Drumbo	Castlereagh	Drumbo
Marl	I	6	E		Lecale	Saul
Marline	I	6	E		Lecale	Saul
Marshall	P	6	15	Bangor	Ards	Bangor
Mawhinney	C	6	I		Lecale	Saul
Maxwell	P	6	21	Newry	Newry	Newry
Mc Allister	P	6	26	Downpatrick	Lecale	Down
Mc Anerny	C	6	I	Bleary	Iveagh	Tullylish
Mc Avers	P	6	S		Lecale	Saul
Mc Bride	C	6	27	Comber	Castlereagh	Comber
Mc Bryer	P	6	I		Lecale	Saul

Surname	R	I	S	Townland	Barony	Place-Parish
Mc Calla	C	6	12	Ballynahinch	Kinelarty	Magheradrool
Mc Camish	C	6	I	Dromore	Iveagh	Warrenspoint
Mc Camon	P	6	I	Market Hill	Fews	Kilclooney
Mc Cann	P	6	15	Newtownards	Ards	Newtownards
Mc Chestney	P	6	S	Drumbo	Castlereagh	Drumbo
Mc Clinshe	C	6	I	Market Hill	Fews	Kilclooney
Mc Cloy	P	6	12		Lecale	Saul
Mc Clurg	P	6	12	Killyleagh	Dufferin	Killyleagh
Mc Comb	P	6	22	Downpatrick	Lecale	Down
Mc Comb	P	6	22		Lecale	Saul
Mc Convil	C	6	I	Bleary	Iveagh	Tullylish
Mc Cormick	C	6	I	Magherally	Iveagh	Magerally
Mc Cosker	C	6	I	Bleary	Iveagh	Tullylish
Mc Cracken	P	6	6		Lecale	Saul
Mc Creevy	C	6	I		Lecale	Saul
Mc Creightt	C	6	I	Market Hill	Fews	Kilclooney
Mc Crisckan	P	6	I	Downpatrick	Lecale	Down
Mc Cullock	P	6	23	Kircubbin	Ards	Inisnargy
Mc Doel	P	6	36	Dromore	Iveagh	Warrenspoint
Mc Fadden	P	6	29	Kircubbin	Ards	Inisnargy
Mc Geean	C	6	I	Downpatrick	Lecale	Down
Mc Gibbon	C	6	I	Bangor	Ards	Bangor
Mc Gibbon	C	6	I	Drumbo	Castlereagh	Drumbo
Mc Gifford	P	6	S	Magheradrool	Kinelarty	Magheradrool
Mc Gill	P	6	7	Newtownards	Ards	Newtownards
Mc Gladry	C	6	I	Dromore	Iveagh	Warrenspoint
Mc Glaughlin	C	6	I	Dromore	Iveagh	Warrenspoint
Mc Glennon	P	6	7		Lecale	Saul
Mc Guffick	P	6	1		Lecale	Saul
Mc Handles	I	6	E		Lecale	Saul
Mc Ilrudd	P	6	6	Armagh	Armagh	Armagh
Mc Ilvine	P	6	21	Drumbo	Castlereagh	Drumbo
Mc Kay	P	6	6		Lecale	Saul
Mc Kee	P	6	26		Lecale	Saul
Mc Keever	I	6	I	Armagh	Armagh	Armagh
Mc Keevers	P	6	I		Lecale	Downpatrick
Mc Kelman	P	6	-		Lecale	Saul
Mc Kenzie	P	6	23		Lecale	Downpatrick

Surname	R	I	S	Townland	Barony	Place-Parish
Mc Keon	C	6	I	Dromore	Iveagh	Warrenspoint
Mc Kibbin	P	6	6	Lisburn	Iveagh	Hillsborough
Mc Knights	P	6	21		Lecale	Saul
Mc Koskran	P	6	S	Dromore	Iveagh	Warrenspoint
Mc Lure	P	6	21	Drumbo	Castlereagh	Drumbo
Mc Math	P	6	22	Kircubbin	Ards	Inisnargy
Mc Mechan	P	6	21	Bangor	Ards	Bangor
Mc Mordie	P	6	I	Lurgan	Iveagh	Seapatrick
Mc Murlan	I	6	E		Lecale	Saul
Mc Murray	P	6	21		Lecale	Saul
Mc Murry	P	6	23	Downpatrick	Lecale	Down
Mc Murty	P	6	25	Dromore	Iveagh	Warrenspoint
Mc Neil	P	6	31		Lecale	Saul
Mc Nish	P	6	22	Drumbo	Castlereagh	Drumbo
Mc Pollan	I	6	S		Iveagh	Anaaclone
Mc Quoid	C	6	I	Kircubbin	Ards	Inisnargy
Mc Watters	P	6	34	Kircubbin	Ards	Inisnargy
Mc Whorc	P	6	21	Kircubbin	Ards	Inisnargy
Menown	P	6	21		Lecale	Saul
Mercer	P	6	20			
Mercer	P	6	4		Lecale	Saul
Millar	I	6	E		Iveagh	Hillsborough
Millar	P	6	12		Lecale	Saul
Millar	P	6	E	Dromore	Iveagh	Warrenspoint
Mind	P	6	S	Drumbo	Castlereagh	Drumbo
Money	I	6	E		Lecale	Saul
Moon	I	6	E		Lecale	Saul
Moorcraft	I	6	E	Drumbo	Castlereagh	Drumbo
Morrison	I	6	E	Downpatrick	Lecale	Down
Muckle	I	6	E	Kircubbin	Ards	Inisnargy
Muldra	P	6	S		Lecale	Downpatrick
Mulligon	P	6	21	Dromore	Iveagh	Warrenspoint
Mullow	C	6	I		Lecale	Saul
Murland	P	6	S	Kircubbin	Ards	Inisnargy
Myars	I	6	E	Dromore	Iveagh	Warrenspoint
Nagons	P	6	F	Lisburn	Castlereagh	Blaris
Nesbit	P	6	17	Bangor	Ards U.	Bangor
Newland	P	6	13	Drumbo	Castlereagh	Drumbo

Surname	R	I	S	Townland	Barony	Place-Parish
Nixon	Q	6	21		Lecale	Saul
Obins	P	6	S	Bleary	Iveagh	Tullylish
Orson	I	6	E	Bleary	Iveagh	Tullylish
Osborne	P	6	1		Lecale	Saul
Palmer	P	6	17		Lecale	Saul
Parker	P	6	4		Lecale	Saul
Parks	I	6	E		Lecale	Saul
Patton	P	6	12	Newtownards	Castlereagh	Newtownards
Peake	I	6	E		Lecale	Saul
Peebles	P	6	23	Dundonald	Castlereagh	Dundonald
Peevers	I	6	E		Lecale	Saul
Pendleton	I	6	E	Kircubbin	Ards	Inisnargy
Pentland	P	6	15	Drumbo	Castlereagh	Drumbo
Perdu	P	6	F	Lisburn	Castlereagh	Blaris
Perry	I	6	E	Ballydugan	Lecale	Down
Perry	I	6	E	Downpatrick	Lecale	Down
Petticrew	P	6	12	Hollywood	Castlereagh	Hollywood
Pollock	P	6	11	Newry	Newry	Newry
Polly	P	6	12		Lecale	Saul
Porter	P	6	12	Drumbo	Castlereagh	Drumbo
Porter	P	6	11	Greyabbey	Ards	Greyabbey
Powell	P	6	W		Lecale	Saul
Pratt	Q	6	1		Lecale	Saul
Presby	P	6	1	Drumbo	Castlereagh	Drumbo
Presley	P	6	1	Drumbo	Castlereagh	Drumbo
Pritchard	P	6	W	Kircubbin	Ards	Inisnargy
Purdy	P	6	12	Newtownards	Ards	Newtownards
Quinton	H	6	F		Lecale	Saul
Rainey	P	6	7	Drumbo	Castlereagh	Drumbo
Ramsey	P	6	7	Bangor	Bangor	Bangor
Reid	P	6	4	Ballywalter	Ards	Ballywalter
Richardson	P	6	4			
Richey	P	6	12	Bangor	Lower Ards	Bangor
Rigby	I	6	E		Lecale	Saul
Roan	P	6	12		Lecale	Down
Robb	P	6	21	Newtownards	Castlereagh	Newtownards
Robinson	I	6	E	Downpatrick	Lecale	Down
Roche	P	6	F	Lisburn	Castlereagh	Blaris

Surname	R	I	S	Townland	Barony	Place-Parish
Rodgers	C	6	I	Newry	Newry	Newry
Rogan	C	6	I	Ballydugan	Lecale	Down
Roney	C	6	I		Lecale	Saul
Ross	P	6	5	Drumbo	Castlereagh	Drumbo
Rowan	P	6	11	Dromore	Iveagh	Dromore
Rowan	P	6	13	Kircubbin	Ards	Inisnargy
Russell	P	6	S	Ballybot*		
Russell	P	6	12	Drumbo	Castlereagh	Drumbo
Sadler	P	6	12		Lecale	Saul
Sanflay	I	6	N	Ballydugan	Lecale	Down
Saul	C	6	N		Lecale	Saul
Savage	P	6	21	Downpatrick	Lecale	Down
Sayers	I	6	E		Lecale	Saul
Scott	P	6	S		Lecale	Saul
Seay	P	6	S		Lecale	Saul
Seeds	P	6	S		Lecale	Saul
Shankey	C	6	I	Ballydugan	Lecale	Down
Shaw	P	6	1	Kircubbin	Ards	Inisnargy
Shepherd	P	6	18		Lecale	Saul
Sherif	P	6	1	Drumbo	Castlereagh	Drumbo
Shields	C	6	20	Downpatrick	Lecale	Down
Shimon	P	6	S		Lecale	Saul
Shimon	P	6	S		Lecale	Saul
Simpson	P	6	1		Lecale	Saul
Singleton	I	6	E	Blaris	Castlereagh	Blaris
Singleton	P	6	15		Lecale	Saul
Skelly	C	6	I	Drumbo	Castlereagh	Drumbo
Skillen	P	6	N	Downpatrick	Lecale	Down
Sloan	P	6	15	Bangor	Lower Ards	Bangor
Sloan	P	6	15		Lecale	Down
Sloan	P	6	15		Lecale	Down
Sloan	C	6	I	Dromore	Iveagh	Dromore
Sloan	P	6	15	Drumbo	Castlereagh	Drumbo
Small	P	6	1		Lecale	Saul
Smith	P	6	E		Lecale	Saul
Speers	P	6	15		Lecale	Saul
Spence	P	6	17		Lecale	Saul
Spittle	P	6	10	Newry	Newry	Newry

Surname	R	I	S	Townland	Barony	Place-Parish
Spratt	P	6	E		Lecale	Saul
St. Sauveur	P	6	F	Lisburn	Castlereagh	Blaris
Stanley	P	6	15	Kircubbin	Ards	Inisnargy
Staples	I	6	E	Dromore	Iveagh	Dromore
Steenson	P	6	11		Lecale	Saul
Stewart	P	6	11	Bangor	Lower Ards	Bangor
Stewart	P	6	4	Donaghadee	Ards	Donaghadee
Strahan	P	6	1		Lecale	Saul
Straiten	P	6	S	Kiecubbin	Ards	Inisnargy
Stuart	P	6	7		Lecale	Down
Sumrall	I	6	E	Dromore	Iveagh	Dromore
Tate	P	6	35	Ballynainch	Kinelarty	Magheradrool
Tate	p	6	35		Lecale	Saul
Tavany	P	6	S		Lecale	Saul
Tea	I	6	E	Dromore	Iveagh	Dromore
Teer	P	6	I		Lecale	Saul
Thompson	P	6	S		Lecale	Saul
Tisdale	P	6	S		Lecale	Saul
Todd	P	6	15		Lecale	Saul
Toman	C	6	I	Bleary	Iveagh	Tullylish
Torney	P	6	E		Lecale	Saul
Torrance	P	6	E		Lecale	Saul
Tremble	P	6	15	Newry	Newry	Newry
Tumelty	P	6	S		Lecale	Saul
Turnbull	P	6	20	Dromore	Iveagh	Dromore
Vance	I	6	E	Kircubbin	Ards	Inisnargy
Wagh	P	6	S	Dromore	Iveagh	Dromore
Walker	P	6	11	Dromore	Iveagh	Dromore
Wallace	P	6	12	Greyabbey	Ards	Greyabbey
Wallace	P	6	11	Hollywood	Castlereagh	Hollywood
Ward	P	6	9	Dromore	Iveagh	Dromore
Warwick	P	6	5		Lecale	Saul
Waterson	P	6	11		Lecale	Saul
Watkins	P	6	W		Lecale	Down
Watt	I	6	E	Dromore	Iveagh	Dromore
Watters	P	6	S		Lecale	Down
Watterson	P	6	S		Lecale	Saul
Weal	I	6	E	Dromore	Iveagh	Dromore

Surname	R	I	S	Townland	Barony	Place-Parish
Welshman	I	6	W	Downpatrick	Lecale	Down
West	I	6	E	Ballydugan	Lecale	Down
Whisker	I	6	E	Downpatrick	Lecale	Down
White	P	6	E	Kircubbin	Ards	Inisnargy
Wilford	P	6	S		Lecale	Saul
Wilkinson	P	6	S		Lecale	Saul
Wilson	P	6	S	Castleregh	Castlereagh	Knockbreda
Windrum	P	6			Lecale	Saul
Winn	P	6		Ballydugan	Lecale	Down

SAVAGE CASTLE
DOWN

Map of Fermangh

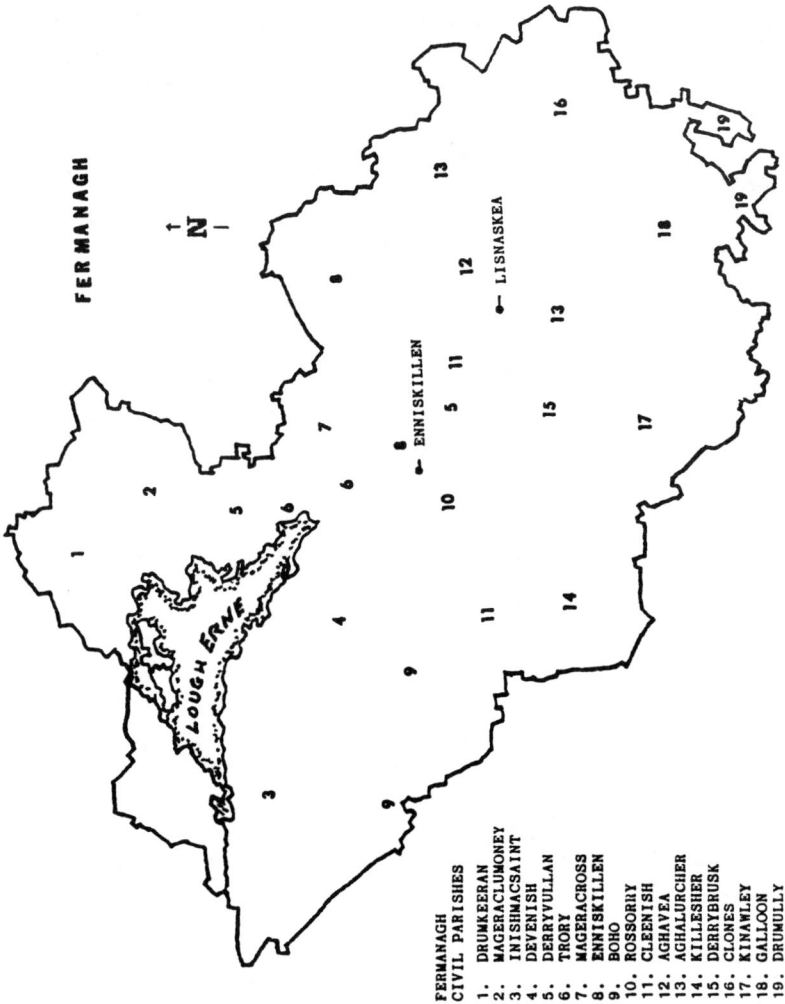

FERMANAGH

N

FERMANAGH
CIVIL PARISHES

1. DRUMKEERAN
2. MAGERACLUMONEY
3. INISHMACSAINT
4. DEVENISH
5. DERRYVULLAN
6. TRORY
7. MAGERACROSS
8. ENNISKILLEN
9. BOHO
10. ROSSORHY
11. CLEENISH
12. AGHAVEA
13. AGHALURCHER
14. KILLESHER
15. DERRYBRUSK
16. CLONES
17. KINAWLEY
18. GALLOON
19. DRUMULLY

LOUGH ERNE

ENNISKILLEN

LISNASKEA

Surname	R	I	S	Townland	Barony	Place-Parish
Acheson	P	7	16	Enniskillen	Magheraboy	Enniskillen
Adams	I	7	E	Enniskillen	Magheraboy	Enniskillen
Aldrich	I	7	S	Enniskillen	Magheraboy	Enniskillen
Alwell		7			Magherstphna	Aghavea
Amoss	I	7	E	Rossory	Magheraboy	Rossory
Archdale	Q	7	E	Enniskillen	Magheraboy	Enniskillen
Archdale *	I	7	E	Tallanal *	Magheraboy	Enniskillen
Archdall ˙	I	7	E	Castl.Archdall	Lurg	Magheramoney
Ardsell	P	7	E	Enniskillen	Magheraboy	Enniskillen
Armstrong	P	7	21	Drummully	Coole	Drummully
Auchinleck	P	7	12	Enniskillen	Magheraboy	Enniskillen
Balfour *	I	7	E	Carrowchee *	Knockninny	Kinawley
Balfour *	I	7	E	Kilspanan *	Knockninny	Kinawley
Balfour *	I	7	E	Montwhany *	Knockninny	Kinwaley
Ballard	I	7	E	Enniskillen	Magheraboy	Enniskillen
Barton *	I	7	E	Drominshin *	Lurg	Derryvullan
Beacum	I	7	E	Enniskillen	Magheraboy	Enniskillen
Beattie	P	7	21	Enniskillen	Magheraboy	Enniskillen
Bedel	P	7	5	Enniskillen	Magheraboy	Enniskillen
Bedine	C	7	I	New Tn Butler	Coole	Galloon
Bell	P	7	21	Derryvullan	Tirkennedy	Derryvullan
Bell	P	7	10	Enniskillen	Magheraboy	Enniskillen
Bell	P	7	21	Enniskillen	Magheraboy	Enniskillen
Bell	P	7	21	Drumbulcan	Tirkennely	Magheracross
Betty	P	7	22	Enniskillen	Magheraboy	Enniskillen
Betty	C	7	I	Killesher	Clanawley	Killesher
Bevish	I	7	E			
Black	I	7	E	Clonfad	Clankelly	Clones
Black	P	7	6	Enniskillen	Magheraboy	Enniskillen
Blakley	C	7	12	Rossory	Magheraboy ˙	Rossory
Blannerhasset *	I	7	E	Banagh *	Lurg	Drumkeeran
Blashford	P	7		Enniskillen	Magheraboy	Enniskillen
Bothwell	C	7	13	Rossory	Magheraboy	Rossory
Boxter	C	7	I	Rossory	Magheraboy	Rossory
Browne	I	7	E	Rossgarn *	Magheraboy	Enniskillen
Browning	P	7	1	Enniskillen	Magheraboy	Enniskillen
Bury	I	7	E	Enniskillen	Magheraboy	Enniskillen
Butler *	I	7	E	Diriany *	Knockninny	Kinawley

Surname	R	I	S	Townland	Barony	Place-Parish
Butler *	I	7	E	Kilspinan *	Knockninny	Kinawley
Campbell	P	7	6	Enniskillen	Magheraboy	Enniskillen
Carothers	P	7	21		Magherstphna	Aghavea
Carrothers	P	7	20	Lowtherstown	Lurg	Derryvallun
Cashell	C	7	I	Enniskillen	Magheraboy	Enniskillen
Cathcart	P	7	11	Enniskillen	Magheraboy	Enniskillen
Chapman	P	7	15		Magherstphna	Aghavea
Clarke	I	7	4	Enniskillen	Magheraboy	Enniskillen
Cole	I	7	E	Enniskillen	Magheraboy	Enniskillen
Cole *	I	7	E	Drumskea	Lurg	Derryvullan
Collyer	P	7	7	Enniskillen	Magheraboy	Enniskillen
Corry	P	7	12	Enniskillen	Magheraboy	Enniskillen
Cosbye	I	7	E	Enniskillen	Magheraboy	Enniskillen
Cox	C	7	I	Lowtherstown	Lurg	Derryvallun
Crozier	I	7	E	Enniskillen	Magheraboy	Enniskillen
Crozier	I	7	E	Enniskillen	Tirkennedy	Enniskillen
Cue	P	7	F	Enniskillen	Magheraboy	Enniskillen
Dane	I	7	E	Enniskillen	Magheraboy	Enniskillen
Davenport	I	7	E	Enniskillen	Magheraboy	Enniskillen
Davies	P	7	W	Carrow *	Clanawley	Killisher
Dean	P	7	12	Enniskillen	Magheraboy	Enniskillen
Deine	P	7	1	Enniskillen	Magheraboy	Enniskillen
Devitt	I	7	E	Enniskillen	Magheraboy	Enniskillen
Dixy	I	7	E	Enniskillen	Magheraboy	Enniskillen
Dobbin	P	7	21	Londonderry	Londonderry	Templemore
Donboro *	P	7	S	Dromcro *	Tirkennedy	Derrybrusk
Dornian	P	7	I	Mullubrack *	Lurg	Derryvullan
Dougkill	P	7	12	Enniskillen	Magheraboy	Enniskillen
Dunbar *	P	7	23	Dromcro *	Magheraboy	
Dunberry	P	7	S	Enniskillen	Magheraboy	Enniskillen
Duncan	P	7	1	Lisneskea	Magerstphana	Aghalurcher
Durning, Chas.	-	7	I	Mullies	Lurg	Derryvullan
Durning,Cath.	-	7	I	Leam	Tirkennedy	Derryvullan
Durning,Chas.	-	7	I	Leam	Tirkennedy	Derryvullan
Durning,James	-	7	I	Mullybrack	Lurg	Derryvullan
Elgun	C	7	I		Magheraboy	Cleenish
Elliott	P	7	17		Clanawley	
Evatt	P	7	4		Magherstphna	Aghavea

Surname	R	I	S	Townland	Barony	Place-Parish
Evatt	P	7	4	Enniskillen	Magheraboy	Enniskillen
Ewart	P	7	20	Enniskillen	Magheraboy	Enniskillen
Fergusson	P	7	7	Enniskellen	Magheraboy	Enniskillen
Fletcher	P	7	5	Ahantra *	Magheraboy	Enniskillen
Follitt	P	7	I	Enniskillen	Magheraboy	Enniskillen
Fowler *	P	7	15	Moyglass	Magheraboy	Rossorry
Frederick,P.	I	7	E		Tirkennedy	Derryvullan
French	P	7	21	Enniskillen	Magheraboy	Enniskillen
Frisell	I	7	E	Enniskillen	Magheraboy	Enniskillen
Frith	I	7	E	Enniskillen	Magheraboy	Enniskillen
Fulton	P	7	12	Enniskillen	Magheraboy	Enniskillen
Gadess	I	7	E	Enniskillen	Magheraboy	Enniskillen
Gibb *	P	7	S	Druma*	Magheraboy	Boho
Glenn	I	7	E	Lisniskea	Magerstphana	Aghalurcher
Goodfellow	I	7	E	Enniskillen	Magheraboy	Enniskillen
Goot	H	7	G	Enniskillen	Magheraboy	Enniskillen
Gore	I	7	E	Enniskillen	Magheraboy	Enniskillen
Grattan		7	I	Enniskillen	Magheraboy	Enniskillen
Grove	I	7	E	Enniskillen	Magheraboy	Enniskillen
Gubbin	I	7	E	Enniskillen	Magheraboy	Enniskillen
Guthrie	P	7	12	Enniskillen	Magheraboy	Enniskillen
Hamilton *	P	7	13	Derrynefogher	Magheraboy	Devenish
Hassard	H	7	F	Enniskillen	Magheraboy	Enniskillen
Heighton	P	7	13	Enniskillen	Magheraboy	Enniskillen
Henning *	P	7	21	Dewress		
Higginbotham	I	7	E	Enniskillen	Magheraboy	Enniskillen
Home *	P	7	10	Dromcoole	Magheraboy	Enniskillen
Hookes	I	7	E	Enniskillen	Magheraboy	Enniskillen
Houston	C	7	5	Rossory	Magheraboy	Rossory
Hudson	I	7	E	Enniskillen	Magheraboy	Enniskillen
Hume *	I	7	17	Ardgart	Magheraboy	Inishmacsaint
Irvine	I	7	12	Enniskillen	Magheraboy	Enniskillen
Irwin	P	7	21	Derrygore	Tirkennedy	Trory
Isaac	H	7	G	Enniskillen	Magheraboy	Enniskillen
Johnston	P	7	21	Brookeborough	Magheraphana	Aghavea
Johnston	P	7	21	Enniskillen	Magheraboy	Enniskillen
Keary	C	7	I	Lisnaskea	Maghersphana	Aghalurcher
Keenan	C	7	I	Derryvullen	Tirkennedy	Derryvullen

Surname	R	I	S	Townland	Barony	Place-Parish
Keenan	C	7	I	Drumbulcan	Tirkennedy	Mahgaracross
Kennedie	P	7	22	Clonkee	Coole	Drummully
Keon	P	7	I	Mullies	Lurg	Derryvullan
Keon	C	7	I	Mullies	Lurg	Derryvullen
Keon	C	7	I	Derryvullen	Tirkennedy	Derryvullen
Kevenay	C	7	W	Rossory	Magheraboy	Rossory
Kewburgh	I	7	E	Castlefin	Magheraboy	Enniskillen
Keyes	I	7	E	Derryvullun	Tirkennedy	Derryvullan
Keyes	I	7	E	Enniskillen	Magheraboy	Enniskillen
Keyes	C	7	I	Drumbulcan	Tirkennedy	Magheracross
Kittle	P	7	7	Enniskillen	Magheraboy	Enniskillen
Knight	I	7	E	Tunnymore	Magheraboy	Enniskillen
Knoght	I	7	E	Tullymore	Magheraboy	Inishmacsaint
Lamon	P	7	6	Ardgart	Magheraboy	Inishmacsaint
Landy	I	7	E	Enniskillen	Magheraboy	Enniskillen
Leathes	I	7	E	Enniskillen	Magheraboy	Enniskillen
Lendrum *	P	7	1	Cleen	Magheraphana	Aghalurcher
Lesley	P	7	1	Enniskillen	Magheraboy	Enniskillen
Letournall	H	7	F	Enniskillen	Magheraboy	Enniskillen
Leturnel	I	7	E	Enniskillen	Magheraboy	Enniskillen
Ligonier	H	7	F	Enniskillen	Magheraboy	Enniskillen
Lindrey *	I	7	E	Dromfkeah*		
Lindsay *	P	7	15	Drumskea	Lurg	Derryvullan
Liturel	I	7	E	Enniskillen	Magheraboy	Enniskillen
Lloyd	I	7	E	Enniskillen	Magheraboy	Enniskillen
Logan	P	7	23	Lowtherstown	Lurg	Derryvullan
Logan	I	7	15	Enniskillen	Magheraboy	Enniskillen
Loghran	C	7	I	Rossory	Magheraboy	Rossory
Love	P	7	11	Lowtherstown	Lurg	Derryvullan
Lucy	I	7		Enniskillen	Magheraboy	Enniskillen
Lyon	C	7	I	Enniskillen	Magheraboy	Enniskillen
Mac Cormick	P	7	S	Enniskillen	Magheraboy	Enniskillen
Mac Cue	C	7	I	Mullies	Lurg	Derryvullan
Mac Dermod	C	7	I	Derryvullen	Tirkennedy	Derryvullen
Mac Dermod	P	7	12	Drumbulcan	Tirkennedy	Magheracross
Mailholm *	I	7	E	Diriany	Knockninny	
March	I	7	E	Rossory	Magheraboy	Rossory
Mc Cusker	P	7	I	Lowtherstown	Lurg	Derryvullan

Surname	R	I	S	Townland	Barony	Place-Parish
Mc Donald	C	7	5	Lisnaskea	Magherstphana	Aghalurcher
Mc Kle	I	7	I	Rossory	Magheraboy	Rossory
Moan	C	7	I	Lisnaskea	Magherstphana	Aghalurcher
Moffit	I	7	21	Enniskillen	Magheraboy	Enniskillen
Moffitt	P	7	21			
Moneypenny *	P	7	7	Kinkell	Knockninny	
Moor	I	7	E	Enniskillen	Magheraboy	Enniskillen
Mulloy	C	7	I	Enniskillen	Magheraboy	Enniskillen
Neper	H	7	E	Enniskillen	Magheraboy	Enniskillen
Nixon	I	7	E	Drumcrow	Magheraboy	Enniskillen
Nixon	I	7	E	Kingstown	Magheraboy	Enniskillen
Nixon *	P	7	20	Nixon Hall		
Pomeroy	I	7	E	Ballycassidy	Tirkennedy	Trory
Pye	P	7	7	Rossory	Magheraboy	Rossory
Rider	I	7	E	Enniskillen	Magheraboy	Enniskillen
Roscrow	I	7	E	Enniskillen	Magheraboy	Enniskillen
Scott	P	7	18	Furnish	Tirkennedy	Enniskillen
Seery	C	7	I	Rossory	Magheraboy	Rossory
Shore	I	7	E	Enniskillen	Magheraboy	Enniskillen
Skelton	I	7	E	Clones	Clankelly	Clones
Slack	I	7	E	Enniskillen	Magheraboy	Enniskillen
Smith	I	7	E	Whitehall	Magheraboy	Enniskillen
Sommes	P	7	S	Enniskillen	Magheraboy	Enniskillen
Spence	P	7	1	Enniskillen	Magheraboy	Devenish
Spence	P	7	I	Moyglass	Magheraboy	Rossorry
Starling	I	7	E	Enniskillen	Magheraboy	Enniskillen
Stevenson	I	7	E	Enniskillen	Magheraboy	Enniskillen
Tenison	I	7	E	Knokbalmor	Magheraboy	Enniskillen
Trotter	P	7	17	Enniskillen	Magheraboy	Enniskillen
Wade	I	7	E	Enniskillen	Magheraboy	Enniskillen
Walmsley	I	7	E	Rossory	Magheraboy	Rossory
Whitten	C	7	I	Rossory	Magheraboy	Rossory
Wisehart	I	7	E	Enniskillen	Magheraboy	Enniskillen

Map Monaghan

MONAGHAN

1

3

2
SCOTSTOWN

MONAGHAN 5

4
CLONES

6 7 8 9 10

11 CASTLEBLANEY

MONAGHAN
CIVIL PARISHES

1. ERRIGAL
2. TEDAVNET
3. DONAGH
4. CLONES
5. MONAGHAN
6. KILLEEVAN
7. AGHABOG
8. TULLYCORBET
9. CLONTIBRET
10. MUCKNO
11. EMATRIS

Surname	R	I	S	Townland	Barony	Place-Parish
Akins	P	8	12			
Alleley	I	8	E	Clones	Dartree	Clones
Allely	I	8	E	Clonkeen	Trough	Errigal T.
Archdecon	I	8	E	Shanmulagh	Monaghan	Tullycorbet
Archer	I	8	E		Cremorne	Muckno
Askin	I	8	E	Legnakelly*		
Barkagh	I	8	E	Lisnagore	Dartree	killeevan
Barkha	I	8	E			
Berren	C	8	I			
Bleakley	P	8	21	Clonkerhill *		
Bog	I	8	E	Drumbenagh	Monaghan	Tedavent
Bourch	P	8	F	Lisnaveane	Cremorne	Tullycorbet
Bowes	I	8	E	Teer	Dartree	Killeevan
Brakey	I	8	E	Drumskelt	Dartree	Killeevan
Brigs	I	8	E	Lisnaveane	Cremorne	Tullycorbet
Burnstep	P	8	S	Teehill	Dartree	Clones
Busby	I	8	E	Analagh *	Trough	Donagh
Carson	P	8	21	Shanroe	Monaghan	Clones
Clegg	I	8	E	Clones	Dartree	Clones
Clindinin	P	8	21	Cornaiaghy	Dartree	Clones
Cloid	I	8	E		Dartree	Aghabog
Coldwill	I	8	E	Crossmoyle	Dartree	Clones
Cotnam	P	8	S	Lisnore *		
Creacy	I	8	E		Cremorne	Clontibret
Crombie	P	8	S	Lisnaveane	Cremorne	Tullycorbet
Dixon	P	8	E	Lisnaveane	Cremorne	Tullycorbet
Dodson	P	8	1	Lisnaveane	Cremorne	Tullycorbet
Egriston	I	8	E		Dartree	Aghabog
Gaddis	P	8	S	Annahagh	Monaghan	Tedavnet
Gallice	P	8	12	Clincorn *		
Gibbs	I	8	E	Clones	Dartree	Clones
Gillanders	C	8	I	Crosses	Monaghan	Monaghan
Gilly	C	8	I	Clonboy	Dartree	Clones
Gluck	I	8	E	Clones	Dartree	Clones
Gordon	P	8	1	Templetate	Dartree	Clones
Gorteen	I	8	E	Clones	Dartree	Clones
Gowan *	C	8	I	Glaslough	Trough	Donagh
Guthree	P	8	12	Clones	Dartree	Clones

Surname	R	I	S	Townland	Barony	Place-Parish
Haddon	I	8	E		Dartree	Aghabog
Hamersly	I	8	E	Clones	Dartree	Clones
Harkness	P	8	S	Lisnaveane	Cremorne	Tullycorbet
Harshaw	P	8	S	Lisnaveane	Cremorne	Tullycorbet
Holdsworth	I	8	E	Caravitragh*		
Honnins	I	8	E	Clones	Dartree	Clones
Hoy	C	8	I	Lisnaveane	Cremorne	Tullycorbet
Jarland	I	8	E	Clones	Dartree	Clones
Jawin	I	8	E	Granshagh		
Kinsalagh	C	8	I	Lattagallon*		
Kinsolagh	I	8	I	Rathmoy*		
Kirk	P	8	S	Lisnaveane	Cremorne	Tullycorbet
Knox *	P	8	11	Glaslough	Trough	Donagh
Larman	I	8	E	Drumulla*		
Lindesay	P	8	7	Killycorran	Trough	Errigal T.
Linster	H	8	G	Lisnaveane	Cremorne	Tullycorbet
Linton	I	8	E	Lisnaveane	Cremorne	Tullycorbet
Lister	H	8	G		Dartree	Ematris
Logan	P	8	S	Lisnaveane	Cremorne	Tullycorbet
Logheed	P	8	S	Lisnaveane	Cremorne	Tullycorbet
Lorrimer	P	8	E	Lisnaveane	Cremorne	Tullycorbet
Lutton	I	8	E		Dartree	Aghabog
Mac Alooney	C	8	I	Carn	Dartree	Clones
Mac Conaghy	C	8	6	Lisnagore	Dartree	Killeevan
Mc Aneany	P	8	S	Coraghbrak	Trough	Donagh
Mc Cabe	C	8	I	Crossreagh	Dartree	Killeevan
Mc Gaw	P	8	12	Corlogharoe	Dartree	Killeevan
Mc Guffy	P	8	I	Lisnaveane	Cremorne	Tullycorbet
Mc Mullan	P	8	6	Lisnaveane	Cremorne	Tullycorbet
Mc Murry	P	8	12	Longfield		
Mc Nemorig	P	8	S		Farney	Magheracloon
Mills	I	8	E	Cappog	Dartree	Killeevan
Morray	P	8	S	Lisnaveane	Cremorne	Tullycorbet
Morrow	I	8	E	Lisnaveane	Cremorne	Tullycorbet
Muir	P	8	S	Lisnaveane	Cremorne	Tullycorbet
Murdock	P	8	S	Glaslough	Trough	Donagh
Napper	I	8	E	Lisnaveane	Cremorne	Tullycorbet
Nixon	Q	8	E	Lisnaveane	Cremorne	Tullycorbet

Map of Cavin

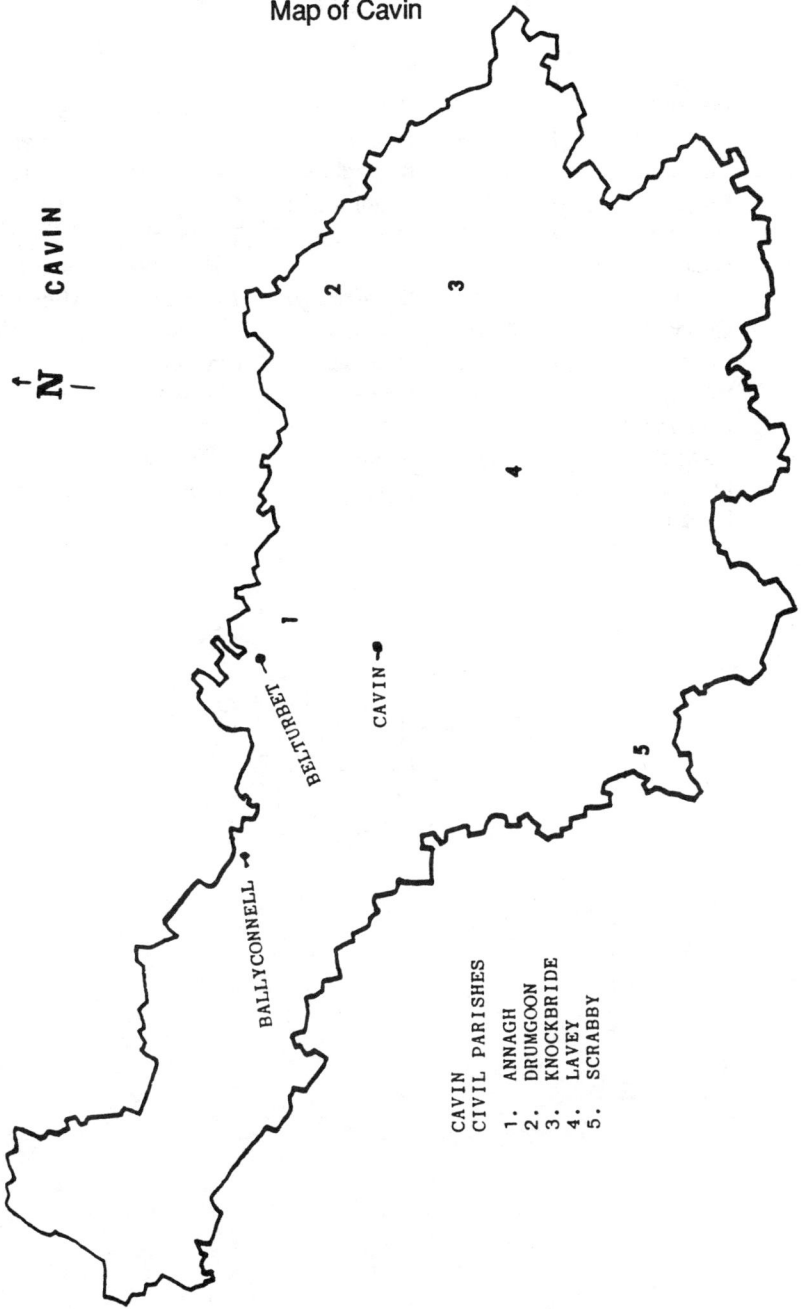

N

CAVIN

CAVIN
CIVIL PARISHES

1. ANNAGH
2. DRUMGOON
3. KNOCKBRIDE
4. LAVEY
5. SCRABBY

BALLYCONNELL

BELTURBET

CAVIN

Name	R	I	S	Townland	Barony	Place-Parish
Achmutie	P	11	15	Drumhillagh	Loughhtee U.	Lavey
Achmutie	P	11	15	Dromheda *	Tallyhunco	Scrabby
Achmutie *	P	11	15	Keylagh *	Tallyhunco	Scrabby
Baillie *	P	11	11	Tonnereghie *	Clankee	Knockbride?
Brown *	P	11	15	Carrodonan *	Tullyhunco	
Buck	I	11	E		Tullygarvey	Annagh
Craig	P	11	15	Drumhillagh	Tallyhunco	Scrabby
Craig *	P	11	S	Achmutie *	Tullyhunco	Scrabby
Dunbar *	P	11	12	Dromack *	Clankee	
Hamilton *	P	11	13	Kilcolgha	Clankee	Drumgoon
Hamilton *	P	11	10	Clonyn *	Tullyhunco	
Keylagh *	I	11	E	Achmutie *	Tullyhunco	
Moorhead	P	11	S	Cavin	Loughtee	Annagh
Nesbitt	I	11	E			

MOUNTJOY CASTLE
TYRONE 1602

Map Sligo

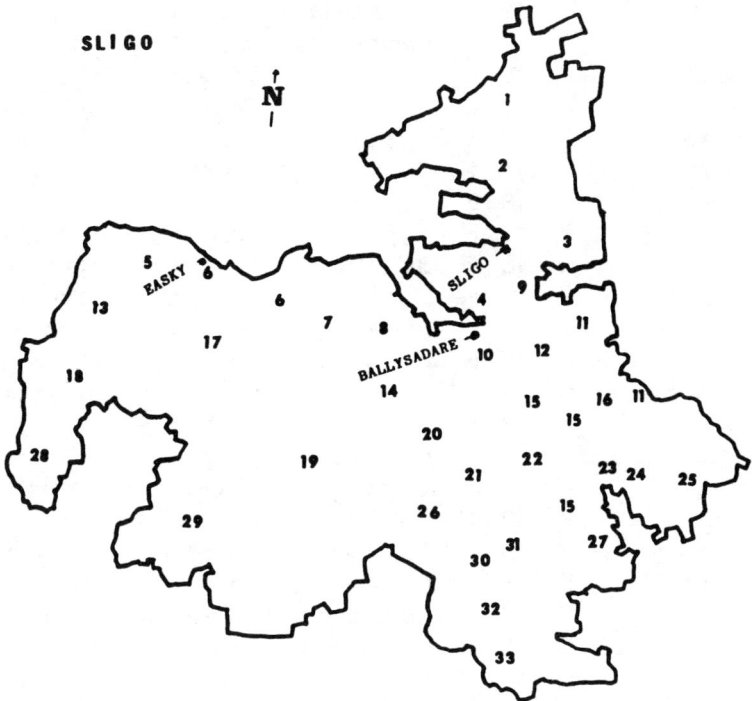

SLIGO

N

SLIGO

EASKY

BALLYSADARE

SLIGO
CIVIL PARISHES

1. AHAMLISH
2. DRUMCLIFF
3. CARLY
4. KILMACOWEN
5. EASKY
6. TEMPLEBOY
7. SKREEN
8. DROMARD
9. ST. JOHN'S
10. BALLYSADARE

11. KILLERRY
12. KILROSS
13. KILGLASS
14. KILLORAN
15. DRUMCOLUMB
16. BALLYNAKILL
17. KILMACSHALGAN
18. CASTLECONOR
19. ACHONRY
20. KILVARNET

21. EMLAGHFAD
22. KILMORGAN
23. KILMACALLAN
24. KILLADOON
25. KILMACTRANNY
26. CLOONOGHIL
27. AGHANAGH
28. KILNORMOY
29. KILMACTEIGE
30. KILSHALVY
31. DRUMRAT
32. KILFREE
33. KILCOLMAN

Surname	R	I	S	Townland	Barony	Place-Parish
Hallas	P	13	14	Kilmacshalgan	Tireragh	Kilmacshalgan
Hart	C	13	I	Ballygrahan	Tireragh	Templeboy
Henry	I	13	E	Sligo	Carbury	Sligo
Higgins	I	13	E	Carrowdurneen	Tireragh	Screen
Hill	P	13	1	Carrownapull	Leyny	Kilmacteige
Hillas	P	13	E		Tireragh	Kilmacshalgan
Holder	I	13	E		Corran	Kilmorgan
Hopps	I	13	E	Collooney	Tirerrill	Killoran
Howe	I	13	1		Corran	Cloonoghil
Humphrey	I	13	E	Sligo	Carbury	Sligo
Irwin	P	13	S		Tireragh	Kilmacshalgan
Joint	H	13	F	Ballyglass	Tireragh	Kilglass
Jones	P	13	W		Tireragh	Skreen
Kean	C	13	I	Ardnaree	Tireragh	Kilmoremoy
King	I	13	E		Corran	Emlaghfad
Lanaghan	C	13	I		Carbury	Drumcliff
Lewis	I	13	E		Tireragh	
Looby	C	13	I	Killadoon	Tirerrill	Killadoon
Low	I	13	E	Collooney	Tirerrill	Killoran
Lynn	P	13	12	Finid	Carbury	Drumcliff
Mac Carrick	P	13	12	Collooney	Tirerrill	Killoran
Mac Keal	I	13	I	Newtown	Carbury	Ahamlish
Mackin	C	13	I	Collooney	Tirerrill	Killoran
Mackin	C	13	I	Grangemore	Tireragh	Templeboy
Magee	C	13	I	Ballyglass	Tireragh	Kilglass
Maguire	C	13	I	Ballintogher	Tirerrill	Killery
Martin	I	13	E	Ardnaree	Tireragh	Kilmoremoy
Martin	I	13	E	Dunmoran	Tireragh	Skreen
Mc Peeter	P	13	S	Ballinafad	Tirerrill	Aghanagh
Mc Pillernane	C	13	I	Ardtermon	Carbury	Drumcliff
Mc Quilkin	C	13	26	Farnmacfrel	Tireragh	Kilmacshalgan
Mc Quyann	C	13	I	Mullaghmore	Tirerrill	Ballynakill
Mc Quyn	C	13	I	Kilmacowen	Carbury	Kilmacowen
Meredith	I	13	E		Corran	Kilshalvey
Moore	I	13	E		Tireragh	Kilglass
Moore	I	13	E	Ardnaree	Tireragh	Kilmoremoy
Morrison	P	13	37	Carrowreagh	Tireragh	Skreen
Mortimer	I	13	E		Tirerrill	Drumcolumb

Surname	R	I	S	Townland	Barony	Place-Parish
Morton	P	13	21	Ardnaree	Tireragh	Kilmoremoy
Murray	C	13	I	Ardnaree	Tireragh	Kilmoremoy
Napier	H	13	F		Tirerrill	Kilmacallan
Nicholson	P	13	S		Tireragh	Castleconor
Nicholson	P	13	S	Drumcliff	Carbury	Drumcliff
Nicholson	P	13	S	Ardnaree	Tireragh	Kilmoremoy
Nicleson *	I	13	E	Larrass		
O 'Quyn	C	13	I	Lugacaha	Corran	Kilmorgan
O' Quickly	C	13	I	Cloonlurg	Corran	Kilmorgan
O' Quillan	C	13	I	Lghnlteen	Carbury	Carly
O' Quyn	C	13	I	Carrowmore	Leyny	Achonry
O' Quynn	C	13	I	Lugacaha	Corran	Kilmorgan
Ormsby	P	13	E	Ballymeeny	Tireragh	Easky
Ormsby	P	13	E	Coolaney	Leyny	Killoran
Ormsby	I	13	E	Ardnaree	Tireragh	Kilmoremoy
Oustan	P	13	S	Rathgran	Leyny	Kilvarnet
Paddock	P	13	S	Rinroe	Tireragh	Castleconor
Parke	I	13	E	Ballytivnan	Carbury	Carly
Parke	I	13	E	Doonycoy	Tireragh	Templeboy
Patchett	I	13	E	Coolaney	Leyny	Killoran
Patron	C	13	S	Lisconny	Tirerrill	Drumcolumb
Pearcy	I	13	E	Cloonameehan	Corran	Cloonoghil
Peathon	I	13	E	Knockbeg	Leyny	Ballysadare
Petterson	P	13	S	Urlar	Carbury	Drumcliff
Phibbs	I	13	E	Ballysadare	Tirerrill	Ballysadare
Phibbs	I	13	E	Ballymote	Corran	Emlaghfad
Piece	I	13	E	Grange	Carbury	Ahamlish
Pierse	I	13	E	Tanrego	Tireragh	Dromard
Pierse	I	13	E	Carowloughlin	Tireragh	Skreen
Pinkard	P	13	5	Knocknahun	Carbury	Kilmacowen
Pirsie	I	13	E	Lisruntagh	Tirerrill	Ballysadare
Power	P	13	15	Ardnaree	Tireragh	Kilmoremoy
Preston	P	13	15	Bunduff	Carbury	Ahamlish
Prew	I	13	E	Carrowkeel	Carbury	Kilmacowen
Pryse	P	13	W	Rathdoonybeg	Corran	Elmaghfad
Quiggley	C	13	I	Cloonacurra	Leyny	Ballysadare
Quirke	C	13	I	Carns	Carbury	St. Johns
Quissoge		13		Carrowlghn	Leyny	Killoran

Surname	R	I	S	Townland	Barony	Place-Parish
Quyn	C	13	I	Carownurlaur*	Coolavin	Killaraght
Quyne	C	13	I	Carrowcashel	Tirerrill	Kilmactranny
Raghnesse	P	13	S		Leyny	Kilvarnet
Raghtagane	P	13	S	Moygara	Coolavin	Kilfree
Raghtegan	C	13	I	Rathlee	Tireragh	Easky
Reed	P	13	4	Ardnaree	Tireragh	Kilmoremoy
Rutledge	I	13	E	Knockahullen*	Corran	Kilshalvy
Scott	P	13	23	Ardnaglass	Carbury	Ahamlish
Scott	I	13	21	Doonowla	Carbury	Drumcliff
Scott	P	13	21	Ballyholan	Tireragh	Kilmoremoy
Scott	P	13	21	Carowdurneen	Tireragh	Skreen
Shannon	P	13	I	Carrowpadeen	Tireragh	Easky
Symson	I	13	E	Sligo	Sligo	Sligo
Taffe	C	13	E	Cashel	Coolavin	Achonry
Talbott	I	13	E	Ballyconnell	Carbury	Drumcliff
Tanist	C	13	I	Killoran	Leyny	Killoran
Till	I	13	E	Doorly	Corran	Kilmorgan
Tingle	I	13	E	Creevagh	Tirerrill	Kilmactranny
Toath		13		Carrowkeel	Tirerrill	Aghanagh
Trench	H	13	F	Kilross	Tirerrill	Kilross
Trumble	I	13	E	Carrowmore	Corran	Emlaghfad
Webb	I	13	E	Ballymote	Corran	Emlaghfad
Wilstead	I	13	E	Lisconry	Corran	Drumrat

RUINS, COUNTY SLIGO

Map of Mayo

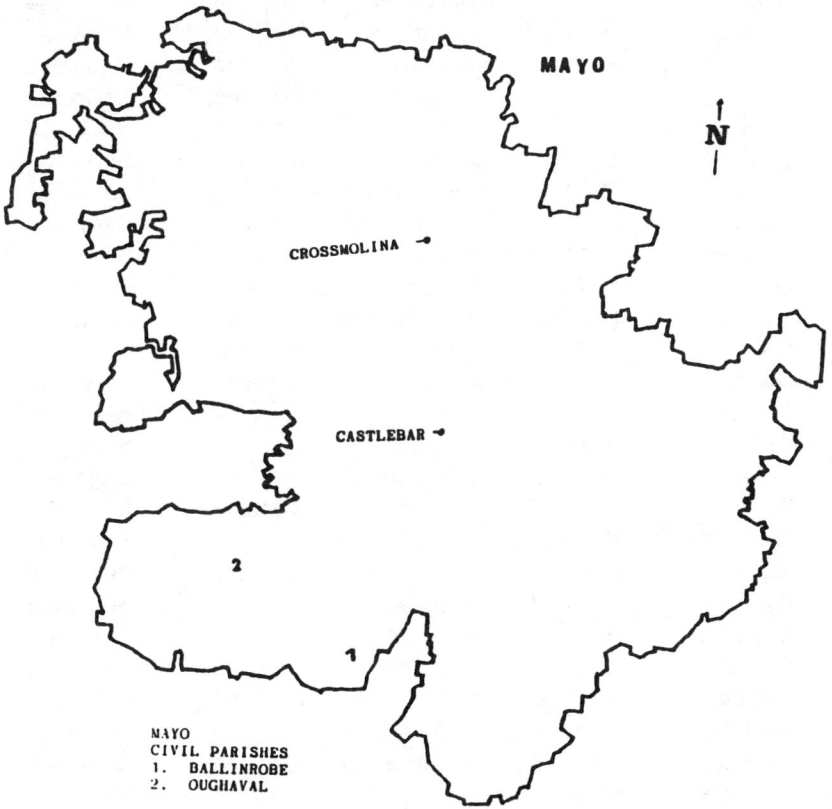

MAYO

CROSSMOLINA ➡

CASTLEBAR ➡

2

1

MAYO
CIVIL PARISHES
1. BALLINROBE
2. OUGHAVAL

N

Name	R	I	S	Townland	Barony	Place-Parish
Hennelly	C	14	I	Kilthrowan *	Kilmaine	Ballinrobe
Higgins	I	14	E	Kilthrowan *	Kilmaine	Ballinrobe
Hirshan	H	14	G	Racareen	Kilmaine	Ballinrobe
Hisham	H	14	G	Racareen	Kilmaine	Ballinrobe
Hoban	P	14	1	Kilthrowan *	Kilmaine	Ballinrobe
Hurdy	I	14	E	Cloongowla	Kilmaine	Ballinrobe
Jennings	I	14	E		Kilmaine	Ballinrobe
Jonnen	Q	14		Cloonluffan	Kilmaine	Ballinrobe
Joyce	C	14	I	Knocklehard	Kilmaine	Ballinrobe
Joyes	C	14	I	Knocklehard	Kilmaine	Ballinrobe
Kirkwood	P	14	S	Killala	Tirawley	Killala
Liddane	I	14	E	Knocklehard	Kilmaine	Ballinrobe
Liviney	I	14	E	Knocklehard	Kilmaine	Ballinrobe
Mellott	I	14	E	Knocklehard	Kilmaine	Ballinrobe
Mellott	I	14	E	Lavally	Kilmaine	Ballinrobe
Morris	P	14	1	Lavally	Kilmaine	Ballinrobe
Murray	P	14	1	Belatogher	Kilmaine	Ballinrobe
Pierse	I	14	E	Carowkeel	Murrisk	Oughaval
Real	C	14	I	Belatogher*	Kilmaine	Ballinrobe
Richison	P	14	12	Belatogher*	Kilmaine	Ballinrobe
Rush	I	14	E	Knockanotish	Kilmaine	Ballinrobe
Rymes	P	14	I	Knockanotish	Kilmaine	Ballinrobe
Saunders	P	14	S	Knockanotish	Kilmaine	Ballinrobe
Sheridan	C	14	I	Knockanotish	Kilmaine	Ballinrobe
Sinnett	I	14	E	Knockanotish	Kilmaine	Ballinrobe
Staunton	I	14	E	Knockanotish	Kilmaine	Ballinrobe
Thornton	I	14	E	Knockanotish	Kilmaine	Ballinrobe
Waldron	C	14	I	Knockanotish	Kilmaine	Ballinrobe
Willis	P	14	E	Knockanotish	Kilmaine	Ballinrobe

Index-II

THE ANCESTRIAL HOMELAND

CHARTS IN THIS SECTION ALSO SERVE AS AN INDEX

First, look for a surname of your choice.

After locating your chosen surname find the column labled "R I S".

"R" designates the religion of an individual of this surname as shown below.

"C" identifies the Catholic faith.
"I" stands for The Church Of Ireland,(Episcopalian). "P" all other protestants.
"Q" Quaker, etc.

The "I" column contains a number representing an Irish county where a person of this surname lived. See the same numbers on the Irish map,(Page 39).

The "S" column is a guide to nationality. Numbers refer to the Scottish map (Page 38). Letters represent nationality. "D" Danish or Norse, "E" English, "F" French, "G" German, "I" Irish, "S' Scot(County unknown),"W" Welsh etc.

Write down the surname you have chosen along with the column headings and the data under each one. This is the basic information required to locate an early immigrant in the North of Ireland.

NEXT,turn to PAGE ONE and read the text before searching furthur.

Note: Baronies are sometimes divided into U=Upper,
M=Middle, L=lower.

Name	R	I	S	Townland	Barony	Place-Parish
Abercromby	P	2	7	Desertmartin	Loughinsholin	Desertmartin
Abernathy	P	4	13	Minterburn*		
Abernethy	P	6	7	Drumbo	Castlereagh	Drumbo
Acheson	P	7	16	Enniskillen	Magheraboy	Enniskillen
Acheson *	P	5	15	Coolmillish	Fews L.	Mullaghbrack
Achey	I	3	7	Derryaghy	Belfast U.	Derryaghy
Achmutie	P	11	15	Drumhillagh	Loughhtee U.	Lavey
Achmutie	P	11	15	Dromheda *	Tallyhunco	Scrabby
Achmutie *	P	11	15	Keylagh *	Tallyhunco	Scrabby
Adair	C	3	23	Ballymena	Toome	Kirkinriola
Adams	P	6	26	Donaghadee	Ards	Donaghadee
Adams	I	2	E	Ballymoney	Coleraine	Dunboe
Adams	I	7	E	Enniskillen	Magheraboy	Enniskillen
Adams	I	2	E	Culmore	Keenaght	Tamlaght O'
Adamson	P	4	17	Omagh	Omagh E.	Drumragh
Agar	I	3	E	Belfast	Belfast	Shankill
Agnew	C	3	23	Larne	Glenarm	Larne
Aidy	C	6	17	Downpatrick	Lecale U.	Down
Aiken	P	3	12	Ballymena	Toome	Kirkinriola
Akins	P	8	12			
Alcorn	P	4	21		Omagh	Drumragh
Alderdice	I	3	E	Derryaghy	Belfast U.	Derryaghy
Aldrich	I	7	S	Enniskillen	Magheraboy	Enniskillen
Alexander	I	4	13	Clogher	Clogher	Clogher
Alexander	I	4	12	Fivemiletown	Clogher	Clogher
Alexander	P	4	12	Dullerton *	Strabane L.	Donaghedy
Alexander	P	1	12		Raphoe	Raphoe
Algier	P	4	12		Strabane L.	Ardstraw
Alleley	I	8	E	Clones	Dartree	Clones
Allely	I	8	E	Clonkeen	Trough	Errigal
Allen	P	4	10	Nurchossy	Clogher	Clogher
Allen	P	6	10	Kircubbin	Ards	Inishargy
Allen	P	6	10	Magheralin	Iveagh	Magheralin
Allen	P	6	10		Lecale	Saul
Allis	P	1	1	Drimahy *	Banagh	Inishkeel
Allisob	I	2	E	Londonderry	Londonderry	Templemore
Allison	P	1	12		Raphoe	Leck
Allot	P	3	S		Dunluce L.	Kilraghts

Name	R	I	S	Townland	Barony	Place-Parish
Alsop	I	6	E		Lecale L.	Ballyculter
Alwell		7			Magherstphna	Aghavea
Amoss	I	7	E	Rossory	Magheraboy	Rossory
Anderson	P	6	21	Aughendarrah	Castlereagh	Killinchy
Anderson	I	1	18	Toome	Boylagh	Lettermcward
Anderson	P	4	1		Omagh	Termonmaguirk
Angle	I	4	E		Dungannon	Derryloran
Anguish	P	4	15		Dungannon	Aghaloo
Annet	I	6	E	Tandragee *	Iveagh U.	Kilbroney
Annett	I	5	E	Tandragee	Orior L.	Ballymore
Anslo	I	6	E		Lecale	Saul
Apton	I	2	E	Londonderry	Londonderry	Templemore
Arbuckle	P	4	13		Strabane	Donaghedy
Arbuthnett	P	6	2	Dromore	Iveagh L.	Dromore
Arbuthnot	P	6	2	Dromore	Iveagh L.	Dromore
Arbutton	I	2	2	Londonderry	Londonderry	Templemore
Archdale	Q	7	E	Enniskillen	Magheraboy	Enniskillen
Archdale *	I	7	E	Tallanal *	Magheraboy	Enniskillen
Archdall	I	7	E	Castl.Archdall	Lurg	Magheramoney
Archdecon	I	8	E	Shanmulagh	Monaghan	Tullycorbet
Archer	I	8	E		Cremorne	Muckno
Archibald	I	4	E		Strabane L.	Ardstraw
Arckley	P	1	3	Portlough	Raphoe	Allsaints
Ardock	I	2	E	Londonderry	Londonderry	Templemore
Ardsell	P	7	E	Enniskillen	Magheraboy	Enniskillen
Arkless	I	1	E	Cloghro	Raphoe	Convoy
Armour	P	1	13	Croghan	Raphoe	Clonleigh
Armour	P	3	17	Bushmills	Dunluce	Dunluce
Armsteed	I	2	E	Londonderry	Londonderry	Templemore
Armstrong	P	3	21	Crumlin	Massereene	Camlin
Armstrong	P	4	20	Dungannon	Dungannon	Drumglass
Armstrong	P	7	21	Drummully	Coole	Drummully
Armstrong	P	4	21	Bogane	Dungannon M.	Killyman
Arnott	P	6	12		Lecale	Saul
Arrell	P	1	4	Monfad	Raphoe	Allsaints
Art	C	4	I	Tullyveagh	Dungannon	Artrea
Art	C	4	I	Dungannon	Dungannon	Drumglass
Asbisson			2	Londonderry	Londonderry	Templemore

Name	R	I	S	Townland	Barony	Place-Parish
Ash	I	1	E		Raphoe	Convoy
Ash	I	2	E	Londonderry	Londonderry	Templemore
Askin	I	8	E	Legnakelly*		
Athenleck		6		Dromore	Iveagh L.	Dromore
Atkinson	I	3	1		Massereene	Derryaghy
Atkinson	I	4	12	Lisgallon	Dungannon	Donaghmore
Atkinson	I	6	E	Dromore	Iveagh L.	Dromore
Auchinleck	P	7	12	Enniskillen	Magheraboy	Enniskillen
Audley *	I	6	E	Brade(Breda)	Castlereagh	Knockbreda
Babington	I	1	E	Portlough	Raphoe	Allsaints
Babington	I	2	E	Londonderry	Londonderry	Templemore
Bailey	P	4	14	Clogher	Clogher	Clogher
Bailey	I	3	13	Derryaghy	Belfast U.	Derryaghy
Bailie	P	6	5	Ardkeen	Ards U.	Ardkeen
Bailie	P	6	14	Inishargy *	Ards	Inishargy
Bailie	P	6	15	Kircubbin	Ards	Inisnargy
Baillie	P	6	15	Bangor	Ards L.	Bangor
Baillie *	P	11	11	Tonnereghie *	Clankee	Knockbride?
Baird	P	4	13	Clogher	Clogher	Clogher
Baker	I	2	E	Moneymore	Loughinsholin	Artrea
Baldrich	I	2	E	Londonderry	Londonderry	Templemore
Balfour	I	2	7	Desertmartin	Loughinsholin	Desertmartin
Balfour *	I	7	E	Carrowchee *	Knockninny	Kinawley
Balfour *	I	7	E	Kilspanan *	Knockninny	Kinawley
Balfour *	I	7	E	Montwhany *	Knockninny	Kinwaley
Balfoure	I	1	E	Kildrum L.	Raphoe	Allsaints
Ballard	I	7	E	Enniskillen	Magheraboy	Enniskillen
Ballentine	P	1	9	Dromore	Raphoe	Leck
Balmann	P	1	2	Portlough	Raphoe	Allsaints
Bane	C	6	I	Dromore	Iveagh L.	Dromore
Banister	I	3	E		Massereene	Derryaghy
Bar	P	2		Lissaghmore	Coleraine	Agivey
Barbor	I	4	E		Strabane L.	Ardstraw
Barclay	I	1	E	Ballybogan	Raphoe	Clonleigh
Barkagh	I	8	E	Lisnagore	Dartree	killeevan
Barkha	I	8	E			
Barkley	P	4	13	Ardstraw	Strabane L.	Ardstraw
Barnett	P	4	15			

Name	R	I	S	Townland	Barony	Place-Parish
Barnett	I	4	15	Ballagh	Clogher	Clogher
Barnett *	P	4	15	Mullybaney*		
Barnhill	P	4	12	Ardstraw	Strabane L.	Ardstraw
Barr	P	3	11	Belfast	Belfast	Shankill
Barrett	I	4	E		Dungannon	Aghaloo
Barron	P	3	21	Antrim	Antrim U.	Antrim
Barrow	I	5	E	Lurgan	Oneilland	Shankill
Barton *	I	7	E	Drominshin *	Lurg	Derryvullan
Bassett	I	6	E	Downpatrick	Lecale U.	Down
Bates	I	1	E	Toome	Kilmacrenan	Clondavaddog
Bateson	P	2	7	Londonderry	Londonderry	Templemore
Baxter	I	4	7	Edernagh	Dungannon	Artrea
Baxter	P	4	7	Fivemiletown	Clogher	Clogher
Baxter	P	4	13	Dungannon	Dungannon	Drumglass
Baxter	P	3	13	Larne	Glenarm	Larne
Baxter	P	1	7	Moness	Raphoe	Taughboyne
Baxter *	I	6	E	Aughentaine *	Lecale	Inch?
Bayers	I	5	E	Armagh	Armagh	Armagh
Bayley	I	2	E	Londonderry	Londonderry	Templemore
Beacum	I	7	E	Enniskillen	Magheraboy	Enniskillen
Beaman	I	2	E	Londonderry	Londonderry	Templemore
Bean	I	4	E	Aughentaine *	Lecale	Inch?
Beattie	P	7	21	Enniskillen	Magheraboy	Enniskillen
Beatty	P	4	21	Dungannon	Dungannon	Drumglass
Beck	P	6	10	Kircubbin	Ards	Inisnargy
Bedel	P	7	5	Enniskillen	Magheraboy	Enniskillen
Bedine	C	7	I	New Tn Butler	Coole	Galloon
Beers	P	6	10	Killyleagh	Duffrin	Killyleagh
Beggs	C	3	I	Carrickfergus	Carrickfergus	Carrickfergus
Beggs	P	6	15	Drumbo	Castlereagh	Drumbo
Bell	P	3	21	Ballinderry	Massereene	Ballinderry
Bell	P	7	21	Derryvullan	Tirkennedy	Derryvullan
Bell	P	7	10	Enniskillen	Magheraboy	Enniskillen
Bell	P	7	21	Enniskillen	Magheraboy	Enniskillen
Bell	P	7	21	Drumbulcan	Tirkennely	Magheracross
Bell	I	6	E		Lecale	Saul
Belshaw	I	3	E	Magheragall	Massereene	Magheragall
Bennard	P	3	4	Bushmills	Dunluce	Dunluce

Name	R	I	S	Townland	Barony	Place-Parish
Bennerman	I	5	E	Market Hill	Fews	Kilclooney
Bennett	P	3	20	Carrickfergus	Carrickfergus	Carrickfergus
Bennett	I	2	20	Colerane	Coleraine	Colerane
Bennett	P	2	20	Londonderry	Londonderry	Templemore
Benson	P	6	7	Drumbo	Castlereagh	Drumbo
Benson	P	6	7		Lecale	Saul
Benson	P	1	7	Drumboe	Raphoe	Stranorlar
Bernard	I	6	E	Drumbo	Castlereagh	Drumbo
Berren	C	8	I			
Betts	P	2	7	Londonderry	Londonderry	Templemore
Betty	C	6	I		Kinelarty	Annahilt
Betty	P	4	E	Lurganboy	Clogher	Donacavey
Betty	P	6	20		Lecale	Down
Betty	P	7	22	Enniskillen	Magheraboy	Enniskillen
Betty	C	6	I	Hillsborough	Iveagh	Hillsborough
Betty	C	7	I	Killesher	Clanawley	Killesher
Betty	C	6	I	Ballykeel	Iveagh	Seapatrick
Bevish	I	7	E			
Bickerstaffe	I	3	E		Massereene	Derryaghy
Bigger	P	4	13		Dungannon	Arboe
Bigham	I	6	E	Banbridge	Iveagh U.	Sea Patrick
Bigley	I	1	E		Tirhugh	Drumhome
Bincher	I	4	E		Omagh	Dromore
Bingham	P	6	12	Rathfryland	Iveagh	Drumgrath
Bingham	P	6	12		Lecale	Saul
Bird	I	4	E			
Birney	P	4	15	Cullenyra *	Magerspthana	Aghalurcher
Birney	P	4	15	Clogher	Clogher	Clogher
Birney	P	4	15	Fivemiletown	Clogher	Clogher
Birrell	P	6	F	Lisburn	Castlereagh	Blaris
Birsben	I	4	E		Strabane L.	Ardstraw
Bisland	P	4	9		Strabane L.	Ardstraw
Bisland	P	4	9		Strabane	Leckpatrick
Black	P	7	15			
Black	I	7	E	Clonfad	Clankelly	Clones
Black	P	7	6	Enniskillen	Magheraboy	Enniskillen
Black	P	2	6	Londonderry	Londonderry	Templemore
Blackburn	I	1	E	Argory *	Raphoe	

Name	R	I	S	Townland	Barony	Place-Parish
Blackburn	P	6	9	Ballylintagh	Iveagh L.	Annahilt
Blackburn	I	3	E	Derryaghy	Belfast U.	Derryaghy
Blackhall	I	3	E		Belfast U.	Derryaghy
Blackly	I	3	E		Belfast U.	Derryaghy
Blackwood	P	6	10	Bangor	Ards L.	Bangor
Blackwood	P	6	13		Lecale	Saul
Blair	P	6	7	Kircubbin	Ards	Inisnargy
Blair	P	1	7		Raphoe	Raphoe
Blair	P	2	7	Londonderry	Londonderry	Templemore
Blakley	P	6	12	Bangor	Ards L.	Bangor
Blakley	C	7	12	Rossory	Magheraboy	Rossory
Blakney	P	3	12	Bushmills	Dunluce	Dunluce
Blannerhasset *	I	7	E	Banagh *	Lurg	Drumkeeran
Blare	P	1	7	Portlough	Raphoe	Allsaints
Blashford	P	7		Enniskillen	Magheraboy	Enniskillen
Bleakley	P	8	21	Clonkerhill *		
Bleakley	I	4	E	Clogher	Clogher	Clogher
Blizard	P	5		Lurgan	Oneilland	Shankill
Bloomfield	I	4	E	Slatmore *	Clogher	Clogher
Bodel	P	6	13	Dromore	Iveagh L.	Dromore
Bog	I	8	E	Drumbenagh	Monaghan	Tedavent
Boggs	I	1	E	Monglass	Raphoe	Allsaints
Boileau	P	6	F	Lisburn	Castlereagh	Blaris
Bole	P	6	15	Bangor	Ards L.	Bangor
Bolton	C	1	21	Toome	Kilmacrenan	Clondavaddog
Bolton	I	3	21	Glenavey	Massereene	Glenavey
Bonar	C	1	I	Ballybofey	Raphoe	Stranorlar
Bonner	Q	1	4	Portlough	Raphoe	Allsaints
Bonner	Q	6	4	Dromore	Iveagh L.	Dromore
Bonner	Q	2	4	Londonderry	Londonderry	Templemore
Booth	I	5	E	Lurgan	Oneilland	Shankill
Bothwell	C	7	13	Rossory	Magheraboy	Rossory
Bounty	P	4	E	Ardstraw	Strabane L.	Ardstraw
Bourch	P	8		Lisnaveane	Cremorne	Tullycorbet
Boveard	P	1	H		Raphoe	Leck
Bowes	I	8	E	Teer	Dartree	Killeevan
Boxter	C	7	I	Rossory	Magheraboy	Rossory
Boyce	I	1	7	Devlin	Kilmacrenan	Mevagh

Name	R	I	S	Townland	Barony	Place-Parish
Boyce	I	1	7	Doagh	Kilmacrenan	Mevagh
Boyce	I	1	7	Tullagh	Kilmacrenan	Mevagh
Boyd	P	4	12	Timpany	Clogher	Aghalurcher
Boyd	P	4	12	Edernagh	Dungannon	Artrea
Boyd	P	6	12	Bangor	Ards L.	Bangor
Boyd	P	4	12	Annagh	Dungannon	Clonfecale
Boyd	P	6	12	Downpatrick	Lecale U.	Down
Boyd	P	4	12	Dungannon	Dungannon	Drumglass
Boyd	P	3	12	Ballygrooby	Toome U.	Drummaul
Boyd	P	3	12	Bushmills	Dunluce	Dunluce
Boyd	P	6	12		Lecale	Saul
Boyd	P	2	12	Londonderry	Londonderry	Templemore
Boyd *	P	4	12	Seein	Strabane	Urney
Boyle	P	4	21	Ballynahone	Dungannon	Artrea
Boyle	P	4	12	Dungannon	Dungannon	Drumglass
Boyle	P	1	12	Drumlackagh	Kilmacrenan	Mevagh
Boys	I	3	E	Derryaghy	Belfast U.	Derryaghy
Brakey	I	8	E	Drumskelt	Dartree	Killeevan
Branah	C	3	I	Derryaghy	Belfast U.	Derryaghy
Brannagh	C	3	I	Ballinderry	Massereene	Ballinderry
Brannon	C	6	I	Bleary	Iveagh	Tullylish
Breadley	P	3	I	Derryaghy	Belfast U.	Derryaghy
Bready	P	1	9	Altacaskin *	Raphoe	Taughboyne
Breedy	P	1	9		Raphoe	Raphoe
Briggs	I	6	E		Iveragh U.	Annaclone
Brigs	I	8	E	Lisnaveane	Cremorne	Tullycorbet
Brisban	P	4	11	Dungannon	Dungannon	Drumglass
Brisben	P	4	11		Strabane L.	Strabane
Brisland	C	1	I		Inishowen	Moville
Brison	C	1	I	Clonmany *	Inishowen	
Britton	I	2	E	Magherafelt	Loughinsholin	Magherafelt
Broadley	C	1	I			
Brogan	C	1	I	Drumies *	Kilmacrenan	Mevagh
Brogton	I	6	E	Dromore	Iveagh L.	Dromore
Brolly	C	2	I		Keenaght	Bovevagh
Broome	I	2	E	Londonderry	Londonderry	Templemore
Brown	P	2	13	Bellaghy	Loughinsholin	Ballyscullion
Brown	P	4	15	Carnteel	Dungannon	Carnteel

Name	R	I	S	Townland	Barony	Place-Parish
Brown	P	3	1	Derryaghy	Belfast U.	Derryaghy
Brown	P	1	17		Raphoe	Raphoe
Brown *	P	11	15	Carrodonan *	Tullyhunco	
Browne	I	7	E	Rossgarn *	Magheraboy	Enniskillen
Browning	P	7	1	Enniskillen	Magheraboy	Enniskillen
Brunett	P	2	18	Londonderry	Londonderry	Templemore
Bruse	P	4	19		Strabane L.	Strabane
Buchanan	P	1	9		Raphoe	Raphoe
Buchanan	P	2	9	Londonderry	Londonderry	Templemore
Buck	I	11	E		Tullygarvey	Annagh
Bulla	P	5	E		Armagh	Kilmore
Bullmer	I	3	E	Derryaghy	Belfast U.	Derryaghy
Bunting	I	4	E		Strabane L.	Strabane
Burch	I	5	E		Armagh	Kilmore
Burd	P	1	1	Croghan	Raphoe	Clonleigh
Burley	I	4	E	Carnteel	Dungannon	Carnteel
Burnes	P	4	12	Carnteel	Dungannon	Carnteel
Burnett	I	2	E		Loughinsholin	Artrea
Burns	P	4	6		Dungannon	Aghaloo
Burns	P	6	6	Lurgan	Oneilland	Shankill
Burnside	P	1	7	Castletorris	Raphoe	Convoy
Burnside	P	1	2		Raphoe	Raphoe
Burnstep	P	8	S	Teehill	Dartree	Clones
Burris	I	3	E	Derryaghy	Belfast U.	Derryaghy
Bury	I	7	E	Enniskillen	Magheraboy	Enniskillen
Busby	I	8	E	Analagh *	Trough	Donagh
Bustard	I	1	E		Tirhugh	Donegal
Butler *	I	7	E	Diriany *	Knockninny	Kinawley
Butler *	I	7	E	Kilspinan *	Knockninny	Kinawley
Buttle	I	3	E	Ballymena L.	Belfast	Ballynure
Caldwell	I	1	E		Raphoe	Raphoe
Calhoone	P	1	10	Letterkenny	Kilmacranan	Conwal
Calkey	I	3	E		Dunluce L.	Billy
Calshinder	I	3	E	Derryaghy	Belfast U.	Derryaghy
Camack	P	5		Lurgan	Oneilland	Shankill
Camble	P	1	6		Raphoe	Raphoe
Campbell	P	4	6		Dungannon	Aghaloo
Campbell	P	6	6	Rathfryland	Iveagh	Drumgrath

Name	R	I	S	Townland	Barony	Place-Parish
Campbell	P	7	6	Enniskillen	Magheraboy	Enniskillen
Campbell	P	2	6	Londonderry	Londonderry	Templemore
Campse	P	2	9	Londonderry	Londonderry	Templemore
Campsie	P	2	9	Londonderry	Londonderry	Templemore
Cannel		3		Derryaghy	Belfast U.	Derryaghy
Canning	I	2	E			
Canning	I	2	E	Lissaghmore	Coleraine	Agivey
Canning	I	2	E	Garvagh	Coleraine	Errigal
Cannon	C	1	I			
Cannon	C	1	I	Ardbane	Kilmacrenan	Mevagh
Cannon	C	1	I	Dundooan	Kilmacrenan	Mevagh
Canny	C	1	I		Inishowen E.	Culdaff
Car	P	9	17		Dundalk	
Care	C	5	I	Market Hill	Fews	Kilclooney
Carmichael	P	4	13	Dungannon	Dungannon	Drumglass
Carothers	P	7	21		Magherstphna	Aghavea
Carr	P	6	17	Kilkeel	Mourne	Kilkeel
Carr	P	2	17	Londonderry	Londonderry	Templemore
Carre	P	1	S	Inver	Banagh	Inver
Carren	C	4	I		Dungannon	Aghaloo
Carroll	C	4	I	Carnteel	Dungannon	Carnteel
Carrothers	P	7	20	Lowtherstown	Lurg	Derryvallun
Carson	P	8	21	Shanroe	Monaghan	Clones
Carson	P	4	10	Dungannon	Dungannon	Drumglass
Carson	P	1	21		Raphoe	Raphoe
Carvill	C	6	I	Downpatrick	Lecale U.	Down
Casement	C	6	I	Downpatrick	Lecale U.	Down
Cashell	C	7	I	Enniskillen	Magheraboy	Enniskillen
Cathcart	P	3	11	Randalstown	Toome	Drummaul
Cathcart	P	7	11	Enniskillen	Magheraboy	Enniskillen
Caughlan	C	1	I		Raphoe	Raphoe
Chaloner	P	5	15	Lurgan	Oneilland	Shankill
Chamberlyn	I	2	E	Lissaghmore	Coleraine	Agivey
Chapman	I	4	E			
Chapman	P	7	15		Magherstphna	Aghavea
Charnor	I	5	E	Lurgan	Oneilland	Shankill
Chartres	P	6	F	Lisburn	Castlereagh	Blaris
Chesnut	I	3	E		Dunluce L.	Derrykeighan

Name	R	I	S	Townland	Barony	Place-Parish
Chisime		1		Momeen	Raphoe	Taughboyne
Chism	P	4	20		Strabane	Donaghedy
Christian	I	3	E	Derryaghy	Belfast U.	Derryaghy
Christie		3	7	Lisburn	Massereene	Blaris
Church	I	2	E	Lissaghmore	Coleraine	Agivey
Clagg	H	3	F	Derryaghy	Belfast U.	Derryaghy
Clandinning	-	2	-	Drummaney	Tirkeeran	Faughanvale
Clapham *	P	4	S	Newton*	Strabane	
Clapham *	I	4	E	Lislapp	Strabane	Cappagh
Clarke	P	4	7	Dungannon	Dungannon	Drumglass
Clarke	I	7	4	Enniskillen	Magheraboy	Enniskillen
Clarke	P	2	7	Londonderry	Londonderry	Templemore
Clegg	I	8	E	Clones	Dartree	Clones
Clements	P	4	10	Dungannon	Dungannon	Drumglass
Clements	P	2	10	Londonderry	Londonderry	Templemore
Clindinin	P	8	21	Cornafaghy	Dartree	Clones
Clingan	P	6	21		Lecale L.	Ballee
Cloid	I	8	E		Dartree	Aghabog
Close	I	3	E	Derryaghy	Belfast U.	Derryaghy
Coates	P	6	1	Blaris	Massereene	Blaris
Cobreth	I	3		Derryaghy	Belfast U	Derryaghy
Coburn	P	3	20	Derryaghy	Belfast U.	Derryaghy
Cock	P	1	13	Cargins *	Raphoe	
Cocken	P	2	7	Londonderry	Londonderry	Templemore
Cohoon	P	3	10	Derryaghy	Belfast U.	Derryaghy
Coken	P	1	4		Raphoe	Raphoe
Coldwill	I	8	E	Crossmoyle	Dartree	Clones
Cole	C	4	I		Dungannon	Aghaloo
Cole	I	7	E	Enniskillen	Magheraboy	Enniskillen
Cole *	I	7	E	Drumskea	Lurg	Derryvullan
Colehy	I	6	E	Dromore	Iveagh L.	Dromore
Colhoun	P	4	10			
Coll	I	1	6		Kilmacrenan	Mevagh
Collins	I	3	E	Derryaghy	Belfast U.	Derryaghy
Collon	P	2		Lissaghmore	Coleraine	Agivey
Collyer	P	7	7	Enniskillen	Magheraboy	Enniskillen
Colquhon *	P	1	10	Corkagh *		
Comberland	I	3	E	Derryaghy	Belfast U.	Derryaghy

Name	R	I	S	Townland	Barony	Place-Parish
Conely	C	4	I		Dungannon	Aghaloo
Conor	C	1	I	Doagh	Kilmacrenan	Mevagh
Conway	P	3	W	Lisburn	Massereene	Blaris
Conyngham	P	1	9	Monargan Glebe	Banagh	Killybegs
Cook	P	4	17	Dungannon	Dungannon	Drumglass
Cooke	I	4	E	Cookstown	Dungannon	Derryloran
Cooper	P	6	7	Killany	Castlereagh	Killaney
Coote	I	4	E	Ballygawley	Clogher	Errigal
Corkin	I	3	E	Derryaghy	Belfast U	Derryaghy
Cormac	C	6	I	Bleary	Iveagh	Tullylish
Cormichil	P	3	13	Derryaghy	Belfast U.	Derryaghy
Cornwall	I	6	E	Ballywilliam	Ards	Donaghadee
Corr	C	3	I	Derryaghy	Belfast U.	Derryaghy
Corry	P	7	12	Enniskillen	Magheraboy	Enniskillen
Cosbye	I	7	E	Enniskillen	Magheraboy	Enniskillen
Cosgrove	C	6	I	Downpatrick	Lecale U.	Down
Cotnam	P	8	S	Lisnore *		
Cott	P	2	4	Londonderry	Londonderry	Templemore
Coulburn	P	2	7	Londonderry	Londonderry	Templemore
Coullow	I	5	E	Lurgan	Oneilland	Shankill
Coulter *	P	6	13	Ballycoulter	Lecale L.	Ballyculter
Courtney	I	3	E	Grange Pk.	Toome	Ballyscullion
Cowan	P	4	12	Dungannon	Dungannon	Drumglass
Cowen	P	1	12	St.Johnstown	Raphoe	Taughboyne
Cowper	I	4	7	Edernagh	Dungannon	Artrea
Cox	C	7	I	Lowtherstown	Lurg	Derryvallun
Coyle	P	4	I	Carnteel	Dungannon	Carnteel
Coyle	I	1	I	Ardbane	Kilmacrenan	Mevagh
Coyle	I	1	I	Dundooan	Kilmacrenan	Mevagh
Coyle	I	1	I	Glenkoe	Kilmacrenan	Mevagh
Coyle	I	1	I	Tullagh	Kilmacrenan	Mevagh
Coyle	C	6	I	Bleary	Iveagh	Tullylish
Craghead	P	4	1		Strabane L.	Strabane
Craig	P	11	15	Drumhillagh	Tallyhunco	Scrabby
Craig *	P	5	15	Magharyetrim*	Fews	
Craig *	P	11	S	Achmutie *	Tullyhunco	Scrabby
Craighead *	P	4	1	Donaghmore	Dungannon	Donaghmore
Crawford	P	4	13	Carnteel	Dungannon	Carnteel

Name	R	I	S	Townland	Barony	Place-Parish
Crawford	C	1	12	Letterkenny	Kilmacrenan	Conwal
Crawford	P	3	12	Donegore	Antrim	Donegore
Creacy	I	8	E		Cremorne	Clontibret
Crickard	C	6	I	Downpatrick	Lecale U.	Down
Croan	C	3	I	Derryaghy	Belfast U.	Derryaghy
Crofton	C	2	I	Londonderry	Londonderry	Templemore
Crogan	C	1	I		Raphoe	Raphoe
Crombie	P	8	S	Lisnaveane	Cremorne	Tullycorbet
Cromie	P	5	1			
Cromlin	Q	3	F	Derryaghy	Belfast U.	Derryaghy
Crommelin	P	6	F	Lisburn	Castlereagh	Blaris
Crooks	P	3	13	Ballykelly	Massereene	Ballinderry
Crooks	P	4	13	Cookstown	Dungannon	Derryloran
Crookshanks	P	1	1	Raphoe	Raphoe	Raphoe
Croskery	C	6	I	Downpatrick	Lecale U.	Down
Crown	I	4	E	Donaghmore	Dungannon M.	Donaghmore
Crozier	I	7	E	Enniskillen	Magheraboy	Enniskillen
Crozier	I	7	E	Enniskillen	Tirkennedy	Enniskillen
Crymble	P	5		Lurgan	Oneilland	Shankill
Cudbertson	P	1	18	Shannon	Raphoe	Taughboyne
Cue	P	7	F	Enniskillen	Magheraboy	Enniskillen
Cullin	C	1	I	Carrickart	Kilmacrenan	Mevagh
Cullin	I	1	I	Dundooan	Kilmacrenan	Mevagh
Cullin	I	1	I	Glenkoe	Kilmacrenan	Mevagh
Cumming	P	3	1	Kilraghts	Dunlance	Kilraghts
Cunningham *	P	3	12	Broadisland*		
Cunningham *	P	1	12	Donboy *	Raphoe	Allsaints
Cunningham *	P	1	12	Portlough	Raphoe	Allsaints
Cuppage		5		Lurgan	Oneilland	Shankill
Curling	P	2	S	Londonderry	Londonderry	Templemore
Cush	P	4	1		Dungannon	Aghaloo
Cushnahan	C	3	I	Derryaghy	Belfast U.	Derryaghy
Cust	I	2	E	Londonderry	Londonderry	Templemore
Cuthbert	C	9	5	Mullabane	Ardee	Clonkeen
Cuthbert	C	5	5	Lurgan	Oneilland	Shankill
Dalzell	I	6	E	Dundonald	Castlereagh	Dundonald
Dane	I	7	E	Enniskillen	Magheraboy	Enniskillen
Darcus	I	2	E	Londonderry	Londonderry	Templemore

Name	R	I	S	Townland	Barony	Place-Parish
Daugherty	C	1	I	Dundooan	Kilmacrenan	Mevagh
Daugherty	I	1	I	Glenkoe	Kilmacrenan	Mevagh
Daugherty	I	1	I	Meenlaragh	Kilmacrenan	Mevagh
Davenport	I	7	E	Enniskillen	Magheraboy	Enniskillen
Davidson	P	4	5	Dungannon	Dungannon	Drumglass
Davies	P	7	W	Carrow *	Clanawley	Killisher
Davis	P	4	W	Dungannon	Dungannon	Drumglass
Davis	P	2	W	Corlackie	Loughinsholin	Killelagh
Davis *	P		W	Granetagh*		
Davison	P	1	20		Raphoe	Raphoe
Davyes	P	2	1	Londonderry	Londonderry	Templemore
Dawson	P	3	5			
De Balquiere	H	3	F	Lisburn	Massereene	Blaris
de Blaquiere	P	2	F	Ardkill	Tirkeeran	Clondermot
de Joncourts	P	9	F	Dundalk	Dundalk U.	Dundalk
De La Cherois	H	3	F	Lisburn	Massereene	Blaris
de la Valade	P	6	F	Lisburn	Castlereagh	Blaris
de Lolme	P	6	F	Lisburn	Castlereagh	Blaris
Dealy	C	5	I		Armagh	Tynan
Dean	P	7	12	Enniskillen	Magheraboy	Enniskillen
Deazley		1			Raphoe	Stranorlar
Debourdieu	P	6	F	Annahilt*		
Deernan E.		9	I		Ardee	Stabannan
Defour	P	6	F	Lisburn	Castlereagh	Blaris
Deglees		2		Londonderry	Londonderry	Templemore
Dein	P	3	1	Derryaghy	Belfast U.	Derryaghy
Deine	P	7	1	Enniskillen	Magheraboy	Enniskillen
dela Brenton	Pe	3	F	Belfast	Belfast	Shankill
Delap	C	4	I		Strabane	Strabane
Delapp	C	4	I	Moylagh	Omagh	Clogherny
Delincourt	P	5	F	Armagh	Armagh	Armagh
Denning	I	1	E	Dromore	Raphoe	Leck
Denning	I	2	E	Londonderry	Londonderry	Templemore
Dennison	P	4	11	Dungannon	Dungannon	Drumglass
Dennison	P	2	11	Londonderry	Londonderry	Templemore
Denniston	I	1	E	Drumdutton	Kilmacrenan	Mevagh
Dent	I	2	E	Londonderry	Londonderry	Templemore
Dent	I	2	E	Londonderry	Londonderry	Templemore

Name	R	I	S	Townland	Barony	Place-Parish
Denvir	I	6	E		Lecale	Bright
Depre	P	6	F	Lisburn	Castlereagh	Blaris
Desbrisay	P	6	F	Lisburn	Castlereagh	Blaris
Devitt	I	7	E	Enniskillen	Magheraboy	Enniskillen
Dewart	P	3	15	Connor	Antrim L.	Connor
Dick	P	6	18	Downpatrick	Lecale U.	Down
Dick	P	1	15		Raphoe	Raphoe
Dilry		4			Dungannon	Clonfeacle
Dimon	I	3	E	Derryaghy	Belfast U.	Derryaghy
Diver	C	1	I	Ardbane	Kilmacrenan	Mevagh
Divers	C	6	I	Bleary	Iveagh	Tullylish
Dixon	I	2	E	Lissaghmore	Coleraine	Agivey
Dixon	P	4	17	Carnteel	Dungannon	Carnteel
Dixon	I	1	E	Rawros	Kilmacrenan	Mevagh
Dixon	P	8	E	Lisnaveane	Cremorne	Tullycorbet
Dixy	I	7	E	Enniskillen	Magheraboy	Enniskillen
Doack	C	1	I		Raphoe	Taughboyne
Doak	C	4	I		Omagh	Ardstraw
Dobbin	P	7	21	Londonderry	Londonderry	Templemore
Dobson	P	5	13	Lurgan	Oneilland	Shankill
Dodson	P	8	1	Lisnaveane	Cremorne	Tullycorbet
Dogan	C	5	I		Oneilland W.	Armagh
Dogherty	C	1	I	Carrickart	Kilmacrenan	Mevagh
Dolling	P	6	F	Magheralin	Iveagh	Magheralin
Dolly	C	4	I	Carnteel	Dungannon	Carnteel
Domville	P	6	F	Lisburn	Castlereagh	Blaris
Donaghy	P	4	6		Dungannon	Agahloo
Donboro *	P	7	S	Dromcro *	Tirkennedy	Derrybrusk
Doran	C	6	I	Bleary	Iveagh	Tullylish
Dornian	P	7	I	Mullybrack	Lurg	Derryvullan
Dougall	P	4	12	Dungannon	Dungannon	Drumglass
Dougkill	P	7	12	Enniskillen	Magheraboy	Enniskillen
Douglas	P	2	21			
Douglas	P	2	21			
Douglass	P	3	13	Broughshane	Antrim L.	Racavan
Dow	P	6	4	Dromore	Iveagh L.	Dromore
Dowey	P	4	4	Edernagh	Dungannon	Artrea
Downing	I	2	E	Bellaghy	Loughinsholin	Ballyscullion

Name	R	I	S	Townland	Barony	Place-Parish
Downing	I	2	E	Londonderry	Londonderry	Templemore
Downing	I	2	E	Londonderry	Londonderry	Templemore
Drainy	C	6	I	Bleary	Iveagh	Tullylish
Drake	I	3	E	Derryaghy	Belfast U.	Derryaghy
Dredan	C	1	15		Raphoe	Raphoe
Drummond	P	1	4	Rathmelton	Kilmacrenan	Aughnish
Drummond *	P	4	4	Ballymagoieth	Strabane	
Drysdale	P	6	1	Portaferry	Ards	Ballyphilip
Dubourdieu	H	3	F	Lisburn	Massereene	Blaris
Duckett	I	2	E	Londonderry	Londonderry	Templemore
Duddle	I	2	E	Londonderry	Londonderry	Templemore
Duff	P	6	26	Drumbo	Castlereagh	Drumbo
Duffin	I	4	26	Dungannon	Dungannon	Dungannon
Duffy	C	4	I	Carnteel	Dungannon	Carnteel
Duffy	C	1	I	Carrickart	Kilmacrenan	Mevagh
Duke	I	5	E	Armagh	Armagh	Armagh
Dunbar *	P	1	23	Kilkerhan *	Boylagh	
Dunbar *	P	11	12	Dromack *	Clankee	
Dunbar *	P	7	23	Dromcro *	Magheraboy	
Dunberry	P	7	S	Enniskillen	Magheraboy	Enniskillen
Duncan	P	7	1	Lisneskea	Magerstphana	Aghalurcher
Duncan	P	3	1	Derryaghy	Belfast U	Derryaghy
Duncan	P	1	31		Raphoe	Raphoe
Dunkin	P	1	17	Portlough	Raphoe	Allsaints
Dunlap	I	3	12	Derryaghy	Belfast U.	Derryaghy
Dunlop	P	3	12	Ballymena	Toome	Kirkinriola
Dunlop	P	6	12	Kilmore	Iveagh	Shankill
Durning, Chas.	C	7	-	Mullies	Lurg	Derryvullan
Durning, Pat.	C	7	-	Mulles	Lurg	Derryvullan
Durning,Cath.		7	I	Leam	Tirkennedy	Derryvullan
Durning,Chas.		1	I		Raphoe	Conwal
Durning,Chas.		7	I	Leam	Tirkennedy	Derryvullan
Durning,Edw.		1	I		Inishowen	Is. of Inch
Durning,Neal	C	-		Drumaran*	Lurg	Derryvullan
Dyermond	I	2	E		Tirkeeran	Cumber
Dysart	P	2	7	Londonderry	Londonderry	Templemore
Eadie	P	6	1	Newtownards	Castlereagh	Newtownards
Eady	P	2	1	Londonderry	Londonderry	Templemore

Name	R	I	S	Townland	Barony	Place-Parish
Eager	I	3	17	Derryaghy	Belfast U.	Derryaghy
Eakin	P	6	S	Bangor	Ards L.	Bangor
Earlie	I	4	E		Dungannon	Kildress
Easter	I	4	E		Omagh	Cappagh
Ebbitt	I	2	E	Londonderry	Londonderry	Templemore
Ectore		4			Strabane	Urney
Edgar	P	6	17	Newtownards	Ards	Newtownards
Edmiston	P	1	13	Trienmullen*	Raphoe	Taughboyne
Egriston	I	8	E		Dartree	Aghabog
Eiles	I	3	E	Derryaghy	Belfast U.	Derryaghy
Elder	P	1	1	Portlough	Raphoe	Allsaints
Elgun	C	7	I		Magheraboy	Cleenish
Elliott	P	7	17		Clanawley	
Ellis	I	6	E	Dromore	Iveagh L.	Dromore
Ellue	H	1	F		Kilmacrenan	Killygarvan
Emery	H	4	G	Castlederg	Omagh	Urney
English	I	6	E	Dromore	Iveagh L.	Dromore
Entrikin		2		Londonderry	Londonderry	Templemore
Eskin	P	4	11	Tullyweery	Dungannon	Artrea
Evatt	P	7	4		Magherstphna	Aghavea
Evatt	P	7	4	Enniskillen	Magheraboy	Enniskillen
Ewart	P	7	20	Enniskillen	Magheraboy	Enniskillen
Ewing	P	1	12		Raphoe	Raphoe
Fall	P	6	10	Dromore	Iveagh L.	Dromore
Falles	P	4	20	Lisboy	Dungannon	Artrea
Falls	P	4	20	Knocknaroy	Dungannon L.	Aghaloo
Faloon	P	6	F	Comber	Castlereagh	Comber
Fane	I	2	E	Londonderry	Londonderry	Templemore
Fane	I	2	E	Londonderry	Londonderry	Templemore
Farril	C	3	I	Derryaghy	Belfast U.	Derryaghy
Faucett	I	1	E	Derrycassan	Kilmacrenan	Mevagh
Faucitt	I	1	E	Meenacross	Kilmacrenan	Mevagh
Faulkner	I	2	E	Londonderry	Londonderry	Templemore
Fawcet	I	5	E	Loughross	Fews	Creggan
Fawcett	I	2	E	Londonderry	Londonderry	Templemore
Fenny	C	2	I	Londonderry	Londonderry	Templemore
Ferguson	P	4	21	Tullyraw	Dungannon	Artrea
Ferguson	P	4	21	Edernagh	Dungannon U.	Artrea

Name	R	I	S	Townland	Barony	Place-Parish
Ferguson	P	4	21	Tullyvegah	Dungannon U.	Artrea
Fergusson	P	7	7	Enniskellen	Magheraboy	Enniskillen
Ferrier	H	2	F	Londonderry	Londonderry	Templemore
Ferry	I	1	E	Carrickart	Kilmacrenan	Mevagh
Ffyliff	I	2	E	Londonderry	Londonderry	Templemore
Fibs		2		Londonderry	Londonderry	Templemore
Fifield	I	2	E	Londonderry	Londonderry	Templemore
Figsby	I	2	E	Londonderry	Londonderry	Templemore
Filson	I	1	E	Maghribue *	Raphoe	Leck
Fisher	I	4	E	Drumlagher	Clogher	Donacavey
Fisher	I	2	E	Londonderry	Londonderry	Templemore
Flemin	Q	2	18	Londonderry	Londonderry	Templemore
Fleming	P	1	18	Drumboy	Raphoe	Clonleigh
Fleming	P	3	18	Glenarm	Glenarm L.	Tickmacrevan
Fletcher	P	7	5	Ahantra *	Magheraboy	Enniskillen
Flood	I	1	E	Meenlaragh	Kilmacrenan	Mevagh
Flood	I	1	E		Raphoe	Raphoe
Flory	I	5	E	Lurgan	Oneilland	Shankill
Follitt	P	7	I	Enniskillen	Magheraboy	Enniskillen
Foreman	I	3	E	Derryaghy	Belfast U.	Derryaghy
Forrest	P	1	21	Gortnesk	Raphoe	Raphoe
Forsythe	P	4	9		Dungannon	Aghaloo
Forsythe	P	3	9	Rosedermot	Kilconway	Dunaghy
Forsythe	P	1	9		Raphoe	Raphoe
Forward	I	2	E	Londonderry	Londonderry	Templemore
Fould	P	1	21	Portlough	Raphoe	Allsaints
Fowler	I	5	E	Meigh	Orior	Killevy
Fowler *	I	7	E			
Fowler *	P	7	15	Moyglass	Magheraboy	Rossorry
Frazier	P	6	31	Bleary	Iveagh	Tullylish
Frederick	I	4	E		Clogher	Clogher
Frederick,J.	I	1	E		Kilmacrenan	
Frederick,P.	I	7	E		Tirkennedy	Derryvullan
French	P	7	21	Enniskillen	Magheraboy	Enniskillen
Frisell	I	7	E	Enniskillen	Magheraboy	Enniskillen
Frith	I	7	E	Enniskillen	Magheraboy	Enniskillen
Frizill	I	3	E	Derryaghy	Belfast U.	Derryaghy
Fuller	P	2	15	Londonderry	Londonderry	Templemore

Name	R	I	S	Townland	Barony	Place-Parish
Fullerton	P	3	12	Ballynure	Belfast	Ballynure
Fullerton	P	2	12	Londonderry	Londonderry	Templemore
Fulsan	I	1	E	Drumerdagh	Raphoe	Leck
Fulton	P	3	12	Carnmoney	Belfast	Carnmoney
Fulton	P	7	12	Enniskillen	Magheraboy	Enniskillen
Fulton	P	2	12	Londonderry	Londonderry	Templemore
Gaddis	P	8	S	Annahagh	Monaghan	Tedavnet
Gadess	I	7	E	Enniskillen	Magheraboy	Enniskillen
Gailbraith	P	2	26	Londonderry	Londonderry	Templemore
Gallagher	C	1	I	Ardbane	Kilmacrenan	Mevagh
Gallagher	I	1	I	Tullagh	Kilmacrenan	Mevagh
Gallaugher	I	1	I	Derrycassan	Kilmacrenan	Mevagh
Galley	I	3	33	Derryaghy	Belfast U.	Derryaghy
Gallice	P	8	12	Clincorn *		
Galtworth	I	2	E	Londonderry	Londonderry	Templemore
Gamble	I	1	E		Raphoe	Raphoe
Gardner	I	2	E	Londonderry	Londonderry	Templemore
Garnet	I	2	E	Londonderry	Londonderry	Templemore
Garven	P	2		Lissaghmore	Coleraine	Agivey
Garvill	H	1	F	Lurgybrack	Kilmacrenan	Clondavaddog
Gayer	I	3	E	Derryaghy	Belfast U.	Derryaghy
Gemett	C	2	I	Londonderry	Londonderry	Templemore
Geneste	H	3	F	Lisburn	Massereene	Blaris
George	P	3	E	Moyrusk	Massereene	Magheragall
Getty	Q	3	E	Belfast	Belfast	Shankill
Gibb *	P	7	S	Droma *		
Gibb *	P	7	S	Drumaa	Magheraboy	Boho
Gibbs	I	8	E	Clones	Dartree	Clones
Gibson	P	4	7	Tullyveagh	Dungannon	Artrea
Gibson	Q	3	21	Belfast	Belfast	Shankill
Gildernue	I	4	E		Dungannon	Aghaloo
Gilgour	P	1	7	Ratein *	Raphoe	Taughboyne
Gill	I	5	E	Armagh	Armagh	Armagh
Gillanders	C	8	I	Crosses	Monaghan	Monaghan
Gilliece	P	1	21	Ballyshannon	Tirhugh	Inishmacsaint
Gillies	P	1	43	Portlough	Raphoe	Allsaints
Gillpin	I	5	E	Portadown	Oneilland	Seagoe
Gilly	C	8	I	Clonboy	Dartree	Clones

Name	R	I	S	Townland	Barony	Place-Parish
Glass	C	6	7	Dromore	Iveagh L.	Dromore
Glenfield	I	3	E	Derryaghy	Belfast U.	Derryaghy
Glenn	I	7	E	Lisniskea	Magerstphana	Aghalurcher
Glenny	I	5	E	Market Hill	Fews	Kilclooney
Gluck	I	8	E	Clones	Dartree	Clones
Godfrey	I	2	E	Londonderry	Londonderry	Templemore
Goffe	C	6	I	Dromore	Iveagh L.	Dromore
Golether	C	3	I	Derryaghy	Belfast U.	Derryaghy
Goodfellow	I	7	E	Enniskillen	Magheraboy	Enniskillen
Goodlett	P	2	7	Londonderry	Londonderry	Templemore
Gooleand	P	1	11	Glassegowen *	Raphoe	
Goot	H	7	G	Enniskillen	Magheraboy	Enniskillen
Gorden	P	4	S		Dungannon	Aghaloo
Gordon	C	3	17	Carnlough	Glenarm	Ardclinis
Gordon	P	8	1	Templetate	Dartree	Clones
Gordon	P	6	17	Comber	Castlereagh	Comber
Gordon	P	2	22	Londonderry	Londonderry	Templemore
Gordon *	P	1	S	Mullaghveagh *	Boylagh	
Gore	I	7	E	Enniskillen	Magheraboy	Enniskillen
Gormley	C	3	I	Magheragall	Massereene	Magheragall
Gorrey	P	2	4	Londonderry	Londonderry	Templemore
Gorteen	I	8	E	Clones	Dartree	Clones
Gould	I	2	E	Lissaghmore	Coleraine	Agivey
Gourland	P	1	S	Momeen	Raphoe	Taughboyne
Gowan *	C	8	I	Glaslough	Trough	Donagh
Goyer	H	3	F	Lisburn	Massereene	Blaris
Goyer	P	5	F	Lurgan	Oneilland	Shankill
Graham	C	3	9			
Graham	P	4	4	Tulluconnell	Dungannon	Artrea
Graham	P	1	9	Carrickart	Kilmacrenan	Mevagh
Graham	P	1	4	Devlin	Kilmacrenan	Mevagh
Graham	P	2	9	Londonderry	Londonderry	Templemore
Grahams	I	3	4	Derryaghy	Belfast U.	Derryaghy
Grainger	P	3	20	Derryaghy	Belfast U.	Derryaghy
Grattan		7	I	Enniskillen	Magheraboy	Enniskillen
Gray	I	1	E		Raphoe	Raphoe
Green	C	3	I	Derryaghy	Belfast U.	Derryaghy
Greenham	I	1	E	Tonage	Raphoe	Taughboyne

Name	R	I	S	Townland	Barony	Place-Parish
Greer	P	4	10	Tullyhurken	Dungannon	Artrea
Greer *	C	2	21	Maghera *	Loughinsholin	Magherafelt
Greg	P	6	7	Newtownards	Ards	Newtownards
Gregg	P	6	7	Dromore	Iveagh L.	Dromore
Gregg	P	2	7	Londonderry	Londonderry	Templemore
Gribib	H	3	F	Derryaghy	Belfast U.	Derryaghy
Grier	P	1	21	Big Park	Tirhugh	Drumhome
Grierson	P	4	21	Tullylagan *	Dungannon	Desertcreat
Griffin	P	4	W	Edernagh	Dungannon	Artrea
Griffith	P	4	W		Dungannon	Aghaloo
Grigson	I	2	E	Londonderry	Londonderry	Templemore
Grimbs	I	3	E	Derryaghy	Belfast U.	Derryaghy
Grogan	C	3	I	Derryaghy	Belfast U.	Derryaghy
Grove	I	7	E	Enniskillen	Magheraboy	Enniskillen
Grove	I	2	E	Londonderry	Londonderry	Templemore
Gubbin	I	7	E	Enniskillen	Magheraboy	Enniskillen
Guest	I	5	E	Armagh	Armagh	Armagh
Guillot	H	3	F	Lisburn	Massereene	Blaris
Gussen	P	6	F	Newry	Newry	Newry
Guthree	P	8	12	Clones	Dartree	Clones
Guthrie	P	7	12	Enniskillen	Magheraboy	Enniskillen
Guy	I	4	E	Carnteel	Dungannon	Carnteel
Haddon	I	8	E			Aghabog
Hagan *	C	2	I		Loughinsholin	Artrea
Haig *	P	4	17	Tiremurtagh*	Strabane	Ardstraw
Hall	P	4	20	Alderwood *	Clogher	Aghalurcher
Hall	P	4	20	Findermore	Clogher	Clogher
Hall	I	2	E	Desertmartin	Loughinsholin	Desertmartin
Hallart	I	2	E	Desertmartin	Louhjinsholin	Desertmartin
Hallas	P	13	14	Kilmacshalgan	Tireragh	Kilmacshalgan
Hallyday	P	6	21	Drumbo	Castlereagh	Drumbo
Hamel	I	3	12		Messereene	Derryaghy
Hamersly	I	8	E	Clones	Dartree	Clones
Hamill *	P	4	I	Aughnaglough*		
Hamilton	P	4	S	Dirrywoon	Strabane	Ardstraw
Hamilton	P	4	13	Tullyveagh	Dungannon	Artrea
Hamilton	P	2	11	Moneymore	Loughinsholin	Artrea
Hamilton	P	4	13	Killycorran	Clogher	Clogher

Name	R	I	S	Townland	Barony	Place-Parish
Hamilton	P	6	23	Comber	Castlereagh	Comber
Hamilton	P	3	23	Bush Mills	Dunluce	Dunluce
Hamilton *	P	5	11	Fdeneveagh?	Fews	
Hamilton *	P	5	11	Magheryetrim*	Fews	
Hamilton *	P	11	10	Clonyn *	Tullyhunco	
Hamilton *	P	4	11	Largie C.	Strabane	Ardstraw
Hamilton *	P	4	13	Teadanekilleny	Strabane	Ardstraw
Hamilton *	P	7	13	Derrynefogher	Magheraboy	Devenish
Hamilton *	P	11	13	Kilcolgha	Clankee	Drumgoon
Hammon	C	2	I	Desertmartin	Loughinsholin	Desertmartin
Hance	P	4	13	Tullybroom	Clogher	Clogher
Hanna	P	4	13	Slatbeg	Clogher	Clogher
Hannah	P	4	12		Clogher	Clogher
Hannah	P	6	23	Comber	Castlereagh	Comber
Hannah	I	3	E		Belfast	Derryaghy
Hansard	I	1	E	Monyn	Raphoe	Raphoe
Haraford	I	6	E	Market Hill	Fews	Kilclooney
Haran	C	1	I	Ballyshannon	Tirhugh	Inishmacsaint
Hardin	I	5	E	Lurgan	Oneilland	Shankill
Hardy	I	4	21	Glenhoy	Clogher	Clogher
Hardy	I	4	21	Eskermore	Omagh E.	Clogherny
Hardy	I	4	21	Kilgreen	Clogher	Errigal
Hardy	P	6	13	Kircubbin	Ards	Inisnargy
Harighty	C	1	I	Derrycassan	Kilmacrenan	Mevagh
Harkness	P	8	S	Lisnaveane	Cremorne	Tullycorbet
Harland	I	5	E	Lurgan	Oneilland	Shankill
Harper	P	6	17	Comber	Castlereagh	Comber
Harper	I	3	E	Bush Mills	Dunluce	Dunluce
Harran *	I	1	E	Carrick	Raphoe	Donaghmore
Harriott	P	4	11	Dungannon	Dungannon	Aghaloo
Harris	I	2	E	Desertmartin	Loughinsholin	Desertmartin
Harris	I	4	E	Dungannon	Dungannon	Drumglass
Harrison	I	3	E	Bush Mills	Dunluce	Dunluce
Harshaw	P	8	S	Lisnaveane	Cremorne	Tullycorbet
Hart	I	3	E	Derryaghy	Belfast	Derryaghy
Hart	P	1	15	Taughboyne	Raphoe	Taughboyne
Hart	C	13	I	Ballygrahan	Tireragh	Templeboy
Harvey	I	6	E	Downpatrick	Lecale	Down

Name	R	I	S	Townland	Barony	Place-Parish
Harvy	I	1	E	Carshoe	Raphoe	Raphoe
Harwood	I	5	E	Armagh	Oneilland	Armagh
Hassard	H	7	F	Enniskillen	Magheraboy	Enniskillen
Hastings	I	3	20		Massereene	Derryaghy
Hatton	I	4	E		Strabane	Ardstraw
Hawthorne	P	6	23	Downpatrick	Lecale	Down
Hay	P	4	4	Ardstraw	Strabane	Ardstraw
Hay	I	3	23	Derryaghy	Belfast	Derryaghy
Heather	I	6	E	Market Hill	Fews	Kilclooney
Heatherton	I	2	E	Desertmartin	Loughinsholin	Desertmartin
Hector	H	4	F		Strabane	Ardstraw
Hedin	C	4	I	Corick	Clogher	Clogher
Heer	C	6	I	Dromore	Iveagh	Warrenspoint
Heidin	C	4	I	Corick	Clogher	Clogher
Heighton	P	7	13	Enniskillen	Magheraboy	Enniskillen
Helan	I	4	E		Strabane	Ardstraw
Henderson	P	1	7	Loughros	Kilmacrenan	Tullyfern
Hendrick	I	4	E	Ardstraw	Strabane	Ardstraw
Hendricks	I	4	E	Ardstraw	Strabane	Ardstraw
Heney	C	1	I	Toome	Kilmacrenan	Clondavaddog
Heney	C	3	I	Moyrusk	Massereene	Magheragall
Hennelly	C	14	I	Kilthrowan	Kilmaine	Ballinrobe
Henning *	P	7	21	Dewress		
Henry	I	13	E	Sligo	Carbury	Sligo
Hepburn *	P	4	S	O'Carragan*		
Heron	C	6	21	Killyleagh	Dufferin	Killyleagh
Heslip	P	6	15	Bangor	Ards	Bangor
Hesson	C	1	I	Toome	Kilmacrenan	Clondavaddog
Heuerat	H	4	G		Strabane	Ardstraw
Hewett	I	5	E			
Hewitt	I	6	E	Bangor	Ards	Bangor
Hicks	I	2	E		Loughinsholin	Desertmartin
Higginbotham	I	7	E	Enniskillen	Magheraboy	Enniskillen
Higgins	I	14	E	Kilthrown	Kilmaine	Ballinrobe
Higgins	I	4	E	Dungannon	Dungannon	Drumglass
Higgins	I	13	E	Carrowdurneen	Tireragh	Screen
Hilhouse	P	2	12	Ballycastle	Keenaght	Aghanloo
Hilhouse	P	2	12	Londonderry	Londonderry	Templemore

Name	R	I	S	Townland	Barony	Place-Parish
Hill	P	4	13	Ardstraw	Strabane	Ardstraw
Hill	I	4	E	Tullyconnell	Dungannon	Artrea
Hill	I	4	E	Dungannon	Dungannon	Drumglass
Hill	P	13	1	Carrownapull	Leyny	Kilmcteige
Hill	I	2	E	Londonderry	Londonderry	Templemore
Hillas	P	13	E		Tireragh	Kilmacshalgan
Hilles	I	4	E	Edernagh	Dungannon	Artrea
Hilles	I	4	E	Dungannon	Dungannon	Drumglass
Hilton	P	2	17		Londonderry	Templemore
Himpol	I	4	E		Strabane	Ardstraw
Hinkell	H	2	G	Londonderry	Londonderry	Templemore
Hinton	I	6	E	Dromore	Iveagh	Warrenspoint
Hipson	P	2	21	Desertmartin	Loughinsholin	Desertmartin
Hirshan	H	14	G	Racareen	Kilmaine	Ballinrobe
Hisham	H	14	G	Racareen	Kilmaine	Ballinrobe
Hitchin	I	2	E	Londonderry	Londonderry	Templemore
Hoard	I	1	E	Portlough	Raphoe	Allsaints
Hoban	P	14	1	Kilthrown	Kilmaine	Ballinrobe
Hobbs	I	5	E	Lurgan	Oneilland	Shankill
Hodsmyth	I	3	E	Derryaghy	Belfast	Derryaghy
Hodson	E	5	E	Armagh	Armagh	Armagh
Hogg	P	4	4	Ballynahone	Dungannon	Artrea
Hogg	P	6	17	Bangor	Ards	Bangor
Hogg	I	3	4	Derryaghy	Belfast	Derryaghy
Hogg	P	6	19		Lecale	Saul
Hogshead	P	1	S	Ballybogan	Raphoe	Clonleigh
Hogsyard *	P	3	11			
Holden	I	3	E	Ballyclare	Antrim U.	Dona Grange
Holder	I	13	E		Corran	Kilmorgan
Holdsworth	I	8	E	Caravitragh*		
Holland	P	6	19	Bangor	Ards	Bangor
Holmes	P	4	12	Ardstraw	Strabane	Ardstraw
Holmes	P	4	12	Clogher	Clogher	Clogher
Home *	P	7	10	Dromcoole	Magheraboy	Enniskillen
Homes	P	4	1		Omagh	Termonmaguirk
Hondwon	P	5	-	Lurgan	Oneilland	Shankill
Hone	P	6	12	Downpatrick	Lecale	Down
Honnins	I	8	E	Clones	Dartree	Clones

Name	R	I	S	Townland	Barony	Place-Parish
Honoff	I	5	E	Lurgan	Oneilland	Shankill
Hood	I	1	E	Portlough	Raphoe	Allsaints
Hood	I	4	E	Mt.Stewart	Clogher	Clogher
Hood	I	1	E	Momein	Raphoe	Taughboyne
Hookes	I	7	E	Enniskillen	Magheraboy	Enniskillen
Hoope	I	5	7	Lurgan	Oneilland	Shankill
Hopps	I	13	E	Collooney	Tirerrill	Killoran
Horner	P	2	12	Desertmartin	Loughinsholin	Desertmartin
Hosh	I	2	E	Desertmartin	Loughinsholin	Desertmartin
Houghy	P	4	12	Tullyconnell	Dungannon	Artrea
Houston	P	2	13	Desertmartin	Loughinsholin	Desertmartin
Houston	C	7	5	Rossory	Magheraboy	Rossory
Houston *	P	4	13	Castlestewart		
How	I	4	E		Strabane	Ardstraw
Howard	I	3	E	Derryaghy	Belfast	Derryaghy
Howard	I	4	E	Lurgiboy	Clogher	Donacavey
Howard	I	4	E	Dungannon	Dungannon	Drumglass
Howat	I	1	E	Tullirapp	Raphoe	Taughboyne
Howden	P	2	20	Desertmartin	Loughinsholin	Desertmartin
Howe	I	13	1		Corran	Cloonoghil
Hoy	C	2	12	Desertmartin	Loughinsholin	Desertmartin
Hoy	C	8	I	Lisnaveane	Cremorne	Tullycorbet
Huddlestone	P	6	21		Lecale	Saul
Hudson	I	3	E	Derryaghy	Belfast	Derryaghy
Hudson	I	7	E	Enniskillen	Magheraboy	Enniskillen
Hues	I	4	E		Strabane	Ardstraw
Hueston	P	3	31	Creggan	Toome U.	Duneane
Huey	P	3	6		Belfast	Derryaghy
Hughes	P	4	W	Dungannon	Dungannon	Aghaloo
Hughes	I	6	E		Lecale	Saul
Hume *	I	7	17	Ardgart	Magheraboy	Inishmacsaint
Humes	P	2	17	Derry	Londonderry	Templemore
Humphrey	I	13	E	Sligo	Carbury	Sligo
Hunter	I	3	11	Derryaghy	Belfast	Derryaghy
Hunter	P	6	12	Moneymore	Iveagh U.	Donaghmore
Hunter	P	3	12	Ballygrooby	Toome	Drummaul
Hunter	P	6	21	Dromore	Iveagh	Warrenspoint
Hurdy	I	14	E	Cloongowla	Kilmaine	Ballinrobe

Name	R	I	S	Townland	Barony	Place-Parish
Hurkles	I	4	N	Ardstraw	Strabane	Ardstraw
Hurst	I	2	E	Desertmartin	Loughinsholin	Desertmartin
Hutcheson	I	4	E	Carnteel	Dungannon	Carnteel
Hutchinson	P	6	1	Dromore	Iveagh	Warrenspoint
Hutchison	P	3	1	Bush Mills	Dunluce	Dunluce
Hutchison	P	6	1	Saintfield	Castlereagh	Saintfield
Hutton	I	6	17	Dromore	Iveagh	Warrenspoint
Hyneman	I	1	E	Beltany L.	Kilmacrenan	
Innis	C	6	I		Lecale	Saul
Irvine	P	4	21	Mullaghmore	Clogher	Clogher
Irvine	P	4	21	Prolusk	Clogher	Clogher
Irvine	I	7	12	Enniskillen	Magheraboy	Enniskillen
Irwin	P	4	S	Carnteel	Dungannon	Carnteel
Irwin	P	4	21	Mullaghmore	Clogher	Clogher
Irwin	I	1	E	Toome	Kilmacrenan	Clondavaddog
Irwin	P	4	21	Drumnamalta	Dungannon	Kildress
Irwin	P	13	S		Tireragh	Kilmacshalgan
Irwin	P	7	21	Derrygore	Tirkennedy	Trory
Isaac	H	7	G	Enniskillen	Magheraboy	Enniskillen
Isaic	H	1	G	Portlough	Raphoe	Allsaints
Islen	I	2	E	Londonderry	Londonderry	Templemore
Jack *	P	-	1	Bullalley*		
Jameson	P	4	1	Shantonagh	Clogher	Clogher
Jamison	P	4	1	Ballyness	Clogher	Clogher
Jarland	I	8	E	Clones	Dartree	Clones
Jawin	I	8	E	Granshagh		
Jellet	P	6	F	Dromore	Iveagh	Warrensport
Jenjins	P	6	15	Bangor	Ards	Bangor
Jennings	I	14	E		Kilmaine	Ballinrobe
Jennings	I	6	E	Downpatrick	Lecale	Down
Jenny	I	2	E	Londonderry	Londonderry	Templemore
Jervis	P	1	9	Donaghmore	Kilmacrenan	Clondavaddog
Jessop	I	1	E	Portlough	Raphoe	Allsaints
Jillets	I	6	E		Lecale	Saul
Johnson	P	4	21	Knocknaroy	Dungannon	Aghaloo
Johnson	P	5	21		Armagh	Armagh
Johnson	P	4	21	Knockinarvoer	Dungannon	Artrea
Johnson	I	3	21	Derryaghy	Belfast	Derryaghy

Name	R	I	S	Townland	Barony	Place-Parish
Johnston	P	4	21	Timpany	Clogher	Aghalurcher
Johnston	P	7	21	Brookeborough	Magheraphana	Aghavea
Johnston	P	2	20	Moneymore	Loughinsholin	Artrea
Johnston	P	4	20	Tulnavert	Clogher	Clogher
Johnston	P	4	21	Tully	Dungannon	Desertcreat
Johnston	P	4	21	Lisgallon	Dungannon	Donaghmore
Johnston	P	7	21	Enniskillen	Magheraboy	Enniskillen
Johnston	P	1	S		Raphoe	Raphoe
Johnston	P	2	21	Derry	Londonderry	Templemore
Johnston *	P	4	20	Annagarvey	Clogher	Clogher
Joint	H	13	F	Ballyglass	Tireragh	Kilglass
Jones	P	13	W		Tireragh	Skreen
Jonken	Q	1	D	Toome	Kilmacrenan	Clondavaddog
Jonnen	Q	14		Cloonluffan	Kilmaine	Ballinrobe
Jordan	I	5	E	Lurgan	Oneilland	Shankill
Joyce	C	14	I	Knocklehard	Kilmaine	Ballinrobe
Joyes	C	14	I	Knocklehard	Kilmaine	Ballinrobe
Kaey	P	2	15	Desertmartin	Loughinsholin	Desertmartin
Kane	C	6	I	Dromore	Iveagh	Warrenspoint
Kavanagh	C	4	I	Ballyscally	Clogher	Clogher
Kean	C	13	I	Ardnaree	Tireragh	Kilmoremoy
Kearnes *	C	4	I	Askragh*	Armagh	
Kearney	C	6	I	Bleary	Iveagh	Tullylush
Keary	C	7	I	Lisnaskea	Clankelly	Lisnaskea
Keenan	C	7	I	Derryvullen	Tirkennedy	Derryvullen
Keenan	C	7	I	Drumbulcan	Tirkennedy	Mahgaracross
Keenan *	C	4	I	Aughnaglough*		
Keene	C	4	I	Ardstraw	Strabane	Ardstraw
Keesh	I	6	E		Lecale	Saul
Keith	P	4	1	Dungannon	Dungannon	Dungannon
Kellips	C	6	32	Dromore	Iveagh	Warrenspoint
Kelly	P	4	I	Dungannon	Dungannon	Aghaloo
Kelly	C	1	I	Ardbane	Kilmacrenan	Mevagh
Kelly	P	6	11		Lecale	Saul
Kelter	H	4	G	Carnteel	Dungannon	Carnteel
Kenitter	P	4	S		Strabane	Ardstraw
Kennedie	P	7	22	Clonkee	Coole	Drummully
Kennedy	P	3	12	Glengormley	Belfast	Carnmoney

Name	R	I	S	Townland	Barony	Place-Parish
Kennedy	P	4	22	Ballymagowan	Clogher	Clogher
Kennedy	P	3	S	Templepatrick	Belfast	Templepatrick
Kennedy	P	6	S	Dromore	Iveagh	Warrenspoint
Kennedy *	P	4	22	Gortnaville*		
Kenner	C	6	I		Lecale	Saul
Keon	P	7	I	Mullies	Lurg	Derryvullan
Keon	C	7	I	Mullies	Lurg	Derryvullen
Keon	C	7	I	Derryvullen	Tirkennedy	Derryvullen
Ker	P	3	20	Ballymoney	Belfast	Shankill
Kernahan	C	3	I	Derryaghy	Belfast	Derryaghy
Kerney	C	3	I	Derryaghy	Belfast	Derryaghy
Kernoghan	C	4	I	Annaloughan	Clogher	Clogher
Kerr	P	4	20	Carnteel	Dungannon	Carnteel
Kevenay	C	7	W	Rossory	Magheraboy	Rossory
Kewburgh	I	7	E	Castlefin	Magheraboy	Enniskillen
Kewon	P	6	I		Lecale	Bright
Keyes	I	4	E	5Mi. Town	Clogher	Clogher
Keyes	I	7	E	Derryvullun	Tirkennedy	Derryvullan
Keyes	I	3	E	Bush Mills	Dunluce	Dunluce
Keyes	I	7	E	Enniskillen	Magheraboy	Enniskillen
Keyes	C	7	I	Drumbulcan	Tirkennedy	Magheracross
Keyes	I	3	E	Belfast	Belfast	Shankill
Keylagh *	I	11	E	Achmutie *	Tullyhunco	
Kibon	I	6	E		Lecale	Saul
Kidd	I	4	E	Tallelar*		
Kidd	P	4	S	Tullyveagh	Dungannon	Artrea
Kidd	P	4	S	Tullyvega	Dungannon	Artrea
Kidd	I	2	E	Moneymore	Loughinsholin	Artrea
Kidd	P	3	E	Derryaghy	Belfast	Derryaghy
Kiell	-	4	-		Strabane	Ardstraw
Killpatrick	I	3	10	Derryaghy	Belfast	Derryaghy
Kinade	P	2	15	Desertmartin	Loughinsholin	Desertmartin
Kinen	C	6	I	Dromore	Iveagh	Warrenspoint
King	P	4	E	Mossfield*		
King	I	13	E		Corran	Emlaghfad
King	I	2	E	Londonderry	Londonderry	Templemore
Kinibrough	I	4	E	Tullyraw	Dungannon	Artrea
Kinibrough	I	4	E	Dungannon	Dungannon	Drumglass

Name	R	I	S	Townland	Barony	Place-Parish
Kinkead	P	1	S		Raphoe	Allsaints
Kinkead	P	6	9	Drumbo	Castlereagh	Drumbo
Kinner	P	6	1		Lecale	Saul
Kinsalagh	C	8	I	Lattagallon*		
Kinsolagh	I	8	I	Rathmoy*		
Kirk	P	6	21	Kircubbin	Ards	Inisnargy
Kirk	P	6	21	Lisburn	Castlereagh	Killaney
Kirk	P	8	S	Lisnaveane	Cremorne	Tullycorbet
Kirkpatrick	P	4	21	Glenhoy	Clogher	Clogher
Kirkwood	P	13	S	Killala	Tirawley	Killala
Kirkwood	I	1	E	Trimra	Raphoe	Leck
Kirrigan	C	3	I	Derryaghy	Belfast	Derryaghy
Kitchen	I	2	E	Desertmartin	Loughinsholin	Desertmartin
Kittle	P	7	7	Enniskillen	Magheraboy	Enniskillen
Kmow	P	2	S	Londonderry	Londonderry	Templemore
Knee	P	1	S		Raphoe	Leck
Knight	I	7	E	Tunnymore	Magheraboy	Enniskillen
Kniland	C	4	I		Strabane	Ardstraw
Knoght	I	7	E	Tullymore	Magheraboy	Inishmacsaint
Knott	I	6	E		Lecale	Saul
Knox	P	3	11	Balleymoney	Dunlance	Ballymoney
Knox	P	1	S		Raphoe	Raphoe
Knox	P	6	11	Dromore	Iveagh	Warrenspoint
Knox *	P	8	11	Glaslough	Trough	Donagh
Kyle	C	1	I		Raphoe	Raphoe
Kyle	C	1	I		Kilmacrenan	Tullyfern
La Vallade	H	3	F	Lisburn	Massereene	Blaris
Laird	P	4	17	Carnahinney	Clogher	Clogher
Laird	P	1	S	Assmoyne*	Raphoe	Raphoe
Lambert	P	6	17		Lecale	Saul
Lamon	P	7	6	Ardgart	Magheraboy	Inishmacsaint
Lamond	P	4	6	Lisboy	Clogher	Clogher
Lamont	P	3	6			
Lamour	I	3	E	Ballinderry	Massereene	Ballinderry
Lanaghan	C	13	I		Carbury	Drumcliff
Land	I	3	E	Derryaghy	Belfast	Derryaghy
Landon	P	6	S		Lecale	Saul
Landy	I	7	E	Enniskillen	Magheraboy	Enniskillen

Name	R	I	S	Townland	Barony	Place-Parish
Lane	C	2	I	Londonderry	Londonderry	Templemore
Large	P	4	1	Ardstraw	Strabane	Ardstraw
Larman	I	8	E	Drumulla*		
Larmock	P	2	1	Desertmartin	Loughinsholin	Desertmartin
Lascelles	P	6	F	Lisburn	Castlereagh	Blaris
Lata		1		Taghboyne	Raphoe	Clonleigh
Latemore	P	4	20	Tullyconnell	Dungannon	Artrea
Latemore	I	4	E	Dungannon	Dungannon	Drumglass
Latimer	P	4	S		Dungannon	Aghaloo
Lauder *	P	5	7	Kilruddan*	Fews	
Laughlin	P	4	1	Ardstraw	Strabane	Ardstraw
Laughlin	P	6	12	Bangor	Ards	Bangor
Laverty	C	3	I	Derryaghy	Belfast	Derryaghy
Law *	P	4	S	Cavanakirk*		
Law *	I	4	E	Latbeg	Clogher	Clogher
Law *	P	2	S	Garvagh	Colerane	Errigal
Lawrence	I	4	E	Ardstraw	Strabane	Ardstraw
Lawrey	P	1	S		Raphoe	Raphoe
Lawson	I	3	21	Derryaghy	Belfast	Derryaghy
le Burt	P	3	F	Belfast	Belfast	Shankill
Leacock	P	2	15	Desertmartin	Loughinsholin	Desertmartin
Leadley	P	6	-	Market Hill	Fews	Kilclooney
Leaky	I	1	E		Bannagh	Inishkeel
Leamond	P	4	4	Lisboy	Dungannon	Artrea
Learman	I	4	E		Strabane	Ardstraw
Leatherdale	I	6	E		Lecale	Saul
Leathers	I	4	E	Tullyraw	Dungannon	Artrea
Leathes	P	4	I	Tullyraw	Dungannon	Artrea
Leathes	I	7	E	Enniskillen	Magheraboy	Enniskillen
Lee	I	2	E	Desertmartin	Loughinsholin	Desertmartin
Leeson	I	2	E	Londonderry	Londonderry	Templemore
Lemon	C	6	I	Drumbo	Castlereagh	Drumbo
Lendrum *	P	4	1	Cullenane*		
Lendrum *	P	4	1	Timpany	Clogher	Aghalurcher
Lendrum *	P	7	1	Cleen	Magheraphana	Aghalurcher
Lennox	P	1	10	Portlough	Raphoe	Allsaints
Lennox	P	3	10	Ballygrooby	Toome	Drummaul
Lenox	P	6	15	Newtownards	Ards	Newtownards

Name	R	I	S	Townland	Barony	Place-Parish
Lesley	P	7	1	Enniskillen	Magheraboy	Enniskillen
Leslie	P	4	7	Clogher	Clogher	Clogher
Leslie	P	4	7		Strabane	Urney
Letch	I	1	E	Cullin	Raphoe	Leck
Letournall	H	7	F	Enniskillen	Magheraboy	Enniskillen
Letty	I	4	E		Strabane	Ardstraw
Leturnel	I	7	E	Enniskillen	Magheraboy	Enniskillen
Lewers	P	6	13		Lecale	Ballee
Lewis	I	13	E		Tireragh	
Ley	P	4	15	Clogher	Clogher	Clogher
Ley	P	4	15	Kilclay	Clogher	Clogher
Liddane	I	14	E	Knocklehard	Kilmaine	Ballinrobe
Lieper		1		Cargins*	Raphoe	
Liggett	P	4	9	Corbo	Clogher	Clogher
Ligonier	H	7	F	Enniskillen	Magheraboy	Enniskillen
Lilburn	I	6	E	Dromore	Iveagh	Warrenspoint
Lilly	I	4	E		Dungannon	Kildress
Lindasy *	P	4	15	Tulloghoge*		
Lindesay	I	4	7	Fardross	Clogher	Clogher
Lindesay	P	8	7	Killycorran	Trough	Errigal
Lindrey *	I	7	E	Dromfkeah*		
Lindsay	P	4	20	Tullyveagh	Dungannon	Artrea
Lindsay	P	4	15	Tullyvega	Dungannon	Artrea
Lindsay	P	6	12	Bangor	Ards	Bangor
Lindsay	P	4	12	Lisnacrieve	Clogher	Donacravey
Lindsay *	P	4	S	Creighballes*		
Lindsay *	P	7	15	Drumskea	Lurg	Derryvullan
Linn	P	4	12	Ardstraw	Strabane	Ardstraw
Linn	P	3	12	Magheragall	Massereene	Magheragall
Linster	H	8	G	Lisnaveane	Cremorne	Tullycorbet
Linton	P	6	20		Lecale	Saul
Linton	I	8	E	Lisnaveane	Cremorne	Tullycorbet
Lister	H	8	G		Dartree	Ematris
Lithgow	P	2	S			Glendermot
Litter	I	3	E	Derryaghy	Belfast	Derryaghy
Little	I	4	E	Slatbeg	Clogher	Clogher
Little	P	3	1	Bush Mills	Dunluce	Dunluce
Liturel	I	7	E	Enniskillen	Magheraboy	Enniskillen

Name	R	I	S	Townland	Barony	Place-Parish
Liviney	I	14	E	Knocklehard	Kilmaine	Ballinrobe
Livingston	P	6	S	Drumbo	Castlereagh	Drumbo
Lloyd	I	7	E	Enniskillen	Magheraboy	Enniskillen
Lloyd	I	6	E		Lecale	Saul
Lochrane	P	4	20	Tullyconnell	Dungannon	Artrea
Lockerby	P	6	21	Drumbo	Castlereagh	Drumbo
Lockhart	P	6	15	Bangor	Ards	Bangor
Lockhart	P	1	15	Creevesmith	Raphoe	Leck
Logan	P	3	13	Carrickfergus	Carrickfergus	Carrickfergus
Logan	P	7	23	Lowtherstown	Lurg	Derryvullan
Logan	I	7	15	Enniskillen	Magheraboy	Enniskillen
Logan	P	2	15	Derry	Londonderry	Templemore
Logan	P	8	S	Lisnaveane	Cremorne	Tullycorbet
Logen	I	3	13	Derryaghy	Belfast	Derryaghy
Loggan	P	3	12	Ahoghill	Toome	Ahoghill
Logheed		8		Lisnaveane	Cremorne	Tullycorbet
Loghran	C	7	I	Rossory	Magheraboy	Rossory
Loghron	P	4	-	Carnteel	Dungannon	Carnteel
Logue	C	1	I	Carrickart	Kilmacrenan	Mevagh
Logue	C	1	I	Downies	Kilmacrenan	Mevagh
Logue	C	1	I	Drimfin	Kilmacrenan	Mevagh
Logue	P	1	I	Dundooan	Kilmacrenan	Mevagh
Lomond	P	4	S	Lisboy	Dungannon	Artrea
Lomond	P	4	S	Lisboy	Clogher	Clogher
Long	P	6	15	Bangor	Ards	Bangor
Long	P	4	21	Augher	Clogher	Clogher
Longmoor	I	3	E	Bush Mills	L. Dunluce	Dunluce
Longpill	I	1	E	Portlough	Raphoe	Allsaints
Loo		5		Lurgan	Oneilland	Shankill
Looby	C	13	I	Killadoon	Tirerrill	Killadoon
Lorrimer	P	8		Lisnaveane	Cremorne	Tullycorbet
Lough	C	2	I	Desertmartin	Loughinsholin	Desertmartin
Lougherbee	P	5	-	Armagh	Armagh	Armagh
Loughlin	C	6	I	Kircubbin	Ards	Inisnargy
Love	P	3	11	Dunlance	Dunlance	Ballymoney
Love	P	7	11	Lowtherstown	Lurg	Derryvullan
Low	P	6	E		Lecale	Downpatrick
Low	I	13	E	Collooney	Tirerrill	Killoran

Name	R	I	S	Townland	Barony	Place-Parish
Lowers	I	6	E		Lecale	Saul
Lowery	I	6	E		Lecale	Saul
Lowry	P	4	S	Knocknaroy	Aghaloo	Aghaloo
Lowry	P	4	21	Ardstraw	Strabane	Ardstraw
Lowry	P	4	1	Knockinarvoer	Dungannon	Artrea
Lowther	I	4	E	Ardstraw	Strabane	Ardstraw
Lucy	I	7		Enniskillen	Magheraboy	Enniskillen
Luggy	P	4	13		Strabane	Ardstraw
Lun	I	3		Derryaghy	Belfast	Derryaghy
Lundy	P	6	7		Lecale	Downpatrick
Lundy	I	2	E	Londonderry	Londonderry	Templemore
Lutton	-	8	-		Dartree	Aghabog
Lyndsie	P	2		Londonderry	Londonderry	Templemore
Lynn	P	4	12	Tullyconnell	Dungannon	Artrea
Lynn	P	13	12	Finid	Carbury	Drumcliff
Lyon	C	7	I	Enniskillen	Magheraboy	Enniskillen
Lyster	I	6	E	Kircubbin	Ards	Inisnargy
Lyttle	I	4	E	Duffsland	Dungannon	Drumglass
Lyttle	I	4	E	Dungannon	Dungannon	Drumglass
Mac Adam	P	4	12	Edernagh	Dungannon	Artrea
Mac Alooney	C	8	I	Carn	Dartree	Clones
Mac Atagart	C	4	I	Lisgallon	Dungannon	Donaghmore
Mac Canna	C	4	I		Omagh	Termonmaguirk
Mac Carran	C	1	I		Raphoe	Raphoe
Mac Carrick	P	13	12	Collooney	Tirerrill	Killoran
Mac Cleery	C	1	I		Raphoe	Raphoe
Mac Clelland	P	3	22	Ballycastle	Cary	Ramoan
Mac Colgan	C	4	I		Omagh	Termonmaguirk
Mac Conaghy	C	8	6	Lisnagore	Dartree	Killeevan
Mac Conway	C	4	I		Omagh	Termonmaguirk
Mac Conwell	P	6	S	Bleary	Iveagh	Tullylish
Mac Corde	P	4	12	Lisnahull	Dungannon	Donaghmore
Mac Corde	P	4	12	Lisnahull	Dungannone	Donaghmore
Mac Cormick	P	7	S	Enniskillen	Magheraboy	Enniskillen
Mac Cory	C	2	I	Moneymore	Loughinsholin	Artrea
Mac Cue	C	7	I	Mullies	Lurg	Derryvullan
Mac Dermod	C	7	I	Derryvullen	Tirkennedy	Derryvullen
Mac Dermod	P	7	12	Drumbulcan	Tirkennedy	Magheracross

Name	R	I	S	Townland	Barony	Place-Parish
Mac Eldoon	C	4	I	Tevena	Dungannon	Artrea
Mac Elhair	C	4	I		Omagh	Termonmaguirk
Mac Elhone	C	2	I	Moneymore	Loughinsholin	Artrea
Mac Erlain	P	1	12	Toome	Kilmacrenan	Clondavaddog
Mac Fadin	P	1	29	Carrickart	Kilmacrenan	Mevagh
Mac Gill	C	1	I	Toome	Kilmacrenan	Clondavaddog
Mac Ginnahty	C	4	I	Duffsland	Dungannon	Artrea
Mac Ginnahty	C	4	I	Dufless	Dungannon	Artrea
Mac Ginnahty	C	4	I	Tevena	Dungannon	Artrea
Mac Ginnahty	C	5	I	Tavanagh	Oneilland W.	Drumcree
Mac Guide	C	2	I	Moneymore	Loughinsholin	Artrea
Mac Guire	C	1	I		Raphoe	Raphoe
Mac Guirk	P	4	S		Omagh	Termonmaguirk
Mac Gulpin	C	2	I	Moneymore	Loughinsholin	Artrea
Mac Henry	C	4	I	Tullyvega	Dungannon	Artrea
Mac Ilbreed	C	4	I		Omagh	Termonmaguirk
Mac Ilduff	P	4	21		Omagh	Termonmaguirk
Mac Keal	I	13	I	Newtown	Carbury	Ahamlish
Mac Kelvey	P	1	12		Raphoe	Raphoe
Mac Lane	P	4	12	Ardstraw	Strabane	Ardstraw
Mac Loinan	C	2	I	Moneymore	Loughinsholin	Artrea
Mac Lorian	P	1		Toome	Kilmacrenan	Clondavaddog
Mac Mahon	C	4	I		Omagh	Termonmaguirk
Mac Manus	C	4	I		Omagh	Termonmaguirk
Mac Murphy	C	4	I		Omagh	Termonmaguirk
Mac Neal	P	2	31	Moneymore	Loughinsholin	Artrea
Mac Neale	P	6	S	Dundrum	Lecale	Kilmegan
Mac Neil	P	2	15	Desertmartin	Loughinsholin	Desertmartin
Mac Peake	C	2	I	Londonderry	Londonderry	Templemore
Mac Quig	P	2	I	Moneymore	Loughinsholin	Artrea
Mac Rory	P	4	22	Tullyveagh	Dungannon	Artrea
Mac Rory	P	4	5	Tullyvega	Dungannon	Artrea
Mac Rory	P	4	5		Omagh	Termonmaguirk
Mac Sparron	C	2	I	Moneymore	Loughinsholin	Artrea
Mac Williams	P	1	23	Toome	Kilmacrenan	Clondavaddog
Mac Wornock	P	4	S		Omagh	Termonmaguirk
Macanally	P	1	10	Toome	Kilmacrenan	Clondavaddog
Machan	P	1	I	Ardchilly	Raphoe	Convoy

Name	R	I	S	Townland	Barony	Place-Parish
Machlin	P	3	S	Derryaghy	Belfast	Derryaghy
Mackedow	P	2	S		Londonderry	Templemore
Mackel	C	6	I	Bleary	Iveagh	Tullylish
Mackey	C	4	I	Clogher	Clogher	Clogher
Mackin	C	13	I	Collooney	Tirerrill	Killoran
Mackin	C	13	I	Grangemore	Tireragh	Templeboy
MacKine	C	3	I	Ballygrooby	Toome	Drummaul
Macklin	P	4	1	Ardstraw	Strabane	Ardstraw
Macool	C	2	I	Desertmartin	Loughinsholin	Desertmartin
Madill	C	6	I		Lecale	Saul
Madole	C	3	I	Bush Mills	L. Dunluce	Dunluce
Magee	C	3	I	Bush Mills	L. Dunluce	Dunluce
Magee	C	13	I	Ballyglass	Tireragh	Kilglass
Maghlin	P	2	I	Londonderry	Londonderry	Templemore
Magill	P	6	S		Lecale	Downpatrick
Magnigain	P	6	I	Bleary	Iveagh	Tullylish
Magorran	C	2	I	Desertmartin	Loughinsholin	Desertmartin
Magory	C	2		Desertmartin	Loughinsholin	Desertmartin
Magovern	P	1	I		Tirhugh	Inishmacsaint
Maguire	C	13	I	Ballintogher	Tirerrill	Killery
Magullion	C	2	I	Desertmartin	Loughinsholin	Desertmartin
Mahon	C	4	I	Findermore	Clogher	Clogher
Mailholm *	I	7	E	Diriany	Knockninny	
Mains	P	3	S	Bush Mills	L. Dunluce	Dunluce
Maize	H	4	F	Tullidonell	Dungannon	Drumglass
Makilly	C	2	I	Desertmartin	Loughinsholin	Desertmartin
Makky	C	6	I	Dromore	Iveagh	Warrenspoint
Maleer	I	2	E	Desertmartin	Loughinsholin	Desertmartin
Mallon	P	2	S	Moneymore	Loughinsholin	Artrea
Mallon	P	4	S	Kilnaheery	Clogher	Clogher
Maloy	C	4	I		Dungannon	Aghaloo
Mandy	P	1	W	Carrickart	Kilmacrenan	Mevagh
Mannis	P	6	20	Drumbo	Castlereagh	Drumbo
Manson	I	2	E	Londonderry	Londonderry	Templemore
March	I	7	E	Rossory	Magheraboy	Rossory
Mardock	I	2	E	Desertmartin	Loughinsholin	Desertmartin
Maris	I	1	E		Raphoe	Raymoghy
Markey	C	4	I	Ardstraw	Strabane	Ardstraw

Name	R	I	S	Townland	Barony	Place-Parish
Marl	I	6	E		Lecale	Saul
Marline	I	6	E		Lecale	Saul
Marmaduke	I	1		Raphoe	Raphoe	Raphoe
Marsden	I	3	E		Belfast	Derryaghy
Marshall	I	4	E		Dungannon	Aghaloo
Marshall	P	6	15	Bangor	Ards	Bangor
Marshall	P	3	15	Bush Mills	L. Dunluce	Dunluce
Martin	P	3	7	Bush Mills	L. Dunluce	Dunluce
Martin	I	13	E	Ardnaree	Tireragh	Kilmoremoy
Martin	I	1	E	Carrickart	Kilmacrenan	Mevagh
Martin	I	13	E	Dunmoran	Tireragh	Skreen
Mason	I	1	E		Raphoe	Raymoghy
Materick	I	4	E		Strabane	Ardstraw
Mathes	I	3	E	Derryaghy	Belfast	Derryaghy
Mathews	P	4	15	Ardstraw	Strabane	Ardstraw
Matters	P	2	1	Desertmartin	Loughinsholin	Desertmartin
Mauleverer	I	2	E	Londonderry	Londonderry	Templemore
Mawhinney	C	6	I		Lecale	Saul
Maxfield	I	1	E	Portlough	Raphoe	Allsaints
Maxwell	P	1	S	Lisskeran*	Raphoe	Bangor
Maxwell	I	1	E	Raforty	Banagh	Inver
Maxwell	P	6	21	Newry	Newry	Newry
Maxwell	I	2	E	Londonderry	Londonderry	Templemore
May	C	3	I	Ballinderry	Massereene	Ballinderry
Maynes	P	4	1	Kilnahushogue	Clogher	Clogher
Maynes	P	4	1	Lungs	Clogher	Clogher
Maziere	H	5	F	Lurgan	Oneilland	Shankill
Mc Adoe	P	1	S	Portrush	Raphoe	Allsaints
Mc Alester	I	3	21		Belfast	Derryaghy
Mc Alister	P	2	6	Desertmartin	Loughinsholin	Desertmartin
Mc Allen	I	4	I	Ardstraw	Strabane	Ardstraw
Mc Allister	P	6	26		Lecale	Downpatrick
Mc Aneany	P	8	S	Coraghbrak	Trough	Donagh
Mc Anerny	C	6	I	Bleary	Iveagh	Tullylish
Mc Ardle	C	4	I	Clogher	Clogher	Clogher
Mc Atagart	C	4	I	Lisgallon	Dungannon	Donaghmore
Mc Aulay	P	1	10	Ballyweagh	Portlough	
Mc Aulay *	P	1	10	Ballyweagh	Raphoe	Allsaints

Name	R	I	S	Townland	Barony	Place-Parish
Mc Avers	P	6	S		Lecale	Saul
Mc Award	P	1	I	Meenlaragh	Kilmacrenan	Mevagh
Mc Bride	C	6	27	Comber	Castlereagh	Comber
Mc Bride	C	3	I	Bush Mills	L. Dunluce	Dunluce
Mc Bride	C	1	I	Ardbane	Kilmacrenan	Mevagh
Mc Bride	P	1	I	Carrickart	Kilmacrenan	Mevagh
Mc Bride	P	1	S	Derrycassan	Kilmacrenan	Mevagh
Mc Bride	P	1	S	Devlinreagh	Kilmacrenan	Mevagh
Mc Bride	C	1	I	Glenoory	Kilmacrenan	Mevagh
Mc Bryer	P	6	I		Lecale	Saul
Mc Cabe	C	8	I	Crossreagh	Dartree	Killeevan
Mc Cadam	P	5	11		Tiranny	Keady
Mc Cafer	C	2	I		Londonderry	Templemore
Mc Caferty	I	1	I	Ardbane	Kilmacrenan	Mevagh
Mc Call	P	3	S	Derryaghy	Belfast	Derryaghy
Mc Calla	C	6	12	Ballynahinch	Kinelarty	Magheradrool
Mc Cames	C	4	I	Edernagh	Dungannon	Artrea
Mc Cames	P	4	25	Edernagh	Dungannon	Artrea
Mc Cames	P	4	10	Lisboy	Dungannon	Artrea
Mc Cames	C	4	I	Lisboy	Clogher	Clogher
Mc Camish	C	6	I	Dromore	Iveagh	Warrenspoint
Mc Camon	P	4	I	Carnteel	Dungannon	Carnteel
Mc Camon	P	5	I	Market Hill	Fews	Kilclooney
Mc Cann	P	6	15	Newtownards	Ards	Newtownards
Mc Cardel	P	4	I	Carnteel	Dungannon	Carnteel
Mc Carney	P	4	15	Altanaverga	Clogher	Clogher
Mc Carney	P	4	15	Fivemiletown	Clogher	Clogher
Mc Carrell	C	4	I			
Mc Carroll	C	4	I	Carntall	Clogher	Clogher
Mc Carroll	C	4	I	Tullybroom	Clogher	Clogher
Mc Cartney	P	3	21			
Mc Caughey	C	4	I	Lismore	Clogher	Clogher
Mc Caugheye	C	4	I	Findermore	Clogher	Clogher
Mc Causland	P	2	10	Dreenagh		
Mc Causland	P	4	10	Tullyconnell	Dungannon	Artrea
Mc Cawell	C	4	I	Newtownsville		
Mc Cawell	C	4	I	Bolies	Clogher	Clogher
Mc Cawell	C	4	I	Lisgorran	Clogher	Clogher

Name	R	I	S	Townland	Barony	Place-Parish
Mc Cayne	P	2	S	Desertmartin	Loughinsholin	Desertmartin
Mc Chesney	P	3	2	Bush Mills	L. Dunluce	Dunluce
Mc Chestney	P	6	S	Drumbo	Castlereagh	Drumbo
Mc Cillin	P	4	11	Ardstraw	Strabane	Ardstraw
Mc Clean	P	4	12	Kilnahushoghe	Clogher	Clogher
Mc Clean	C	3	12	Derryaghy	Belfast	Derryaghy
Mc Clelland	P	4	12	Clogher	Clogher	Clogher
Mc Clemens	P	3	S	Bush Mills	L. Dunluce	Dunluce
Mc Clery	P	4	I		Dungannon	Agahloo
Mc Clhenny	P	2	S	Londonderry	Londonderry	Templemore
Mc Clinchy	P	5	I	Lurgan	Oneilland	Shankill
Mc Clinshe	C	5	I	Market Hill	Fews	Kilclooney
Mc Clintoc	P	1	S		Raphoe	Raphoe
Mc Cloy	P	3	10	Carrickfergus	Carrickfergus	Carickfergus
Mc Cloy	P	6	12		Lecale	Saul
Mc Cloyster	P	3	I	Derryaghy	Belfast	Derryaghy
Mc Clune	P	3	12	Bush Mills	L. Dunluce	Dunluce
Mc Clure	P	1	23	Drumlackagh	Kilmacrenan	Mevagh
Mc Clure	P	1	23		Raphoe	Raphoe
Mc Clurg	P	3	12	Bush Mills	L. Dunluce	Dunluce
Mc Clurg	P	6	12	Killyleagh	Dufferin	Killyleagh
Mc Coach	P	1		Rawros	Kilmacrenan	Mevagh
Mc Cobe	P	4	S		Strabane	Ardstraw
Mc Colgah	I	4	I	Ardstraw	Strabane	Ardstraw
Mc Collum	P	4	S	Clogher	Clogher	Clogher
Mc Comb	P	6	22		Lecale	Downpatrick
Mc Comb	P	6	22		Lecale	Saul
Mc Comb	P	3	23	Belfast	Belfast	Shankill
Mc Come	P	5	S		Armagh	Armagh
Mc Connel	C	1	I	Island Roy	Kilmacrenan	Mevagh
Mc Connell	C	1	I		Raphoe	Raphoe
Mc Convil	C	6	I	Bleary	Iveagh	Tullylish
Mc Corkill	P	1	S	Portlough	Raphoe	Allsaints
Mc Corkle	P	1	S	Ballehesky	Raphoe	
Mc Cormick	C	6	I	Magherally	Iveagh	Magerally
Mc Cosker	C	6	I	Bleary	Iveagh	Tullylish
Mc Cowy	P	4	I	Carnteel	Dungannon	Carnteel
Mc Coy	C	4	I	Cess *		

Name	R	I	S	Townland	Barony	Place-Parish
Mc Coy	C	4	I	Altanaverga	Clogher	Clogher
Mc Crabb	P	4	1	Ardstraw	Strabane	Ardstraw
Mc Cracken	P	3	I	Derryaghy	Belfast	Derryaghy
Mc Cracken	P	6	6		Lecale	Saul
Mc Crea	P	4	12	Townagh	Clogher	Clogher
Mc Creery	P	3	5	Belfast	Belfast	Shankill
Mc Creevy	P	4	12	Corcreevy	Clogher	Clogher
Mc Creevy	C	6	I		Lecale	Saul
Mc Creight	C	3	23		Massereene	Derryaghy
Mc Creightt	C	5	I	Market Hill	Fews	Kilclooney
Mc Crisckan	P	6	I	Downpatrick	Lecale	Down
Mc Crusky	P	3	23	Lisburn	Belfast	Lambeg
Mc Cublagh	I	3	S	Derryaghy	Belfast	Derryaghy
Mc Cue	C	1	I	Glenkoe	Kilmacrenan	Mevagh
Mc Culer	P	4	E		Strabane	Ardstraw
Mc Culloch	P	1	23	Mullaghveagh	Boylagh & B.	
Mc Culloch	P	2	6	Londonderry	Londonderry	Templemore
Mc Culloch *	P	1	23	Cargie	Boylagh	
Mc Cullock	P	6	23	Kircubbin	Ards	Inisnargy
Mc Cusker	P	7	I	Lowtherstown	Lurg	Derryvallun
Mc Cutchon	C	1	32	Portlough	Raphoe	Allsaints
Mc Dade	P	1	4	Killarhel		
Mc Dermond	P	4	12	Gravaghey	Clogher	Clogher
Mc Doel	P	6	36	Dromore	Iveagh	Warrenspoint
Mc Donald	C	7	5	Lisnaskea	Clankelly	Lisnaskea
Mc Dowell	C	4	38	Ardstraw	Strabane	Ardstraw
Mc Dowell	C	4	38	Augher	Clogher	Clogher
Mc Dowell	C	4	38	Clogher	Clogher	Clogher
Mc Dowell	C	4	38	kilrudden	Clogher	Clogher
Mc Elhar	C	1	I	Devlin	Kilmacrenan	Mevagh
Mc Elhar	I	1	I	Devlinreagh	Kilmacrenan	Mevagh
Mc Elhar	C	1	I	Glenoory	Kilmacrenan	Mevagh
Mc Elhenney	C	4	I	Shanco	Clogher	Clogher
Mc Elhinney	C	1	I	Island Roy	Kilmacrenan	Mevagh
Mc Elhinney	C	1	I	Maghera Beg	Kilmacrenan	Mevagh
Mc Elhir	C	1	I	DerryCassan	Kilmacrenan	Mevagh
Mc Elrath	C	4	I	Beltiny	Strabane	Cappagh
Mc Elroy	P	4	I	Springtown		

Name	R	I	S	Townland	Barony	Place-Parish
Mc Elroy	P	4	I	Clogher	Clogher	Clogher
Mc Elroy	P	5	I	Drumgaw	Fews	Lisnadill
Mc Fadden	P	6	29	Kircubbin	Ards	Inisnargy
Mc Fadin	I	1	I	Carrickart	Kilmacrenan	Mevagh
Mc Fadin	I	1	I	Doagh	Kilmacrenan	Mevagh
Mc Fadin	C	1	I	Glenieragh	Kilmacrenan	Mevagh
Mc Farlan	P	1	10	Portlough	Raphoe	Allsaints
Mc Farlan	P	4	10	Ardstraw	Strabane	Ardstraw
Mc Farlin	P	3	10	Bush Mills	L. Dunluce	Dunluce
Mc Fee	I	3	6	Derryaghy	Belfast	Derryaghy
Mc Fetridge	P	4	21	Clogher	Clogher	Clogher
Mc Gahey	C	4	I	Lurgaboyn	Dungannon	Drumglass
Mc Gaogy	I	4	I	Cormore	Clogher	Clogher
Mc Gaogy	I	4	I	Lisnarable	Clogher	Clogher
Mc Garvey	I	1	I	Drimfin	Kilmacrenan	Mevagh
Mc Garvey	C	1	I	Mgrymagrn	Kilmacrenan	Mevagh
Mc Gauggey	C	4	I	Fernaghandrum	Clogher	Clogher
Mc Gauvern	P	4	12	Ballymagowan	Clogher	Clogher
Mc Gaw	P	8	12	Corlogharoe	Dartree	Killeevan
Mc Gee	C	4	I	Clogher	Clogher	Clogher
Mc Geean	C	6	I	Downpatrick	Lecale	Down
Mc Getigan	P	1	S	Drumlackagh	Kilmacrenan	Mevagh
Mc Getigan	C	1	I	Glenieragh	Kilmacrenan	Mevagh
Mc Gibbon	C	6	I	Bangor	Ards	Bangor
Mc Gibbon	C	6	I	Drumbo	Castlereagh	Drumbo
Mc Gifford	P	6	S	Magheradrool	Kinelarty	Magheradroll
Mc Gilahattan	I	2	I		Londonderry	Templemore
Mc Gill	P	6	7	Newtownards	Ards	Newtownards
Mc Ginly	C	1	I	Derrycassan	Kilmacrenan	Mevagh
Mc Ginly	C	1	I	Meenformal	Kilmacrenan	Mevagh
Mc Ginn	C	4	I	Malabaney	Clogher	Clogher
Mc Ginnahty	C	3	I	Ballygrooby	Toome	Drummaul
Mc Ginnelly	C	4	I	Tullybroom *		
Mc Ginnelly	C	4	I	Beltiny	Strabane	Cappagh
Mc Girr	P	4	21	Clarmore	Clogher	Clogher
Mc Gladry	C	6	I	Dromore	Iveagh	Warrenspoint
Mc Glaggan	C	2	I	Londonderry	Londonderry	Templemore
Mc Glaughlin	C	6	I	Dromore	Iveagh	Warrenspoint

Name	R	I	S	Townland	Barony	Place-Parish
Mc Glennon	P	6	7		Lecale	Saul
Mc Golphin	P	3	I	Derryaghy	Belfast	Derryaghy
Mc Grady	C	4	I	Carnteel	Dungannon	Carnteel
Mc Grane	C	5	I	Armagh	Armagh	Armagh
Mc Gregor	P	3	4	Bush Mills	L. Dunluce	Dunluce
Mc Grody	P	1	S	Ardbane	Kilmacrenan	Mevagh
Mc Guckin	C	3	6	Ballygrooby	Toome	Drummaul
Mc Guffick	P	6	1		Lecale	Saul
Mc Guffin	P	3	1	Bush Mills	L. Dunluce	Dunluce
Mc Guffy	P	8	I	Lisnaveane	Cremorne	Tullycorbet
Mc Guire	C	4	I	Altnacerney *		
Mc Gunshenon	P	4	-		Dungannon	Aghaloo
Mc Handles	I	6	E		Lecale	Saul
Mc Hatten	C	2	I	Londonderry	Londonderry	Templemore
Mc Hilbrown		2		Londonderry	Londonderry	Templemore
Mc Hugh	C	1	I	Tullagh	Kilmacrenan	Mevagh
Mc Ilduff	P	5	21	Lurgan	Oneilland	Shankill
Mc Ilgallogly	C	5	I	Armagh	Armagh	Armagh
Mc Ilroy	I	3	12	Derryaghy	Belfast	Derryaghy
Mc Ilrudd	P	6	6	Armagh	Armagh	Armagh
Mc Ilvaney	C	4	I	Ardstraw	Strabane	Ardstraw
Mc Ilvine	P	6	21	Drumbo	Castlereagh	Drumbo
Mc Intire	C	1	I	Dundooan	Kilmacrenan	Mevagh
Mc Kasby	P	4	I		Strabane	Ardstraw
Mc Kay	P	6	6		Lecale	Saul
Mc Kee	P	3	26	Bush Mills	L. Dunluce	Dunluce
Mc Kee	P	6	26		Lecale	Saul
Mc Kee*	P	1	12	Cargie	Boylagh & B.	
Mc Keever	I	6	I	Armagh	Armagh	Armagh
Mc Keever	p	4	I	Gortin	Strabane	Bodoney
Mc Keevers	P	6	I		Lecale	Downpatrick
Mc Kelman	P	6	-		Lecale	Saul
Mc Kelvey	P	2	21	Desertmartin	Loughinsholin	Desertmartin
Mc Kelvey	P	3	21	Bush Mills	L. Dunluce	Dunluce
Mc Kenna	P	4	21	Altnacarney *		
Mc Kenna	P	4	21	Norchossy		
Mc Kenna	C	4	I	Tulnavert *		
Mc Kenna	P	4	I		Dungannon	Aghaloo

Name	R	I	S	Townland	Barony	Place-Parish
Mc Kenzie	P	6	23		Lecale	Downpatrick
Mc Keon	P	3	S	Lisabany		
Mc Keon	C	6	I	Dromore	Iveagh	Warrenspoint
Mc Keowan	C	4	I	Ballynaguragh*		
Mc Keown	C	4	I	Ballymagowan	Clogher	Clogher
Mc Kever	P	4	S	Carnteel	Dungannon	Carnteel
Mc kever	I	3	I	Derryaghy	Belfast	Derryaghy
Mc Kibbin	P	6	6	Lisburn	Iveagh	Hillsborough
Mc Kibbin	P	3	6		Lecale	Saul
Mc Kinney	P	1	11	Glenoughly	Raphoe	Leck
Mc Kinney	P	4	22		Omagh	Termonmaguirk
Mc Kinsey	P	4	S		Omagh	Termonmaguirk
Mc Kitrick	P	3	21	Belfast	Belfast	Shankill
Mc Kle	I	7	I	Rossory	Magheraboy	Rossory
Mc Knight	P	4	12	Clogher	Clogher	Clogher
Mc Knight	P	4	12	Glenhoy	Clogher	Clogher
Mc Knight *	P	4	12	Omagh		
Mc Knights	P	6	21		Lecale	Saul
Mc Koskran	P	6	S	Dromore	Iveagh	Warrenspoint
Mc Laferty	P	1	26	Derrycassan	Kilmacrenan	Mevagh
Mc Lane	I	5	E	Tavanagh	Oneilland W.	Drumcree
Mc Langly	I	5	E	Lurgan	Oneilland	Shankill
Mc Laren	P	4	4			
Mc Laurin	P	4	4	Latbeg		
Mc Lean	P	2	29	Moneymore	Loughinsholin	Artrea
Mc Lean	P	3	29		Massereene	Derryaghy
Mc Leane	P	4	6	Tevena	Dungannon	Artrea
Mc Levenny	I	3	I		Belfast	Derryaghy
Mc Linnan	C	2	S	Desertmartin	Loughinsholin	Desertmartin
Mc Loan	I	3	S	Derryaghy	Belfast	Derryaghy
Mc Loghlin	C	2	I	Desertmartin	Loughinsholin	Desertmartin
Mc Lorinan	C	2	I	Moneymore	Loughinsholin	Artrea
Mc Lough	P	4	S		Strabane	Ardstraw
Mc Lroy	P	3	12	Derryaghy	Belfast	Derryaghy
Mc Lure	P	3	12	Derryaghy	Belfast	Derryaghy
Mc Lure	P	6	21	Drumbo	Castlereagh	Drumbo
Mc Mackin	C	5	I	Armagh	Armagh	Armagh
Mc Mahon	P	4	I		Dungannon	Agahloo

Name	R	I	S	Townland	Barony	Place-Parish
Mc Mahon	C	4	I		Omagh	Termonmaguirk
Mc Manis	P	3	S	Derryaghy	Belfast	Derryaghy
Mc Martin	P	4	21		Omagh	Termonmaguirk
Mc Math	P	6	22	Kircubbin	Ards	Inisnargy
Mc Mechan	P	6	21	Bangor	Ards	Bangor
Mc Minn	I	4	I			Killeman
Mc Mopne	P	5	-	Armagh	Armagh	Armagh
Mc Mordie	P	6	I	Lurgan	Iveagh	Seapatrick
Mc Mullan	P	8	6	Lisnaveane	Cremorne	Tullycorbet
Mc Mullen	C	3	S	Derryaghy	Belfast	Derryaghy
Mc Murlan	I	6	E		Lecale	Saul
Mc Murran	I	3	23	Derryaghy	Belfast	Derryaghy
Mc Murray	P	6	21		Lecale	Saul
Mc Murry	P	8	12	Longfield		
Mc Murry	P	6	23	Downpatrick	Lecale	Down
Mc Murty	P	6	25	Dromore	Iveagh	Warrenspoint
Mc Nabs	P	3	4	Derryaghy	Belfast	Derryaghy
Mc Neale	P	1	15	Toome	Kilmacrenan	Clondavaddog
Mc Neevein	P	1	S	Tullyrap	Raphoe	Taughboyne
Mc Neil	P	6	31		Lecale	Saul
Mc Nemorig	P	8	S		Farney	Magheracloon
Mc Nevin	I	1	E		Raphoe	Raphoe
Mc Nichol	P	4	31	Tullyveagh	Dungannon	Artrea
Mc Nichol	P	4	32	Tullyvega	Dungannon	Artrea
Mc Night	P	3	22	Bush Mills	L. Dunluce	Dunluce
Mc Night	C	3	I	Glenavey	Massereene	Glenavey
Mc Nish	P	6	22	Drumbo	Castlereagh	Drumbo
Mc Nulty	C	1	I	Carrickart	Kilmacrenan	Mevagh
Mc Peeter	P	13	S	Ballinafad	Tirerrill	Aghanagh
Mc Pillernane	C	13	I	Ardtermon	Carbury	Drumcliff
Mc Pollan	I	6	S		Iveagh	Anaclone
Mc Quade	C	4	I		Dungannon	Agahloo
Mc Quaffye	C	5	I	Armagh	Armagh	Armagh
Mc Quilkin	C	13	26	Farnmacfrel	Tireragh	Kilmacshalgan
Mc Quoid	C	6	I	Kircubbin	Ards	Inisnargy
Mc Quyann	C	13	I	Mullaghmore	Tirerrill	Ballynakill
Mc Quyn	C	13	I	Kilmacowen	Carbury	Kilmacowen
Mc Robb	P	1	4	Drumenan	Raphoe	Conwal

Name	R	I	S	Townland	Barony	Place-Parish
Mc Roly	P	5	S	Lurgan	Oneilland	Shankill
Mc Sherry	C	5	I	Armagh	Armagh	Armagh
Mc Tyre	P	4	S		Strabane	Ardstraw
Mc Ward	C	1	I	Glenkoe	Kilmacrenan	Mevagh
Mc Watters	P	3	S	Rasham		
Mc Watters	P	6	34	Kircubbin	Ards	Inisnargy
Mc Whiney	P	3	12	Derryaghy	Belfast	Derryaghy
Mc Whorc	P	6	21	Kircubbin	Ards	Inisnargy
Mc Williams	P	4	23	Kilnahushogue		
Mealary	C	8	I	Lisnaveane	Cremorne	Tullycorbet
Means	C	4	S	Dufless*	Dungannon	Artrea
Mecue	C	2	I	Desertmartin	Loughinsholin	Desertmartin
Meculloch	P	3	21		Belfast	Derryaghy
Meegan	C	4	I	Mountstewart	Clogher	Clogher
Megart	P	2	21	Desertmartin	Loughinsholin	Desertmartin
Megue	C	2	I	Desertmartin	Loughinsholin	Desertmartin
Mellon	C	4	I		Clogher	Clogher
Mellott	I	14	E	Knocklehard	Kilmaine	Ballinrobe
Mellott	I	14	E	Lavally	Kilmaine	Ballinrobe
Menaul		4		Clogher	Clogher	Clogher
Menown	P	6	21		Lecale	Saul
Menzes	P	1	S		Bannagh	Inishkeel
Mephet	I	3	E	Derryaghy	Belfast	Derryaghy
Mercer	P	6	20			
Mercer	Q	3	E	Whiteabbey	Belfast	Carnmoney
Mercer	P	3	4	Bush Mills	L. Dunluce	Dunluce
Mercer	P	6	4		Lecale	Saul
Meredith	I	13	E		Corran	Kilshalvey
Merwin	I	4	E	Trilick *		
Mexwell	P	3	S	Derryaghy	Belfast	Derryaghy
Meyring	I	4	E	Ardstraw	Strabane	Ardstraw
Mickey	P	1	S		Raphoe	Conwal
Middleton	P	4	2	Ardstraw	Strabane	Ardstraw
Millar	P	4	12	Daisey Hill		
Millar	P	6	E	Dromore		
Millar	I	6	E		Iveagh	Hillsborough
Millar	P	6	12		Lecale	Saul
Miller	I	4	E	Ardstraw	Strabane	Ardstraw

Name	R	I	S	Townland	Barony	Place-Parish
Miller	I	4	E	Knockinarvoer	Dungannon	Artrea
Miller	I	4	E	Dungannon	Dungannin	Drumglass
Milligan	P	4	11	Kell		
Mills	P	4	1	Carntall	Clogher	Clogher
Mills	P	4	1	Clogher	Clogher	Clogher
Mills	I	8	E	Cappog	Dartree	Killeevan
Mills	P	1	1		Raphoe	Raymoghy
Milygan	P	4	S		Dungannon	Aghaloo
Mind	P	6	S	Drumbo	Castlereagh	Drumbo
Mitchel	P	2	12	Moneymore	Loughinsholin	Artrea
Mitchell	P	4	1	Ardstraw	Strabane	Ardstraw
Mitchell	P	1	S		Raphoe	Raphoe
Mitcheltree	P	4	S	Rahack	Clogher	Aghalurcher
MMcCausland	I	4	10	Ardstraw	Strabane	Ardstraw
Moan	C	7	I	Lisnaskea	Clankelly	Lisnasken
Moderwell	I	4	E		Strabane	Clogher
Moffat	P	4	21	Cormore	Clogher	Clogher
Moffett	P	2	21	Londonderry	Londonderry	Templemore
Moffit	I	7	21	Enniskillen	Magheraboy	Enniskillen
Moffitt	P	7	21			
Moggs	P	5	S	Lurgan	Oneilland	Shankill
Moncreiff	P	2	S	Londonderry	Londonderry	Templemore
Monday	C	2	I		Tirkeeran	Cumber
Money	I	6	E		Lecale	Saul
Moneypenny *	P	7	7	Kinkell	Knockninny	
Monry	I	2	E	Londonderry	Londonderry	Templemore
Montcriff	P	4	S		Strabane	Ardstraw
Montgomery	P	4	12	Slatbeg	Clogher	Clogher
Montgomery	P	2	11	Desertmartin	Loughinsholin	Desertmartin
Montgomery	P	3	11	Belfast	Belfast	Shankill
Moody	I	1	E		Raphoe	Raphoe
Moody	P	2	E	Londonderry	Londonderry	Templemore
Moon	I	6	E		Lecale	Saul
Moor	I	7	E	Enniskillen	Magheraboy	Enniskillen
Moorcraft	I	6	E	Drumbo	Castlereagh	Drumbo
Moorcroft	P	4	E	Newtownstewart		
Moore	P	4	S		Dungannon	Aghaloo
Moore	P	4	E	Augher	Clogher	Clogher

Name	R	I	S	Townland	Barony	Place-Parish
Moore	I	4	E	Ballymacan	Clogher	Clogher
Moore	I	4	E	Deanery	Clogher	Clogher
Moore	I	4	E	Donaghmoyne	Clogher	Clogher
Moore	P	4	13	Glenhoy	Clogher	Clogher
Moore	I	4	E	Lislane	Clogher	Clogher
Moore	P	4	I	Lislane	Clogher	Clogher
Moore	I	13	E		Tireragh	Kilglass
Moore	I	13	E	Ardnaree	Tireragh	Kilmoremoy
Moore	P	1	I	Carrickart	Kilmacrenan	Mevagh
Moore	I	1	E	Island Roy	Kilmacrenan	Mevagh
Moore	I	4	E	Corkhill	Dungannon	Pomeroy
Moore	I	2	E	Londonderry	Londonderry	Templemore
Moorhead	P	11	S	Cavin	Loughtee	Annagh
Moorhead	P	4	S	Lisgallon	Dungannon	Donaghmore
Morgan	P	2	W	Londonderry	Londonderry	Templemore
Morison	I	3	E	Derryaghy	Belfast	Derryaghy
Morovonagh	P	2	S	Desertmartin	Loughinsholin	Desertmartin
Morray	P	8	S	Lisnaveane	Cremorne	Tullycorbet
Morrell	I	3	E	Belfast	Belfast	Shankill
Morris	P	14	1	Lavally	Kilmaine	Ballinrobe
Morrison	I	6	E	Downpatrick	Lecale	Down
Morrison	P	13	37	Carrowwreagh	Clanmorris	Kilcolman
Morrow	I	4	E	Kilrudden	Clogher	Clogher
Morrow	I	3	E	Bush Mills	L. Dunluce	Dunluce
Morrow	I	2	E	Londonderry	Londonderry	Templemore
Morrow	I	8	E	Lisnaveane	Cremorne	Tullycorbet
Mortimer	I	13	E		Tirerrill	Drumcolumb
Morton	P	13	21	Ardnaree	Tireragh	Kilmoremoy
Moryson	P	1	37	Portlough	Raphoe	Allsaints
Mossey	I	4	E	Augher	Clogher	Clogher
Muckle	I	6	E	Kircubbin	Ards	Inisnargy
Mucklewrath	C	4	1	Carnteel	Dungannon	Carnteel
Mudd	I	4	E		Strabane	Ardstraw
Muddy	I	4	E		Strabane	Ardstraw
Muir	P	8	S	Lisnaveane	Cremorne	Tullycorbet
Muldra	P	6	S		Lecale	Downpatrick
Mulholland	C	2	I	Londonderry	Londonderry	Templemore
Mullan	C	2	I	Desertmartin	Loughinsholin	Desertmartin

Name	R	I	S	Townland	Barony	Place-Parish
Mulligan	C	4	21	Orchard Hill*		
Mulligon	P	6	21	Dromore	Iveagh	Warrenspoint
Mullow	C	6	I		Lecale	Saul
Mulloy	C	7	I	Enniskillen	Magheraboy	Enniskillen
Munagh	-	4	-	Aughamullan	Dungannon M.	Clone
Murdock	P	8	S	Glaslough	Trough	Donagh
Murgan	I	3	E	Derryaghy	Belfast	Derryaghy
Murland	P	6	S	Kircubbin	Ards	Inisnargy
Murphy	C	2	I	Moneymore	Loughinsholin	Artrea
Murra	P	3	1		Belfast	Derryaghy
Murray	P	1	S	Mullaghveagh	Boylagh & B.	
Murray	P	14	1	Belatogher	Kilmaine	Ballinrobe
Murray	C	13	I	Ardnaree	Tireragh	Kilmoremoy
Murray	P	1	S		Raphoe	Raphoe
Murray *	P	1	23		Boylagh	
Murray *	P	1	S	Kilkerhan	Boylagh	
Murrey	P	4	4	Ardstraw	Strabane	Ardstraw
Musen	H	3	G	Massereene	Massereene	Derryaghy
Musgrave	I	3	E	Bush Mills	L. Dunluce	Dunluce
Mussen	H	3	G	Derryaghy	Belfast	Derryaghy
Myars	I	6	E	Dromore	Iveagh	Warrenspoint
Myegah	I	1		Carshoe	Raphoe	Raphoe
Nagons	P	6	F	Lisburn	Castlereagh	Blaris
Napier	H	13	F		Tirerrill	Kilmacallan
Napper	I	8	E	Lisnaveane	Cremorne	Tullycorbet
NcGahey	C	4	I	Lurgiboy	Clogher	Donacavey
Nearne	C	1	I	Tullyrap	Raphoe	Taughboyne
Neely	C	4	I	Ballymagowan	Clogher	Clogher
Neesson	C	1	I	Toome	Kilmacrenan	Clondavaddog
Nelson	P	5	12			
Nelson	I	4	E	Carnteel	Dungannon	Carnteel
Nelson	I	4	E	Killyfaddy	Clogher	Clogher
Nelson *	I	4	E	Townagh *		
Nelson *	I	4	E	Carntall	Clogher	Clogher
Neper	H	7	E	Enniskillen	Magheraboy	Enniskillen
Nesbit	P	4	17	Ardstraw	Strabane	Ardstraw
Nesbit	P	6	17	Bangor	Ards U.	Bangor
Nesbit	I	1	E		Raphoe	Raphoe

Name	R	I	S	Townland	Barony	Place-Parish
Nesbitt	I	11	E			
Nesbitt	I	3	E	Glenarm	Glenarm	Tickmcrevan
Nesmith	I	4	E		Strabane	Ardstraw
Nevel	I	3	E	Derryaghy	Belfast	Derryaghy
Nevin	I	1	E		Raphoe	Raphoe
Nevins	I	2	E	Moneymore	Loughinsholin	Artrea
Newcomb	I	2	E	Londonderry	Londonderry	Templemore
Newell	P	3	22	Bush Mills	L. Dunluce	Dunluce
Newland	P	6	13	Drumbo	Castlereagh	Drumbo
Newton	I	2	E	Londonderry	Londonderry	Templemore
Nicholl	P	4	13	Ardstraw	Strabane	Ardstraw
Nicholson	P	13	S		Tireragh	Castleconor
Nicholson	P	13	S	Drumcliff	Carbury	Drumcliff
Nicholson	P	13	S		Tirerrill	Kilmacallan
Nicholson	P	13	S	Ardnaree	Tireragh	Kilmoremoy
Nicleson *	I	13	E	Larrass		
Nixon	I	7	E	Drumcrow	Magheraboy	Enniskillen
Nixon	I	7	E	Kingstown	Magheraboy	Enniskillen
Nixon	Q	1	S		Tirhugh	Inishmacsaint
Nixon	Q	6	21		Lecale	Saul
Nixon	Q	8	E	Lisnaveane	Cremorne	Tullycorbet
Nixon *	P	7	20	Nixon Hall		
Noble	P	4	10	Carnahinney	Clogher	Clogher
Noble	P	2	10	Desertmartin	Loughinsholin	Desertmartin
Noble	I	1	E	Cashell	Raphoe	Kilteevoge
Noble	I	2	E	Londonderry	Londonderry	Templemore
Nogher	C	2	I	Desertmartin	Loughinsholin	Desertmartin
Norret	P	3	S	Bush Mills	L. Dunluce	Dunluce
O' Brainighan	C	5	I	Armagh	Fews	Armagh
O' Coogan	C	4	I		Omagh	Termonmaguirk
O' Dailly	C	5	I	Armagh	Fews	Armagh
O' Donnell	C	1	I	Meenformal	Kilmacrenan	Mevagh
O' Donnell	C	1	I	Meenlaragh	Kilmacrenan	Mevagh
O' Donnelly	C	4	I		Omagh	Termonmaguirk
O' Gorman	C	4	I		Omagh	Termonmaguirk
O' Green	I	3	I		Belfast	Lambeg
O' Heartye	C	5	I	Armagh	Fews	Armagh
O' Heir	P	4	I	Carnteel	Dungannon	Carnteel

Name	R	I	S	Townland	Barony	Place-Parish
O' Hourisky	C	4	I		Omagh	Termonmaguirk
O' Hoyne	C	4	I		Omagh	Termonmaguirk
O' Kain	P	2	I	Desertmartin	Loughinsholin	Desertmartin
O' Kane	C	2	I	Moneymore	Loughinsholin	Artrea
O' Kelly	C	4	I	Ardstraw	Strabane	Ardstraw
O' Lafferty	C	4	I		Omagh	Termonmaguirk
O' Larkion	C	2	I	Moneymore	Loughinsholin	Artrea
O' Lavery	I	3	I	Derryaghy	Belfast	Derryaghy
O' Lavvan	C	5	I	Armagh	Fews	Armagh
O' Lue	C	5	I	Armagh	Fews	Armagh
O' Mackill	C	1	I	Toome	Kilmacrenan	Clondavaddog
O' Merran	C	3	I	Carrickfergus	Carrickfergus	Carrickfergus
O' Moony	I	5	I	Armagh	Oneilland	Armagh
O' Mullen	P	4	I	Carnteel	Dungannon	Carnteel
O' Mulroomey	C	4	I		Omagh	Termonmaguirk
O' Neale	C	1	I	Toome	Kilmacrenan	Clondavaddog
O' Neill	C	4	I		Omagh	Termonmaguirk
O' Quickly	C	13	I	Cloonlurg	Corran	Kilmorgan
O' Quillan	C	13	I	Lghnlteen	Carbury	Carly
O' Quyn	C	13	I	Carrowmore	Leyny	Achonry
O' Quyn	C	13	I	Lugacaha	Corran	Kilmorgan
O' Quyn	C	13	I	Lugacaha	Corran	Kilmorgan
O' Quyne	C	5	I	Armagh	Fews	Armagh
O' Rugan	C	5	I	Armagh	Fews	Armagh
O' Shiel	C	4	I		Omagh	Termonmaguirk
O' Tanny	C	4	I		Omagh	Termonmaguirk
O' Teigue	C	4	I		Omagh	Termonmaguirk
O' Tonner	C	5	I	Armagh	Fews	Armagh
Obins	P	6	S	Bleary	Iveagh	Tullylish
Ogle	I	5	E	Lurgan	Oneilland	Shankill
Oliver	I	4	E		Dungannon	Aghaloo
Oliver	I	5	E	Markethill	Fews L.	Kilclooney
Ore	P	4	S	Ardstraw	Strabane	Ardstraw
Ormsby	P	13	E	Ballymeeny	Tireragh	Easky
Ormsby	P	13	E	Coolaney	Leyny	Killoran
Ormsby	I	13	E	Ardnaree	Tireragh	Kilmoremoy
Orr	P	2	12	Desertmartin	Loughinsholin	Desertmartin
Orr	P	2	11	Londonderry	Londonderry	Templemore

Name	R	I	S	Townland	Barony	Place-Parish
Orr *	P	4	12	Prolusk	Clogher	Clogher
Orr *	P	4	12	Tullybroom	Clogher	Clogher
Orr *	P	4	11	Drumhirk	Dungannon	Donaghmore
Orson	I	6	E	Bleary	Iveagh	Tullylish
Osborn	I	4	E	Brigh	Dungannon	Ballylcog
Osborne	P	6	1		Lecale	Saul
Osbourah	I	3	E	Derryaghy	Belfast	Derryaghy
Otterson	P	4	17	Ballynahone	Dungannon	Artrea
Ourvis	P	2	S	Desertmartin	Loughinsholin	Desertmartin
Oustan	P	13	S	Rathgran	Leyny	Kilvarnet
Owens	C	4	I	Dromore	Dungannon	Arboe
Owns	P	2	W	Desertmartin	Loughinsholin	Desertmartin
Packenham	I	1	E	Kilbarron	Tirhugh	Kilbarron
Paddock	P	13	S	Rinroe	Tireragh	Castleconor
Palmer	P	6	17		Lecale	Saul
Park	P	1	17	Devlin	Kilmacrenan	Mevagh
Parke	I	13	E	Ballytivnan	Carbury	Carly
Parke	I	13	E	Doonycoy	Tireragh	Templeboy
Parker	P	6	4		Lecale	Saul
Parks	I	6	E		Lecale	Saul
Patchett	I	13	E	Coolaney	Leyny	Killoran
Patrick	P	4	12	Carnteel	Dungannon	Carnteel
Patron	C	13	S	Lisconny	Tirerrill	Drumcolumb
Patten	P	3	7	Derryaghy	Belfast	Derryaghy
Patterson	P	3	1	Lisburn	Massereene	Blaris
Patterson	P	3	1	Derryaghy	Belfast	Derryaghy
Patterson	P	3	9	Bushmills	Dunluce	Dunluce
Patterson	P	4	S	Ballygawley	Clogher	Errigal K.
Patton	P	6	12	Newtownards	Castlereagh	Newtownards
Paul	P	4	7	Ardstraw	Strabane	Ardstraw
Peake	I	3	E	Derryaghy	Belfast	Derryaghy
Peake	I	6	E		Lecale	Saul
Pearcy	I	13	E	Cloonameehan	Corran	Cloonoghil
Peathon	I	13	E	Knockbeg	Leyny	Ballysadare
Pedin	I	1	E	Cloghfin	Raphoe	Clonleigh
Peebles	P	1	7	Lifford	Raphoe	Clonleigh
Peebles	P	6	23	Dundonald	Castlereagh	Dundonald
Peel	P	3	21	Bushmills	Dunluce	Dunluce

Name	R	I	S	Townland	Barony	Place-Parish
Peet	P	4	1	Ardstraw	Strabane	Ardstraw
Peevers	I	6	E		Lecale	Saul
Pendleton	I	6	E	Kircubbin	Ards	Inisnargy
Pentland	P	6	15	Drumbo	Castlereagh	Drumbo
Peoples	P	1	S	Maghera Beg	Kilmacrenan	Mevagh
Pepper	P	3	11	Derryaghy	Belfast	Derryaghy
Perdu	P	6	F	Lisburn	Castlereagh	Blaris
Perrin	I	3	E	Lisburn	Massereene	Blaris
Perry	I	6	E	Ballydugan	Lecale	Down
Perry	I	6	E	Downpatrick	Lecale	Down
Perry	I	4	E		Omagh	Termonmaguirk
Peticrue	H	4	F		Dungannon	Aghaloo
Petterson	P	13	S	Urlar	Carbury	Drumcliff
Petticrew	P	3	13	Bushmills	Dunluce	Dunluce
Petticrew	P	6	12	Hollywood	Castlereagh	Hollywood
Pettigrew	H	1	F	Glassegowan*	Raphoe	
Phelan	C	2	I	Moneymore	Loughinsholin	artrea
Phibbs	I	13	E	Ballysadare	Tirerrill	Ballysadare
Phibbs	I	13	E	Ballymote	Corran	Emlaghfad
Philips	P	3	21	Derryaghy	Belfast	Derryaghy
Phillips	I	3	E	Derryaghy	Belfast	Derryaghy
Phillips	I	2	21	Londonderry	Londonderry	Templemore
Phynas		6		Ballydugan	Lecale	Down
Piece	I	13	E	Grange	Carbury	Ahamlish
Pierse	I	13	E	Tanrego	Tireragh	Dromard
Pierse	I	14	E	Carowkeel	Murrisk	Oughaval
Pierse	I	13	E	Carowloughlin	Tireragh	Skreen
Pillow	I	5	E	Armagh	Fews	Armagh
Piner	I	8	E	Aghabog	Dartree	Aghabog
Pinkard	P	13	5	Knocknahun	Carbury	Kilmacowen
Pirsie	I	13	E	Lisruntagh	Tirerrill	Ballysadare
Pock	I	4	E	Ardstraw	Strabane	Ardstraw
Pohgue	I	3	E	Derryaghy	Belfast	Derryaghy
PoKe	P	4	11	Ardstraw	Strabane	Ardstraw
Polke	P	8	S	Liseggerton	Dartree	Clones
Pollock	P	6	11	Newry	Newry	Newry
Pollock	P	2	11	Londonderry	Londonderry	Templemore
Polly	P	6	12		Lecale	Saul

Name	R	I	S	Townland	Barony	Place-Parish
Pomeroy	I	7	E	Ballycassidy	Tirkennedy	Trory
Ponsonby	C	2	E	Londonderry	Londonderry	Templemore
Pooler	P	5	21	Markethill	Fews L.	Mullaghbrack
Porse	P	8	S	Clonmore	Dartree	Clones
Porter	I	4	11	Derrygonigan	Dungannon	Artrea
Porter	I	4	E	Clogher	Clogher	Clogher
Porter	P	6	12	Drumbo	Castlereagh	Drumbo
Porter	P	6	11	Greyabbey	Ards L.	Greyabbey
Porterfield	I	1	E	Ballylennon	Raphoe	Taughboyne
Portus	P	2	18	Desertmartin	Loughinsholin	Desertmartin
Poslitt	P	2	E	Londonderry	Londonderry	Templemore
Pots	P	2	15	Desertmartin	Loughinsholin	Desertmartin
Potter	P	4	12	Ardstraw	Strabane	Ardstraw
Potter	I	4	E	Carnteel	Dungannon	Carnteel
Potter	P	4	12	Freughmore	Clogher	Donacavey
Pottinger	P	3	35	Larne	Glenarm	Larne
Potts	I	3	E	Derryaghy	Belfast	Derryaghy
Poulton	I	2	E	Londonderry	Londonderry	Templemore
Powell	P	6	W		Lecale	Saul
Power	P	13	15	Ardnaree	Tireragh	Kilmoremoy
Pratt	Q	6	1		Lecale	Saul
Preistman	P	3	18	Derryaghy	Belfast	Derryaghy
Presby	P	6	1	Drumbo	Castlereagh	Drumbo
Presley	P	6	1	Drumbo	Castlereagh	Drumbo
Preston	P	13	15	Bunduff	Carbury	Ahamlish
Prew	I	13	E	Carrowkeel	Carbury	Kilmacowen
Pringle	P	4	S		Dungannon	Aghaloo
Pritchard	P	6	W	Kircubbin	Ards	Inisnargy
Provan	P	4	12	Augher	Clogher	Clogher
Prunty	I	8	N	Annagilly	Monaghan	Telavent
Prushoes		8		Bulgbrean*		
Pryse	P	13	W	Rathdoonybeg	Corran	Elmaghfad
Purdon	C	4	N	Ardstraw	Strabane	Ardstraw
Purdy	P	6	12	Newtownards	Ards	Newtownards
Purvey	C	2	17	Moneymore	Loughinsholin	Artrea
Purvice	P	4	17	Derrygonigan	Dungannon	Artrea
Purvice	P	4	17	Tullyvega	Dungannon	Artrea
Pye	P	7	7	Rossory	Magheraboy	Rossory

Name	R	I	S	Townland	Barony	Place-Parish
Quale	C	1	I	Raphoe	Raphoe	Raphoe
Quiggley	C	13	I	Cloonacurra	Leyny	Ballysadare
Quigley	C	2	I	Moneymore	Loughinsholin	Artrea
Quigley	P	4	19	Carnteel	Dungannon	Carnteel
Quigley	C	8	I	Drumloo	Dartree	Killeevan
Quinton	H	6	F		Lecale	Saul
Quirke	C	13	I	Carns	Carbury	St. Johns
Quissoge		13		Carrowlghn	Leyny	Killoran
Quyn	C	13	I	Carownurlaur*	Coolavan	Killaraght
Quyne	C	13	I	Carrowcashel	Tirerrill	Kilmactranny
Rae	P	4	34	Ardstraw	Strabane	Ardstraw
Raghnesse	P	13	S		Leyny	Kilvarnet
Raghtagane	P	13	S	Moygara	Coolavan	Kilfree
Raghtegan	C	13	I	Rathlee	Tireragh	Easky
Rainey	P	6	7	Drumbo	Castlereagh	Drumbo
Ramsay	P	4	17	Waterhill*		
Ramsay	P	4	17	Gunnell	Clogher	Clogher
Ramsay	P	4	17	Mullaghtinny	Clogher	Clogher
Ramsay	P	4	17	Beagh	Omagh East	Clogherny
Ramsey	P	2	3	Moneymore	Loughinsholin	Artrea
Ramsey	P	6	7	Bangor	Bangor	Bangor
Ramsey	P	2	3	Londonderry	Londonderry	Templemore
Ramsey	P	4	S	Castlegore	Omagh	Urney
Rankin	P	4	12	Ardstraw	Strabane	Ardstraw
Rankin	P	2	12	Desertmartin	Loughinsholin	Desertmartin
Rankin	P	1	1	Corcamon	Raphoe	Donaghmore
Rankin	P	2	S	Londonderry	Londonderry	Templemore
Ransay	P	4	3	Castletown	Strabane	Leckpatrick
Ray	P	4	23		Dungannon	Aghaloo
Ray	P	3	9	Derryaghy	Belfast	Derryaghy
Ray	P	3	34	Derryaghy	Belfast	Derryaghy
Ray	P	4	12	Lisgallon	Dungannon	Donaghmore
Rea	I	3	1	Carrickfergus	Carrickfergus	Carrickgergus
Read	I	4	E	Ardstraw	Strabane	Ardstraw
Read	I	5	E	Armagh	Oneilland	Armagh
Real	C	14	I	Belatogher*	Kilmaine	Ballinrobe
Reed	I	2	E	Aghadowey	Coleraine	Aghadowey
Reed	P	13	4	Ardnaree	Tireragh	Kilmoremoy

Name	R	I	S	Townland	Barony	Place-Parish
Rees	P	1				
Reid	P	6	4	Ballywalter	Ards	Ballywalter
Reily	P	4	I	Carnteel	Dungannon	Carnteel
Rennet	H	3	F	Derryaghy	Belfast	Derryaghy
Rennick	I	8	E	Clones	Dartree	Clones
Renny	P	4	16	Aedstraw	Strabane	Ardstraw
Resnison	P	3		Derryaghy	Belfast	Derryaghy
Reston	P	2	12	Desertmartin	Loughinsholin	Desertmartin
Reynalds	C	4	I	Ardstraw	Strabane	Ardstraw
Rice	P	4	W	Augher	Clogher	Clogher
Rice	P	3	W	Derryaghy	Belfast	Derryaghy
Rice	P	2	W	Londonderry	Londonderry	Templemore
Richardson	P	6	4			
Richardson	P	4	1	Farnetra*		
Richardson	P	4	1	Augher	Clogher	Clogher
Richardson	P	4	1	Springtown	Clogher	Clogher
Richardson	P	3	10	Derryaghy	Belfast	Derryaghy
Richey	P	4	12	Clarmore	Omagh West	Ardstraw
Richey	P	6	12	Bangor	Lower Ards	Bangor
Richey	P	4	12	Carnahinney	Clogher	Clogher
Richey	P	4	12	Fivemiletown	Clogher	Clogher
Richey	P	3	12	Derryaghy	Belfast	Derryaghy
Richey	P	4	12	Freughmore	Clogher	Donacavey
Richison	P	14	12	Belatogher*	Kilmaine	Ballinrobe
Riddle	P	8	12	Corramegan	Dartree	Anhabog
Riddle	P	2	12	Londonderry	Londonderry	Templemore
Rider	I	7	E	Enniskillen	Magheraboy	Enniskillen
Rigby	I	6	E		Lecale	Saul
Rines	P	3	I	Derryaghy	Belfast	Derryaghy
Roan	P	6	12		Lecale	Down
Robb	P	6	21	Newtownards	Castlereagh	Newtownards
Robinson	P	4	17	Ardstraw	Strabane	Ardstraw
Robinson	P	2	7	Moneymore	Loughinsholin	Artrea
Robinson	I	6	E	Downpatrick	Lecale	Down
Robinson	P	3	4	Bushmills	Dunluce	Dunluce
Robinson	P	2	11	Londonderry	Londonderry	Templemore
Robison	P	3	21	Bushmills	Dunluce	Dunluce
Roche	P	6	F	Lisburn	Castlereagh	Blaris

Name	R	I	S	Townland	Barony	Place-Parish
Rockbourah	I	3	E	Derryaghy	Belfast	Derryaghy
Rod	I	2	E	Aghadowey	Coleraine	Aghadowey
Roddy	C	8	I	Clones	Dartree	Clones
Rodgers	P	3	4	Derryaghy	Belfast	Derryaghy
Rodgers	C	6	I	Newry	Newry	Newry
Rogan	C	6	I	Ballydugan	Lecale	Down
Rogers	C	2	E	Londonderry	Londonderry	Templemore
Roland	I	8	E	Drumskelt	Dartree	Killeevan
Rolland	I	8	E	Lisnavane	Cremorne	Tullycorbet
Roney	C	6	I		Lecale	Saul
Roper	I	8	E	Shantonagh	Cremorne	Aghnamullen
Roper	I	1	E	Knockfare	Raphoe	Stranorlar
Roragh	P	8	S	Drumee	Dartree	Killevan
Rosbothom	I	3	E	Derryaghy	Belfast	Derryaghy
Roscrow	I	7	E	Enniskillen	Magheraboy	Enniskillen
Ross	P	6	5	Drumbo	Castlereagh	Drumbo
Rossbotham	I	3	E	Derryaghy	Belfast	Derryaghy
Rossgrow	I	2	E	Desertmartin	Loughinsholin	Desertmartin
Rowan	I	3	E	Dunaghy	Dunluce	Ballymoney
Rowan	P	3	12	Lisburn	Massereene	Blaris
Rowan	P	6	11	Dromore	Iveagh	Dromore
Rowan	P	6	13	Kircubbin	Ards	Inisnargy
Rowley	P	2	20	Londonderry	Londonderry	Templemore
Ruddagh	P	3	1	Ballygrooby	Toome	Drummaul
Ruddell	I	5	E	Lurgan	Oneilland	Shankill
Rule	P	8	S	Glasslough	Trough	Donagh
Rullack	P	2	E	Londonderry	Londonderry	Templemore
Rush	I	14	E	Knockanotish	Kilmaine	Ballinrobe
Russel	P	3	1	Bushmills	Dunluce	Dunluce
Russell	P	6	S	Ballybot*		
Russell	P	4	1	Ardstraw	Strabane	Ardstraw
Russell	P	3	S	Lisburn	Massereene	Blaris
Russell	P	4	S	Dunnamany	Strabane	Donaghedy
Russell	P	6	12	Drumbo	Castlereagh	Drumbo
Russell	P	5	17	Lurgan	Oneilland	Shankill
Rutherford	P	2	5	Moneymore	Loughinsholin	Artrea
Rutherford	P	3	20	Bushmills	Dunluce	Dunluce
Rutledge	I	4	E	Collumbrone*		

Name	R	I	S	Townland	Barony	Place-Parish
Rutledge	I	13	E	Knockahullen	Corran	Kilshalvy
Rymes	P	14	I	Knockanotish	Kilmaine	Ballinrobe
Sadler	P	6	12		Lecale	Saul
Sadler	P	2	20	Londonderry	Londonderry	Templemore
Sampson	P	4	13	Carntall	Clogher	Clogher
Sanderson	P	2	5	Londonderry	Londonderry	Templemore
Sandiford	P	4	7	Ballynahone	Dungannon	Artrea
Sands	C	1	7	Moneymore	Raphoe	Raymoghy
Sanflay	I	6	N	Ballydugan	Lecale	Down
Saul	C	6	N		Lecale	Saul
Saunders	P	14	S	Knockanotish	Kilmaine	Ballinrobe
Saurin	P	3	F	Ardagh	Cary	Ramoan
Savage	P	6	21	Downpatrick	Lecale	Down
Savage	P	6	N		Lecale	Saul
Sayers	I	4	E	Omagh	Omagh East	Drumragh
Sayers	I	6	E		Lecale	Saul
Schoales	I	2	E	Londonderry	Londonderry	Templemore
Schofield	I	8	E	Anahagh	Trough	Monaghan
Scholay	C	8	S	Mullaghgrena	Farney	Magheraclone
Scot	P	3	7	Derryaghy	Belfast	Derryaghy
Scott	P	13	23	Ardnaglass	Carbury	Ahamlish
Scott	P	4	12	Augher	Clogher	Clogher
Scott	I	13	21	Doonowla	Carbury	Drumcliff
Scott	P	3	12	Ballygrooby	Toome	Drummaul
Scott	P	7	18	Furnish	Tirkennedy	Enniskillen
Scott	P	1	15	Tullymore	Kilmacrenan	Gartan
Scott	P	1	S	Ardara	Banagh	Killybegs
Scott	P	13	21	Ballyholan	Tireragh	Kilmoremoy
Scott	P	6	S		Lecale	Saul
Scott	P	3	12	Belfast	Belfast	Shankill
Scott	P	13	21	Carowdurneen	Tireragh	Skreen
Scott	P	4	12		Omagh	Termonmaguirk
Seate	I	4	E	Clogher	Clogher	Clogher
Seaton	I	4	E	Lisnahull	Dungannon	Donaghmore
Seay	P	6	S		Lecale	Saul
Seeds	I	3	E	Derryaghy	Belfast	Derryaghy
Seeds	I	3	E		Massereene	Derryaghy
Seeds	P	6	S		Lecale	Saul

Name	R	I	S	Townland	Barony	Place-Parish
Seery	C	7	I	Rossory	Magheraboy	Rossory
Sefton	I	3	E	Magheragall	Massereene	Magheragall
Semple	P	1	E	Letterkenny	Kilmacrenan	Conwal
Semple	P	2	E	Londonderry	Londonderry	Templemore
Shankey	C	6	I	Ballydugan	Lecale	Down
Shannon	P	13	I	Carrowpadeen	Tireragh	Easky
Sharp	P	2	4	Desertmartin	Loughinsholin	Desertmartin
Shaw	P	3	12	Gemeway		
Shaw	P	3	12	Ahoghill	Toome Lower	Ahoghill
Shaw	P	3	20	Carnmoney	Belfast L.	Carnmoney
Shaw	P	3	S	Bushmills	Dunluce	Dunluce
Shaw	P	6	1	Kircubbin	Ards	Inisnargy
Shean	P	3	12	Derryaghy	Belfast	Derryaghy
Shearer	P	3	12	Belfast	Belfast	Carnmoney
Shepherd	I	4	18	Clogher	Clogher	Clogher
Shepherd	P	6	18		Lecale	Saul
Sheridan	C	4	I		Dungannon	Aghaloo
Sheridan	C	14	I	Knockanotish	Kilmaine	Ballinrobe
Sherif	P	6	1	Drumbo	Castlereagh	Drumbo
Sherry	P	4	I		Dungannon	Aghaloo
Shiel	I	3	E	Ballygrooby	Toome	Drummaul
Shields	P	4	15	Clogher	Clogher	Clogher
Shields	C	6	20	Downpatrick	Lecale	Down
Shiels	P	1	20	Ardbane	Kilmacrenan	Mevagh
Shiels	C	1	20	Drumies	Kilmacrenan	Mevagh
Shiels	C	1	15	Derrycassan	Kilmacrennan	Mevagh
Shimon	P	6	S		Lecale	Saul
Shiry	I	2	E	Desertmartin	Loughinsholin	Desertmartin
Shore	I	7	E	Enniskillen	Magheraboy	Enniskillen
Short	P	4	21	Clogher	Clogher	Clogher
Short	H	5	S	Lurgan	Oneilland	Shankill
Short	P	5	21	Lurgan	Oneilland	Shankill
Shoyough		2		Londonderry	Londonderry	Templemore
Shugog	C	8	I		Cremorne	Aughanumulen
Sidney	I	2	E	Londonderry	Londonderry	Templemore
Simms	I	1	E	Rawros	Kilmacrenan	Mevagh
Simpson	I	4	E	Daisey Hill*		
Simpson	P	2	12	Moneymore	Loughinsholin	Artrea

Name	R	I	S	Townland	Barony	Place-Parish
Simpson	P	3	35	Ballyclare	Belfast	Ballynure
Simpson	P	2	15	Toome	Kilmacrenan	Clondavaddog
Simpson	P	4	15	Drumhirk	Dungannon	Donaghmore
Simpson	P	3	1	Bushmills	Dunluce	Dunluce
Simpson	P	4	1	Bloomhill	Clogher	Errigal K.
Simpson	P	4	15	Keady	Clogher	Errigal K.
Simpson	P	4	15	Cullentra	Dungannon L.	Kileeshil
Simpson	P	3	12	Ballymena	Lower Toome	Kirkinriola
Simpson	P	6	1		Lecale	Saul
Simson	P	3	15	Toome	Kilmacrenan	Clondavaddog
Sinclair	P	5	34			
Sincler	P	3	34	Derryaghy	Belfast	Derryaghy
Singleton	I	6	E	Blaris	Castlereagh	Blaris
Singleton	P	6	15		Lecale	Saul
Sinnett	I	14	E	Knockanotish	Kilmaine	Ballinrobe
Sitt	P	4	S	Knockinarvoer	Dungannon	Artrea
Skelly	C	6	I	Drumbo	Castlereagh	Drumbo
Skelly	P	3	I	Bushmills	Dunluce	Dunluce
Skelton	I	7	E	Clones	Clankelly	Clones
Skelton	I	3	E	Derryaghy	Belfast	Derryaghy
Skillen	P	6	N	Downpatrick	Lecale	Down
Skinner	P	2	20	Londonderry	Londonderry	Templemore
Skipton	I	2	E	Londonderry	Londonderry	Templemore
Slack	I	8	E	Clones	Dartree	Clones
Slack	I	7	E	Enniskillen	Magheraboy	Enniskillen
Slavin	C	2	E	Desertmartin	Loughinsholin	Desertmartin
Slevan	C	8	I	Crossreagh	Dartree	Killevan
Sloan	P	6	15	Bangor	Lower Ards	Bangor
Sloan	P	6	15		Lecale	Down
Sloan	C	6	I	Dromore	Iveagh	Dromore
Sloan	P	6	15	Drumbo	Castlereagh	Drumbo
Sloan	P	6	15		Lecale	Saul
Sloane	P	4	15	Tullyconnell	Dungannon	Artrea
Slowey	C	8	I	Annagilly	Monaghan	Telavnet
Small	P	6	1		Lecale	Saul
Smith	I	4	E	Ardstraw	Strabane	Ardstraw
Smith	P	2	E	Moneymore	Loughinsholin	Artrea
Smith	I	4	15	Carnteel	Dungannon	Carnteel

Name	R	I	S	Townland	Barony	Place-Parish
Smith	P	4	15	Lisnamaghery	Clogher	Clogher
Smith	P	8	1	Clonmore	Dartree	Clones
Smith	I	2	E	Desertmartin	Loughinsholin	Desertmartin
Smith	I	7	E	Whitehall	Magheraboy	Enniskillen
Smith	P	7	E	Whitehall	Magheraboy	Enniskillen
Smith	P	6	E		Lecale	Saul
Smith	I	4	E		Omagh	Termonmaguirk
Smyth	I	4	E	Augher	Clogher	Clogher
Smyth	P	2	1	Londonderry	Londonderry	Templemore
Snodgrass	P	1	S	Beltany	Raphoe	Raphoe
Somervil	I	4	17	Ardstraw	Strabane	Ardstraw
Somerville	I	4	E	Augher	Clogher	Clogher
Somerville	I	4	17	Bolies	Clogher	Clogher
Sommes	P	7	S	Enniskillen	Magheraboy	Enniskillen
Souter	I	8	E	Corkeeran	Dartree	Killevan
Speers	P	6	15		Lecale	Saul
Speir(Speer)	P	1	4	Kill	Kilmacrenan	Mevagh
Spence	P	7	1	Enniskillen	Magheraboy	Devenish
Spence	P	7	4	Enniskillen	Magheraboy	Devenish
Spence	P	7	I	Moyglass	Magheraboy	Rossorry
Spence	P	6	17		Lecale	Saul
Spence	P	11	1	Ballyconnell	Tallyhaw	Tomregan
Spire	I	2	E	Aghadowey	Coleraine	Aghadowey
Spittle	P	6	10	Newry	Newry	Newry
Spottswood	P	2	17	Londonderry	Londonderry	Templemore
Spratt	I	2	E	Moneymore	Loughinsholin	Artrea
Spratt	P	6	E		Lecale	Saul
Spraule	P	2	13	Londonderry	Londonderry	Templemore
Squire	I	2	E	Londonderry	Londonderry	Templemore
St. Sauveur	P	6	F	Lisburn	Castlereagh	Blaris
Stanley	P	6	15	Kircubbin	Ards	Inisnargy
Staples	I	6	E	Dromore	Iveagh	Dromore
Starling	I	7	E	Enniskillen	Magheraboy	Enniskillen
Starrit	I	1	E	Drumlackagh	Kilmacrenan	Mevagh
Staunton	I	14	E	Knockanotish	Kilmaine	Ballinrobe
Steel	P	4	21	N.Tn.Stewart	Strabane	Ardstraw
Steele	P	4	12	Ardstraw	Strabane	Ardstraw
Steen	C	4	I	Tiercar*		

Name	R	I	S	Townland	Barony	Place-Parish
Steen	P	4	I	Clogher	Clogher	Clogher
Steen	C	4	I	Skelgagh	Clogher	Clogher
Steen	P	4	I	Cornmullagh	Dungannon M.	Clonfeacle
Steenson	P	6	11		Lecale	Saul
Stephenson	P	4	12	Findermore	Clogher	Clogher
Stevenson	I	7	E	Enniskillen	Magheraboy	Enniskillen
Stewart	P	4	15	Aughentain*		
Stewart	P	4	15	Aughnaglough*		
Stewart	P	4	11	Daisey Hill*		
Stewart	P	4	7		Dungannon	Aghaloo
Stewart	P	6	11	Bangor	Lower Ards	Bangor
Stewart	P	4	15	Clogher	Clogher	Clogher
Stewart	P	4	11	Knocknacarny	Clogher	Clogher
Stewart	P	4	20	Lislane	Clogher	Clogher
Stewart	P	4	7	Killemoonan	Omagh	Donacavey
Stewart	P	6	4	Donaghadee	Ards	Donaghadee
Stewart	P	4	13	Lisgallon	Dungannon	Donaghmore
Stewart	P	2	11	Londonderry	Londonderry	Templemore
Stiles	I	2	E	Londonderry	Londonderry	Templemore
Stincean	P	1	S	Leganathraw	Raphoe	Taughboyne
Stinson	I	4	E	Travenmore*		
Stockdale	I	4	E	Beechill*		
Stockdale	I	4	E	Clogher	Clogher	Clogher
Stockman	I	2	E	Desertmartin	Loughinsholin	Desertmartin
Stoller	H	2	G	Londonderry	Londonderry	Templemore
Stoope	P	2	E	Londonderry	Londonderry	Templemore
Storrett	P	1	S	Gortlush	Raphoe	All Saints
Story	P	4	1	Corick	Clogher	Clogher
Stout	I	2	E	Londonderry	Londonderry	Templemore
Stoyle		2		Londonderry	Londonderry	Temolemore
Strahan	P	6	1		Lecale	Saul
Strain	C	8	I	Lisnagore	Dartree	Killeevan
Strain	C	1	I	Downies	Kilmacrenan	Mevagh
Straiten	P	6	S	Kiecubbin	Ards	Inisnargy
Strowde	P	3	S	Lisburn	Massereene	Blaris
Stuart	P	6	7		Lecale	Down
Stueart	P	3	7	Derryaghy	Belfast	Derryaghy
Sturdyr	P	2	G	Desertmartin	Loughinsholin	Desertmartin

Name	R	I	S	Townland	Barony	Place-Parish
Sturgeon	I	2	E	Londonderry	Londonderry	Templemore
Suden	P	2	N	Londonderry	Londonderry	Templemore
Sullivan	C	2	I	Desertmartin	Loughinsholin	Desertmartin
Sumrall	I	6	E	Dromore	Iveagh	Dromore
Swain	P	8	22	Teer	Dartree	Killeevan
Sweeney	C	1	I	Carrickart	Kilmacrenan	Mevagh
Sweeney	C	1	I	Glenkoe	Kilmacrenan	Mevagh
Sweeney	P	1	I	Meenformal	Kilmacrenan	Mevagh
Syms	I	1	E	Baractcla*		
Symson	I	13	E	Sligo	Sligo	Sligo
Taffe	C	13	E	Cashel	Coolavan	Achonry
Taggart	P	4	21	Clogher	Clogher	Clogher
Talbott	I	13	E	Ballyconnell	Carbury	Drumcliff
Tanahill	P	4	12	Ardstraw	Strabane	Ardstraw
Tanist	C	13	I	Killoran	Leyny	Killoran
Tassy	I	8	S	Lisnavane	Cremorne	Tullycorbet
Tate	P	3	35	Derryaghy	Belfast	Derryaghy
Tate	P	6	35	Ballynainch	Kinelarty	Magheradrool
Tate	p	6	35		Lecale	Saul
Tavany	P	6	S		Lecale	Saul
Taylor	P	2	6			
Taylor	P	4	21	Cranbrooke*		
Taylor	P	4	21	Norchossy*		
Tea	I	6	E	Dromore	Iveagh	Dromore
Tearney	C	4	I	Corleaghan	Clogher	Clogher
Teer	P	6	I		Lecale	Saul
Tenison	I	7	E	Knokbalmor	Magheraboy	Enniskillen
Thirkhill	P	3	N		Massereene	Derryaghy
Thobrar	I	8	E	Lisnavane	Cremorne	Tullycorbet
Thompson	I	3	E	Lisburn	Massereene	Blaris
Thompson	P	4	21	Augher	Clogher	Clogher
Thompson	P	3	21	Derryaghy	Belfast	Derryaghy
Thompson	P	6	S		Lecale	Saul
Thornton	I	14	E	Knockanotish	Kilmaine	Ballinrobe
Tichburn	I	2	E	Desertmartin	Loughinsholin	Desertmartin
Tilford	I	2	E	Londonderry	Londonderry	Templemore
Till	I	13	E	Doorly	Corran	Kilmorgan
Tingle	I	13	E	Creevagh	Tirerrill	Kilmactranny

Name	R	I	S	Townland	Barony	Place-Parish
Tinsly	I	5	E	Lurgan	Oneilland	Shankill
Tisdale	P	6	S		Lecale	Saul
Toath		13		Carrowkeel	Tirerrill	Aghanagh
Tobias	I	2	E	Londonderry	Londonderry	Templemore
Todd	P	4	17	Ballynaguragh*		
Todd	P	8	15	Newbliss	Dartree	Killeevan
Todd	P	6	15		Lecale	Saul
Toman	C	6	I	Bleary	Iveagh	Tullylish
Tome	I	2	E	Londonderry	Londonderry	Templemore
Tomkins	I	2	E	Londonderry	Londonderry	Templemore
Toomouth	I	2	E	Desertmartin	Loughinsholin	Desertmartin
Torenline	I	1	E	Drumore	Raphoe	Leck
Torney	P	6	E		Lecale	Saul
Torrance	P	6	E		Lecale	Saul
Tracy	C	2	I	Desertmartin	Loughinsholin	Desertmartin
Treanor	P	4	I	Aughnacloy	Dungannon L.	Carnteel
Treanor	P	4	I	Killaney	Clogher	Clogher
Treanor	P	4	I	Mount Stewart	Clogher	Clogher
Tremble	P	4	13	Gartmore*		
Tremble	P	6	15	Newry	Newry	Newry
Trench	H	13	F	Kilross	Tirerrill	Kilross
Trimble	P	4	E	Lisgawsey?		
Trimble	I	4	E	Tullyweery	Dungannon	Artrea
Trimble	P	4	15	Ballymacan	Clogher	Clogher
Trimble	P	4	15	Clogher	Clogher	Clogher
Trimble	P	4	E	Shanco	Clogher	Clogher
Trimble	P	4	15	Ballagh	Clogher	Clougher
Trimble	I	6	E		Lecale	Saul
Triwews	I	1	E	Carnshannagh	Raphoe	Taughboyne
Trotter	P	7	17	Enniskillen	Magheraboy	Enniskillen
Truman	I	5	E	Lurgan	Oneilland	Shankill
Truman	I	2	E	Londonderry	Londonderry	Templemore
Trumble	I	13	E	Carrowmore	Corran	Emlaghfad
Tuck	I	2	E	Londonderry	Londonderry	Templemore
Tucker	P	3	E	Derryaghy	Belfast	Derryaghy
Tuckey	I	2	E	Londonderry	Londonderry	Templemore
Tumelty	P	6	S		Lecale	Saul
Tummin	I	8	E	Crossmoyle	Dartree	Clones

Name	R	I	S	Townland	Barony	Place-Parish
Turbett	I	5	E	Lurgan	Oneilland	Shankill
Turnbull	P	6	20	Dromore	Iveagh	Dromore
Turner	P	5	1	Lurgan	Oneilland	Shankill
Twigg	I	4	E	Clogher	Clogher	Clogher
Tyford	I	1	E	Raphoe	Raphoe	Raphoe
Upton	I	4	E	Knockinarvoer	Dungannon	Artrea
Upton	I	3	E	Templepatrick	Belfast U.	Templepatrick
Usher	I	5	E	Lurgan	Oneilland	Shankill
Vance	P	3	S	Bushmills	Dunluce	Dunluce
Vance	I	6	E	Kircubbin	Ards	Inisnargy
Vaughn	P	1	W	Buncrana	Inishowen W.	Fahan L.
Veach	I	2	E	Desertmartin	Loughinsholin	Desertmartin
Venables	P	3	W		Massereene	Derryaghy
Venart		8		Ramany	Monaghan	Monaghan
Vicars	I	3	E	Derryaghy	Belfast	Derryaghy
Vildone	H	2	G	Desertmartin	Loughinsholin	Desertmartin
Wade	I	7	E	Enniskillen	Magheraboy	Enniskillen
Wagh	P	6	S	Dromore	Iveagh	Dromore
Waldron	C	14	I	Knockanotish	Kilmaine	Ballinrobe
Walke	H	4	G	Carnteel	Dungannon	Carnteel
Walker	P	3	15	Derryaghy	Belfast	Derryaghy
Walker	P	6	11	Dromore	Iveagh	Dromore
Walker	I	3	E	Bushmills	Dunluce	Dunluce
Walker	I	2	E	Londonderry	Londonderry	Templemore
Walker	P	2	17	Londonderry	Londonderry	Templemore
Wallace	P	4	12	Carnteel	Dungannon	Carnteel
Wallace	P	6	12	Greyabbey	Ards L.	Greyabbey
Wallace	P	6	11	Hollywood	Castlereagh	Hollywood
Wallis	P	4	5	Ardstraw	Strabane	Ardstraw
Wallis	P	2	5	Desertmartin	Loughinsholin	Desertmartin
Walmsley	I	7	E	Rossory	Magheraboy	Rossory
Ward	I	2	E	Aghadowey	Coleraine	Aghadowey
Ward	P	6	9	Dromore	Iveagh	Dromore
Ward	C	1	I	Glenkoe	Kilmacrenan	Mevagh
Warde	I	8	E	Munilly	Dartree	Clones
Waring	I	3	E	Derryaghy	Belfast	Derryaghy
Warke	I	1	E	Drumore	Raphoe	Leck
Warwick	P	6	5		Lecale	Saul

Name	R	I	S	Townland	Barony	Place-Parish
Wat	P	4	1	Ardstraw	Strabane	Ardstraw
Waterson	P	2	12	Desertmartin	Loughinsholin	Desertmartin
Waterson	P	6	11		Lecale	Saul
Watkins	P	6	W		Lecale	Down
Watson	P	4	7	Ardstraw	Strabane	Ardstraw
Watson	P	3	E	Bushmills	Dunluce	Dunluce
Watson	P	1	7	Rawros	Kilmacrenan	Mevagh
Watson	P	4	E		Omagh	Termonmaguirk
Watt	P	3	E			
Watt	I	8	E	Drumulla*		
Watt	I	4	11	Carnteel	Dungannon	Carnteel
Watt	I	6	E	Dromore	Iveagh	Dromore
Watt	P	3	E	Bushmills	Dunluce	Dunluce
Watters	P	6	S		Lecale	Down
Watterson	P	6	S		Lecale	Saul
Watts	Q	3	E	Whiteabbey	Belfast	Carnmoney
Waugh	P	4	S	Carnteel	Dungannon	Carnteel
Weal	I	6	E	Dromore	Iveagh	Dromore
Webb	I	13	E	Ballymote	Corran	Emlaghfad
Webb	I	5	E	Lurgan	Oneilland	Shankill
Weir	P	3	13			
Weir	P	3	13	Bushmills	Dunluce	Dunluce
Wells	I	5	E	Lurgan	Oneilland	Shankill
Welshman	I	6	W	Downpatrick	Lecale	Down
Welshman	P	6	S		Lecale	Saul
Wenn	P	4	S	Ardstraw	Strabane	Ardstraw
West	P	6	S		Lecale	Down
West	I	6	E	Ballydugan	Lecale	Down
Wetsor	P	2	S	Desertmartin	Loughinsholin	Desertmartin
Whisker	I	6	E	Downpatrick	Lecale	Down
White	P	4	E	Derrygonigan	Dungannon	Arerea
White	I	3	E	Derryaghy	Belfast	Derryaghy
White	P	6	E	Kircubbin	Ards	Inisnargy
White	I	2	E	Londonderry	Londonderry	Templemore
White *	P	3	S	Fannet*		
Whitley	P	5	S	Markethill	Fews L.	Kilclooney
Whitten	C	7	I	Rossory	Magheraboy	Rossory
Whittlo	I	2	E	Londonderry	Londonderry	Templemore